The Illustrated Guide to the Mass Communication Research Project

This book makes mass communication research projects more accessible to the new student researcher through a balance between an academically rigorous guide and an informal and humorous student-centered approach.

The Illustrated Guide to the Mass Communication Research Project's unique, visual approach brings to life concepts and tactics under discussion through vivid illustrations. The book follows the universal format of the academic research paper: abstract, introduction, literature review, methodology, hypotheses/research questions, quantitative and qualitative analysis/findings, discussion, and conclusion. It guides the reader through using key methods central to much of mass communication research: observation, interviews, focus groups, case studies, content analysis, surveys, experiments, and sampling. Each chapter contains examples of the segment under discussion, using excerpted research studies that provide writing models for the student's own research report.

Ideal for students in research-centered courses in mass media, communication studies, marketing, and public relations, whether at the undergraduate or graduate level, this text will continue to serve as a valuable resource into a future communications and marketing career.

Online resources are provided to support the book: examples of an in-depth interview guide, a focus group moderator guide, a content analysis coding form, observation field notes and an experiment cover story; templates for a personal SWOT analysis and an informed consent form; a research topic worksheet; a literature review matrix; and coding exercises. Please visit www.routledge.com/9781032080758.

Patricia Swann, former Dean of the School of Business and Justice Studies, is a Professor of Public Relations and Management at Utica University, USA. She is the Executive Director of the Raymond Simon Institute for Public Relations and Journalism and the former head of the Public Relations Division of the Association for Education in Journalism and Mass Communication. She is the author of *Cases in Public Relations Management* and *The Illustrated Guide to the Content Analysis Research Project*.

Figure 0.0 Pat Swann.

The Illustrated Guide to the Mass Communication Research Project

Patricia Swann

Routledge
Taylor & Francis Group

NEW YORK AND LONDON

Cover image: ©Patricia Swann

First published 2023
by Routledge
605 Third Avenue, New York, NY 10158

and by Routledge
4 Park Square, Milton Park, Abingdon, Oxon, OX14 4RN

Routledge is an imprint of the Taylor & Francis Group, an informa business

ISBN: 978-1-032-10263-4 (hbk)
ISBN: 978-1-032-08075-8 (pbk)
ISBN: 978-1-003-21448-9 (ebk)

DOI: 10.4324/9781003214489

Typeset in Adobe Garamond
by KnowledgeWorks Global Ltd.

Access the Support Material: www.routledge.com/9781032080758

Dedicated to my husband, John.

Thanks for stomping out my passive voice!

Contents

Figure 1 An online focus group screen showing individuals.

Online Focus Group

Figure 2 An online focus group of laptops discussing stuff.

Figure 3 A sensory tasting lab.

Figure 4 Group dynamics includes people who dominate the discussion.

"Vaping Associated with Healthy Food Words: A Content Analysis of Twitter" (Basáñez et al., 2018).

Figure 5 Content analysis that analyzed marketing language of vape products.

Figure 6 Communication research can include social media communication.

I suppose you're wondering why I've gathered you all here today...

RESEARCH CON

Figure 7 Research is often presented publicly to peers.

The Illustrated Guide
to the Mass Communication
Research Project

1

Getting Started

Research Cat Beckons You

Figure 1.0 The Japanese beckoning cat (maneki-neko) offers you good luck as you start your research project.

DOI: 10.4324/9781003214489-1

What This Book Offers: HELP!

To the beginning researcher: This book is an essential guide to help you design, carry out, and complete a research project, including its written report. Every page tries to help make the whole research process easier for you and to show how research really is, well, cool! It's interesting, powerful, and something anyone can do – and do *well*.

Help for New Researchers – This book assumes that you are new to research, so it breaks down the process into easy-to-manage chunks using (mostly) plain language. It focuses on the essential elements that you need to do a research project. Twenty years of helping actual students do actual research really informed this book. (Thanks, former students!)

Help for Writing the Research Report – New researchers are often confused by what they need to do for a research report, how to write it, and what goes in each section, so this book focuses on those essentials. Examples of a typical research report's sections provide models you can adapt to write your own research report, and a resource website provides additional models, including examples of published research using various data collection methods.

Many chapters of the book focus on the research process itself, and the all-important research report, following this common structure (Figure 1.1):

Abstract – What did you find out and how did you do it? While it's the first thing in your paper, the abstract is the last thing you write. Usually, about 250–300 words long, it sums up how the data was selected and analyzed and what the key results revealed (Chapter 10).

Introduction – Why should someone reading your report care? The start of the report introduces your research topic, explains why it's important, and summarizes main concepts and definitions (Chapter 5).

Literature Review – What do we already know? This section brings together what academic researchers and other experts have already found about your research topic, including relevant theories (Chapter 5).

Methodology – What is your overall approach and why? The methodology section explains and justifies the overall approach for your research design (Chapter 3). When determining the approach, researchers also consider the ethical consequences of their research (Chapter 4).

Hypothesis and/or Research Question – What do you predict? What question do you want to answer? A *hypothesis* is a proposed speculation, written as a statement, about

Figure 1.1 Seven parts of a research paper.

what the researcher (that's you!) thinks will happen in a relationship between two or more variables. Common in *quantitative* projects, a hypothesis is confirmed or disproved. A hypothesis is not as common in *qualitative* projects. Every research project, however, needs a research question or questions to guide the structure and management of your data collection and analysis (Chapter 6).

Method – What is your data collection technique? *Research method* means the way you collect data, but there are other things besides just *method*. What kind of data? Where did you get it? How much did you collect? This section shows you how you set up your whole data collection scheme (Chapter 7).

Results – What did you find out? This section describes what you discovered after carefully analyzing the data you collected (Chapter 8) to create results.

Discussion – What does it mean? This section explains what the findings/results might mean and how they fit in with other research findings. What's next? The conclusion, linked to the discussion section, provides some final thoughts and mentions suggestions for future researchers. The conclusion should mention the research's limitations, since no research is perfect (Chapter 9).

References – List your sources. This guide uses American Psychological Association (APA) style. Most electronic databases automatically create references in the style needed, but they usually need some editing to meet particular style requirements (Chapter 10).

Supplemental Materials – More stuff. Optional but common. Researchers often share elements of their research such as a focus group moderator's guide or a survey instrument in a supplemental materials section (Chapter 10).

More...

Helpful Textbook Resources – Easy-to-understand research studies, guides, templates, tips, and other informational sources are provided to help you with your research project.

Helpful Internet Resources – Yes, "everything's online," but it's not always easy to find. Each chapter presents some of the best online resources, including YouTube videos, guides, and research examples.

Helpful Illustrations – Some people think of "research" as kind of, well, not fun – something that only really serious people (aka "boring" people) do. Not true! Research can be interesting, useful, and easy to do if you put in the time. The cartoons in this book are intended to illustrate the research process or inject a little humor into a usually serious academic subject.

What's in It for You?

Maybe you're thinking: Why do I have to do research? Good question! At first, it might seem boring – even pointless. But learning how to do research can deliver some fantastic

Figure 1.2 Your efforts learning research come with real benefits.

benefits. It trains your mind to think critically – assess evidence, consider other possibilities, and express it, so that it makes sense. Understanding research and possessing the skills are résumé-worthy. Employers respect and pursue applicants with those abilities. Honestly, there's no downside to completing a simple research project. Just opportunities for you (Figure 1.2).

Here are some benefits of doing a research project:

Understanding Research – Whether or not you ever do anything with your academic research, from now on you'll notice research is everywhere! Research forms the basis for news media reports, laws, policies, and product development and marketing, so understanding how research happens can help you judge and understand your world better.

Job Search Leverage – Pick a research topic that relates to your career interests and you can use it when looking for a job. In an interview, you can impress a potential employer by showing knowledge and a level of interest in a career-related topic that you researched.

Résumé Builder – A research project listed on your résumé shows potential employers that you're a critical thinker who can make data-driven decisions. You don't have to put a lot on your résumé, just the research project title, a basic description, and the key findings (results) are enough to show that research is one of your academic (and career-building!) qualifications.

Résumé Skills – Employers want applicants with skills and experience, and research gives you both. You should include specific skills and experience you got from doing research, like focus group moderation or notetaking; knowledge of focus group method design protocols; analytic coding/analysis; and academic research writing.

Master's and Ph.D. Degrees – If you are thinking about a master's degree program, research experience helps prepare you for the program's research expectations and requirements. The Ph.D. dissertation is a much deeper and complex research experience training you on how to conduct research at a professional level.

Campus Research Jobs – At every level of higher education, student jobs in research are available, including lab assistant, undergraduate, and graduate assistant positions. Beyond academic research positions, most colleges and universities have a research office. When you're looking for research possibilities, start on campus.

Research Career – If you have a knack for research, go for it! Lots of industry and academic jobs require research skills or just a good working knowledge of the research process.

Conference Presentations – Presenting your research at academic or professional conferences connects you to other researchers in a community of mutual support. And if you get to present, put that on your résumé – an organization's acceptance of you as a presenter is "peer-reviewed" and sets you apart from other job-seekers who haven't had that experience.

Publication Opportunities – Newsletters, newspapers, websites, blogs, podcasts, and media outlets publish research. Even your college's student run-media could be potential outlets for your research.

Developing a Research Mindset

Many entertaining high-quality media are covering research today. Checking them out is an easy way to get comfortable with the basics of research. Good science reporting breaks down the terminology and processes, so you don't have to be an expert to figure out what's being described. Here are just a few sources:

National News Media – Most national news outlets have dedicated coverage of science news.

- The New York Times – https://www.nytimes.com/section/science
- The Wall Street Journal – https://www.wsj.com/news/science
- The Guardian – https://www.theguardian.com/science

- Science Focus (BBC) – https://www.sciencefocus.com/news/
- National Public Radio – https://www.npr.org/sections/research-news/
- National Geographic – https://www.nationalgeographic.com/science/

Science Websites – Here's a selection of websites that offer news and articles, written in easy-to-understand language, about new research and research tips:

- The British Psychological Society's Research Digest – https://digest.bps.org.uk/
- The Conversation – https://theconversation.com/us/technology
- Discover – https://www.discovermagazine.com/
- EurekaAlert! – https://www.eurekalert.org/
- Futurity – https://www.futurity.org/
- Live Science – www.livescience.com
- Medical News Today – https://www.medicalnewstoday.com/
- Nature – https://www.nature.com/
- National Geographic – https://www.nationalgeographic.com/science/
- PNAS (Proceedings from the National Academy of Sciences) – https://www.pnas.org
- Science Alert – https://www.sciencealert.com/
- Science News – https://www.sciencenews.org/
- Science Daily – https://www.ScienceDaily.com
- Science X – https://sciencex.com/news/
- Scientific American – https://www.scientificamerican.com/
- U.S. National Science Foundation – https://www.nsf.gov/
- Wired – https://www.wired.com/category/science/

Science Podcasts – Don't like to read? No problem. There are many entertaining and informative science-related podcasts (Figure 1.3).

- BrainStuff – https://www.iheart.com/podcast/brainstuff-20922291/
- Curiosity – https://www.curiositydaily.com/
- Discovery (BBC) – https://www.bbc.co.uk/programmes/p002w557/episodes/downloads
- Hidden Brain – https://www.npr.org/series/423302056/hidden-brain
- The Naked Scientists – https://www.thenakedscientists.com/podcasts/naked-scientists-podcast

Figure 1.3 Hidden Brain podcast provides a fascinating look at social science research today.

- Nature Podcast – https://www.nature.com/nature/articles?type=nature-podcast
- Ologies – https://www.alieward.com/ologies
- Overheard (National Geographic) – https://www.nationalgeographic.com/podcasts/overheard/
- Radiolab – https://www.wnycstudios.org/podcasts/radiolab
- Science Friday – https://www.sciencefriday.com/
- The Science Show – https://www.abc.net.au/radionational/programs/scienceshow/
- Science VS – https://gimletmedia.com/shows/science-vs
- Science Weekly (The Guardian) – https://www.theguardian.com/science/series/science
- Scientific American, 60-Second Science – https://www.scientificamerican.com/podcasts/
- The Skeptics' Guide to the Universe – https://www.theskepticsguide.org/podcasts
- The Story Collider – https://www.storycollider.org/podcasts/
- Talk Nerdy – https://www.carasantamaria.com

Science Blogs – Here are some popular science blogs:

- Everyday Research Methods Blog – https://www.everydayresearchmethods.com/
- The Guardian – https://www.theguardian.com/science/series/science-blog-network
- It's Ok to be Smart – https://itsokaytobesmart.tumblr.com/
- Nautilus – http://nautil.us/blog
- PLOS Blogs Network – https://plos.org/blogs/
- Scientific American – https://blogs.scientificamerican.com/

Science YouTube Videos:

- AsapSCIENCE – https://www.youtube.com/user/AsapSCIENCE
- BrainCraft – https://www.youtube.com/user/braincraftvideo/videos
- TheBrainScoop – https://www.youtube.com/user/thebrainscoop/videos
- Earth Lab (BBC) – https://www.youtube.com/channel/UCdsOTr6SmDrxuWE7sJFrkhQ
- Gross Science (PBS) – https://www.youtube.com/user/grossscienceshow/featured
- In a Nutshell (Kurzgesagt) – https://www.youtube.com/c/inanutshell/featured
- Naked Science – https://www.youtube.com/user/PioneerProductionsUK/videos
- Nova (PBS) – https://www.youtube.com/user/NOVAonline/videos
- Opinion Science: A Psychology Podcast – https://www.ted.com/talks?topics%5B%5D=science
- Physics Girl – https://www.youtube.com/user/physicswoman
- Science Magazine – https://www.youtube.com/user/ScienceMag/videos
- Scientific American – https://www.youtube.com/user/SciAmerican/videos
- SciShow – https://www.youtube.com/channel/UCZYTClx2T1of7BRZ86-8fow

Figure 1.4 Communication can be as simple as a tin can call!

- Seeker – https://www.youtube.com/user/DNewsChannel/videos
- SmarterEveryDay – https://www.youtube.com/user/destinws2
- TED Talks (Science) – https://www.ted.com/talks?topics%5B%5D=science
- Two Minute Papers – https://www.youtube.com/user/keeroyz/videos
- Veritasium – https://www.youtube.com/user/1veritasium/videos
- Vsauce – https://www.youtube.com/user/Vsauce/videos

Developing an Academic Writing Mindset – Don't let the prospect of writing a research paper discourage you. This book's goal is to eliminate confusion about the research process and the research report. And plenty of online resources provide help with writing research papers (Figure 1.4).

- **APA Style Blog** – This blog provides good writing tips and help for writing your research paper and explains some of the trickier APA style issues: https://apastyle.apa.org/blog
- **Learn Higher – Academic Writing** – While intended as a resource for teachers, this website is helpful for students, too. The "What is Academic Writing?" is a good lesson to start with at: http://www.learnhigher.ac.uk/writing-for-university/academic-writing/
- **GradHacker** – This blog from Inside Higher Ed provides wise advice for research writing, time management, and better organizing skills: https://www.insidehighered.com/blogs/gradhacker
- **Explorations of Style** – Dr. Rachael Cayley's blog provides useful advice for academic writing. Be sure to read "Can You Write Too Early?" to motivate you to just start writing when you feel intimidated or otherwise unmotivated. Check her out at https://explorationsofstyle.com/.

- **AcademicsWrite** – Dr. Kim Mitchell's blog discusses insightful academic writing in a supportive way. Posts like "Student Peer Review Process? Here's My Version" explain how research writing is graded, and "Inspired by Trauma: The Things Our Students Write About… if You Let Them" demonstrates that selecting your research topic can be very meaningful. Her blog is at https://academicswrite.ca/.
- **Finish Your Thesis** – An ideal blog for procrastinators, since one of the common pitfalls of doing a project like this is … finishing it. Dr. Dora Farkas tackles academic writing for students. She offers great writing advice such as "Literature Review Tips: Five Steps to an Outstanding Paper" and "5 Steps to Stop Distractions from Derailing Your Theses Writing" and much more. Her blog is at https://finishyourthesis.com/blog/.
- **The Thesis Whisperer** – The Thesis Whisperer blog focuses on getting research projects completed. https://thesiswhisperer.com/
- **Writing for Research** – Dr. Patrick Dunleavy provides useful tips and good resources for improving academic writing. https://blogs.lse.ac.uk/writingforresearch/
- **Ph.D. Comics** – The funny side of research is presented by Jorge Cham. It's guaranteed to produce a smile. http://phdcomics.com/comics/archive.php?comicid=2037

Activities

Develop a Research Mindset

1. Take one of the suggested resources from this chapter and read, listen, or watch an article or episode. Be ready to discuss in class what you find out.
2. Provide the title and a web link to the resource you chose.
3. Briefly summarize the key points.
4. What did you like about the item you selected? Be specific.

Examine an Academic Research Study

Using your library databases, find a communication-related journal or do a topic search for a peer-reviewed study that interests you. You can also access the Elon Journal of

Figure 1.5 Your author likes feedback so send an email to pswann@utica.edu!

Undergraduate Research in Communications (https://www.elon.edu/u/academics/communications/journal/) to view a communication study written by an undergraduate student.

With your selected research study, read and answer the following:

1. What did the researchers want to find out?
2. How did they select the participants? How would you describe the participants' overall characteristics?
3. How did the researchers gather data? Describe this data collection process. What did the researchers find out?
4. What did the researchers conclude about their research?
5. Were there any problems (weaknesses) in the research?
6. What terms or other aspects of the study confused you?
7. Write the reference citation of the article, video or podcast in the appropriate APA style.

Connect with Me

I welcome feedback from you – good or bad! I can be reached via LinkedIn or by email at pswann@utica.edu (Figure 1.5). I'm especially interested in your suggestions for:

- Research illustrations
- Explanations of certain research concepts
- Helpful learning activities and resources

Do you have feedback to improve this book? I'd like to hear them! Feel free to contact me, Patricia Swann, at pswann@utica.edu.

2

Finding a Research Topic You Like

Figure 2.0 Don't avoid starting your research project. Procrastination, while enjoyable, is to be avoided!

DOI: 10.4324/9781003214489-2

How to Find a Research Topic

A research project's first step is picking (carefully) a *research topic* – something important *and* interesting – for you and others. And "important" doesn't mean boring! Case in point, society considers the entire entertainment industry – including sports, computer gaming, movies, TV, music – important because millions of people spend billions of dollars and lots of time to participate in it. Big money and big impact on our everyday lives. Bottom line, you need to find a good topic that's right for you – one that will help motivate you to do a great research project.

Step 1: What's Your Passion?

What do you really, *really* care about? Think about how you spend your spare time, and you're on your way to finding a research topic that inspires curiosity and makes you want to learn more about it. And since doing a research project requires bulking up on your topic by reading research articles, books, industry reports, and other sources, consider all this work an opportunity to pursue new avenues of growth for you. This kind of learning can better position you for the career you want – as a sports communication professional, nutritional communication expert in vegetarianism, or working for a nonprofit organization's communication team. You can even mix it up a bit: think about a research topic that combines *two* things you love.

To find your "passion," start identifying some things that fascinate you. (Don't think right away about your research project) (Figure 2.1).

List your favorite things. Ask yourself:

- How would I spend my time if I could do anything I wanted?
- If money didn't matter, what job would I want?
- What subject could I read about without getting bored?

List your top five dream jobs. Think big. Go beyond the entry-level job you imagine getting after graduation. If you're stuck for ideas, try the U.S. Department of Labor's CareerOneStop (https://www.careeronestop.org). A good way to determine potential jobs is to list both your talents and passions. Connecting the two could describe your ideal job or career.

- What are your passions, hobbies, and strong interests?

Figure 2.1 All aspects of music, including lyrics, can be rich sources of communication research.

- What are your true talents, skills or abilities?
- Think about what you'd like to do in 10 or 15 years.

Finally, if you don't know your passions or your dream job, answer these questions to get clues:

- What do you talk about with friends?
- How do you spend your free time?
- What shows do you stream most on TV?

Step 2: Link Your Passion Pick to Other Interests

Once you have some topics you'd like to pursue, link them to something else that interests you, such as a career interest. In Example #1, football is the passion, and the other area of interest is communication – marketing and public relations work. Social media is the main topic in Example #2, and the secondary interest is features or uses of social media

Example #1

Passion: *I love sports, especially football!*
Career Choice: *I want to be a professional communicator in marketing or public relations*

Figure 2.2 One way to find an interesting research topic is to combine your passions with your career interests.

Combine the Two: "Football and ... (communication job functions) *(Figure 2.2).*

- team website content
- podcasts
- live game broadcasts
- player/fan traditions
- advertising content
- social media content
- sports news coverage content
- NFL or team communication content
- mass media depictions (movies, TV, books, radio, etc.)
- player communication
- fan messages
- logos
- images
- gaming
- storytelling techniques

Lots of interesting communication-related topics connect with football and other sports. A research project, for example, could explore why people follow certain football players' social media posts and what they like about their social media content. A focus group could discuss fan family traditions or game day traditions, important information for sports marketing and public relations professionals trying to better connect a team with its fans.

Example #2

Career Interest: *I want to be a social media coordinator. (Social media is also a passion!)*

Who Needs it: *How is social media used within a business setting; what's new?*

Combine Two Things and Narrow Your Search: *"Social media and ...*

- small businesses
- innovations
- marketing
- advertising
- celebrities
- influencers (micro/macro)
- public relations
- activists
- stories/storytelling
- live video
- user generated content
- augmented reality

Or try this: Social media and _____ (fill in the blank…music, sports, health, etc.)

Any of these topics could be discussed in research: how small local businesses use social media to promote products, what social media innovations are useful, or why businesses follow social media influencers.

Step 3: Preliminary Research: What's Being Said About Your Topic?

Next, take your topic and start reading about it. In Example #1's "football and fan traditions," an internet search on "game day traditions" reveals what fans do on game days: eating, drinking, wearing team colors/jersey, playing games, cheering/ singing or chanting, face and body painting, tailgating, etc. A mind map is a way to visually represent your main topic and various components that relate to it. Envision a wagon wheel with spokes. Digging deeper into tailgating and food traditions could be interesting. Or it might be useful to understand why some families love to watch football. Another topic, understanding the fan experience at live games, could produce valuable intel (Figure 2.3).

Finding and Using Authoritative Sources – Your first internet searches hopefully spark interest and lead to more refined topic ideas. You'll want to learn everything you can about the topic. Like brainstorming, these first searches should collect anything and everything about the topic.

Once you settle on a topic you love, start focusing on what authoritative sources have to say – information that comes from people or institutions recognized in the field.

Authoritative means credible information based on evidence. Even information that comes from a respected source is suspect unless evidence backs it up. A source without proof is just an opinion. Credible authoritative sources use current

Mind Map

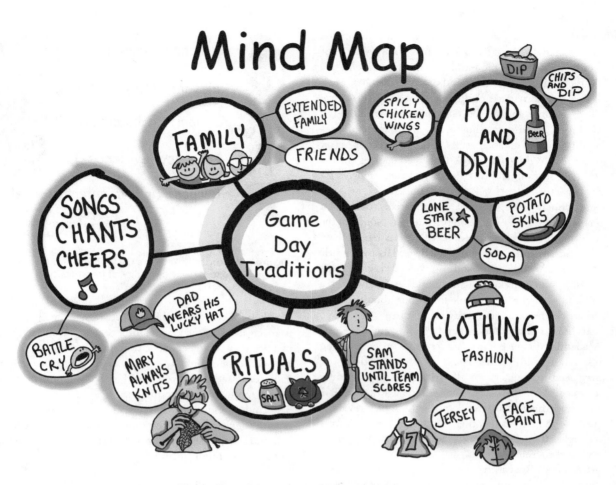

Figure 2.3 A mind map of game day traditions.

established facts, primary (original) sources, peer-reviewed scientific research, and first-person experiences based on direct observation (Evaluating Sources, 2012).

Recognized experts in a particular field represent another type of authoritative source. Experts may have awards from respected institutions that acknowledge their expertise, and their work might be cited by other experts, peer recognition. Experts often have professional experience and related educational achievements in their area. Plus, researchers whose peer-reviewed articles are approved for publication by other recognized researchers in their field have established their expertise.

Journalists use expert interviews for stories, and those published in well-respected news publications are usually safe bets. But sometimes news organizations identify with social-political agendas. The Fox News Channel, for example, is considered politically and socially conservative while the *Washington Post* is considered liberal. Some media outlets emphasize certain topics and perspectives more than others or ignore them completely.

Be sure to look at information from unfamiliar websites carefully. Anyone with the right software can create a professional-looking site. Just because a website lands at the top of a Google search doesn't mean it's authoritative. Use the website's "about" section to see who operates it and how it establishes credibility in a particular area. A number of acronym tools have been developed over the years to help students keep uppermost important evaluative methods for assessing information quality. A popular one is CRAAP (currency, relevance, authority, accuracy, and purpose) (Blakeslee, 2004). There are many others such as SIFT (stop, investigated, find, and trace) for fact checking information quality (Figure 2.4).

Business websites operating in the domain you're researching might publish useful information, such as facts and statistics. Businesses, however, are not obligated to provide information that does not benefit their competitive interests. In other words, you may get just one point of view. It's a good idea to see what competitors also say about a given topic so you get the full picture.

Quick Search Suggestions – Initial internet searches for topic sources might bring up Wikipedia, Google Scholar, ResearchGate, Academia.edu, and JSTOR. These sites and many others can power your search for interesting information. (Library database searches are discussed in Chapter 5.)

Wikipedia – Students wonder if it's okay to use Wikipedia for research. Wikipedia can be helpful if you're not familiar with your topic and/or you need terminology to aid more advanced internet and database searches. Most researchers do not use Wikipedia as a credited source. That's because anyone can post information, although Wikipedia's self-correcting peer editing process does produce mostly reliable results (Giles, 2005). It's better to go to a Wikipedia entry's footnoted sources (in the reference section) and link directly to those sources for further scrutiny.

Google Scholar – Google Scholar is a quick way to check for scholarly research available on the internet. Not all of the results will be peer reviewed. Some articles require payment for access. Don't pay to play. Instead, copy the title of the article and author and use your library website's one-stop search engine, usually WorldCat Discovery. If a full-text version is unavailable from your library, request the article through interlibrary loan for free.

ResearchGate and Academia.edu – ResearchGate and Academia.edu are popular academic social networking research repository sites. To access research articles you may need to register; not all articles are automatically downloadable. Be aware, though, that ResearchGate and Academia.edu articles do not require peer review.

JSTOR – JSTOR is another repository for academic research. It provides open access to mostly peer-reviewed content.

Open-Access Research Sites – Open-access (OA) journals are growing and they offer academic, peer-reviewed studies. They provide peer-reviewed research free to anyone. Some open access academic journals for communication include *Frontiers in Communication, American Communication Journal, Case Studies in Strategic Communication, the International Journal of Communication, PRism, and the Journal of Computer-Mediated Communication.*

Never Pay for Research! – Online searches may take you to academic journal websites operated by SAGE Publishing, Elsevier, Taylor and Francis, and many others. These publishers charge fees to access tens of thousands of journal articles that university libraries can provide free to students. You must be logged into your library system to get this free access, and don't try to get a journal article directly from the publisher's website – you'll hit a paywall. Never pay for research articles (Figure 2.5). Instead, copy the article's author name(s), date, article title, and publication name. Your campus library can get you free access to virtually any published research.

Step 4: Formulate Tentative Questions About Your Topic

Based on your topic and your readings, start to consider how you could narrow the topic. Understanding the fan experience, for instance, could be narrowed to in-person game day traditions.

Figure 2.4 Sarah Blakeslee's CRAAP Test is a good way to examine the quality of information.

One helpful tool to thinking expansively about your passion is to create a mind map or other visual diagram. A mind map visually represents your thinking. It takes a central concept and creates links to related items. With the concept of game day traditions, you could visually represent all ways people might engage in different types of activities on game day. Understanding the fan's experience is valuable to sports organizations that use communication strategies to encourage maximum enjoyment and growth of the sport. Tentative questions for fans might include:

- Can you describe what you like most about attending a game?
- Can you describe your favorite game day tradition?
- Can you explain what you like least about attending a game?
- What are your favorite memories of attending a game or watching from home?
- What could your team to do to enhance the fan experience?
- How does your family watch a game on TV?
- What are your favorite family traditions at home on game day?
- What foods are most associated with watching football?
- What team merchandise would you like as a fan?

These questions demonstrate how narrowing a topic can still give you lots to explore. More work would need to be done conducting a literature review and creating formal research questions (see Chapters 5 and 6). At this early stage, though, keep an open mind and explore possibilities. It's important your research topic really interests you.

Moving On

Your research topic should excite you. If it doesn't, stop and give yourself more time to consider ideas. Don't rush this, because your project will take a lot of time and energy. Be sure you ask your teacher for feedback. Research teachers are

Figure 2.5 A stone commandment that says never pay for research.

experienced at developing good research projects and know the challenges students run into.

Again, your topic selection is important. A well-executed research project can lead to all sorts of benefits and opportunities – in-demand career skills, research conference presentations and publishing opportunities that look great on your résumé, in-depth knowledge (about your topic) that you can brag about in a job interview, and preparation for a future graduate degree.

What if You Change Your Mind? – It can be discouraging when your topic doesn't work out because there's not a lot of research already out there to draw on, or you realize that it's not as interesting as you first thought. Or maybe you just change your mind while doing the beginning research assignments – a completely new topic idea pops into your head. Students realize they want a different topic but wonder if it's too late to change. If this happens talk with your teacher as soon as possible.

Why? Most research projects start with a demanding first assignment – creating a literature review (a written synthesis of what's already known about a topic). That's a time consuming and lengthy part of the overall research effort. As time goes on, it gets harder to switch your topic as research work and assignment deadlines loom. The earlier you commit to a research topic, the better. Don't procrastinate. Explore and read as much as possible and quickly. The sooner you dive into your topic's possibilities the sooner you will settle on a topic that's right for you (Figure 2.6).

Activities

Picking a Research Topic - Define Your Passions

Developing a research topic requires some careful consideration because you will be stuck with it for a semester or more.

1. List your true passions (sports, gaming, watching TV, music, protecting the environment, etc.)
2. List your career interests.
3. List issues in the news that catch your attention (climate change, #BlackLivesMatter, #MeToo, political elections, etc.)
4. List possible communication elements of your top three ideas.
5. What might be some questions you have about the communication related to these ideas?
6. Do a quick Google search on your top three ideas, including some type of communication with your search ("social media and police departments," for example).
7. Discuss your top three ideas and what you think might make a good research project with your classmates.

Mind Map Development

1. Visually brainstorm ideas for your topic by creating a simple mind map. Draw a circle in the center of your page. Write your topic in the circle.

Figure 2.6 Television has long been studied by communication researchers. Its effects on viewers and how TV portrays reality and certain groups of people are rich areas for researchers even today.

2. Draw additional circles orbiting your center circle. Fill those with ideas connected to the topic in the center circle. Example: The topic is gameday traditions. Orbiting circles are filled with: eating, drinking, wearing team colors/jersey, playing games, cheering/singing or chanting, face and body painting, tailgating, etc.
3. Add additional circles to further develop ideas. Example: Center circle – gameday traditions; additional connected circles – tailgating; tailgating vehicle, tailgating games, and tailgating foods.

Evaluating Information

1. Find 10 articles that relate to your research topic.
2. Use the CRAAP Test (https://library.csuchico.edu/sites/default/files/craap-test.pdf) to evaluate each article.
3. Briefly explain any potential information issues.

Analyze a Peer-Reviewed Academic Study

Pick a peer-reviewed academic study that relates to your topic. Write a short response to each of the following:

1. How was the research article structured? What were the main sections?
2. What were the hypotheses and/or research questions?
3. How did the researchers define the study's concepts?

4. Describe the sampling size and method.
5. What was measured/observed in the study?
6. What were the study's key findings (results)?
7. What were the study's limitations?

Resources

- CareerOneStop U.S. Department of Labor
  https://www.careeronestop.org/
- Developing a Research Topic, MATC Libraries
  https://www.youtube.com/watch?v=R_V1LMaD1e4
- Evaluating Sources, Western University
  https://www.youtube.com/watch?v=EyMT08mD7Ds
- How to Carry Out a Personal SWOT Analysis, Mind ToolsVideos
  https://www.youtube.com/watch?v=PBOtnyt7BP4&t=135s
- Interest Assessment, CareerOneStop U.S. Department of Labor
  https://www.careeronestop.org/toolkit/careers/interest-assessment.aspx
- Mind Mapping Your Research Topic, Hudlibrary
  https://www.youtube.com/watch?v=WW-iO-SsId0
- Skills Matcher, CareerOneStop U.S. Department of Labor
  https://www.careeronestop.org/toolkit/Skills/skills-matcher.aspx
- Work Values Matcher, CareerOneStop U.S. Department of Labor
  https://www.careeronestop.org/Toolkit/Careers/work-values-matcher.aspx

References

Blakeslee, S. (2004). The CRAAP Test. *LOEX Quarterly, 31* (3), 6–7. https://commons.emich.edu/cgi/viewcontent.cgi?article=1009&context=loexquarterly

CareerOneStop (n.d.) U.S. Department of Labor. https://www.careeronestop.org

Developing a research topic (2013, Jan.14). MATC Libraries [Video]. https://www.youtube.com/watch?v=R_V1LMaD1e4

Evaluating sources (2012, Jan. 13). Western University https://www.youtube.com/watch?v=EyMT08mD7Ds

Giles, J. (2005). Internet encyclopedias go head to head. *Nature, 438,* 900–901. https://doi.org/10.1038/438900a

How to carry out a personal SWOT analysis (2014, March 14). MindToolsVideos [Video]. https://www.youtube.com/watch?v=PBOtnyt7BP4&t=135s

Interest assessment (n.d.). CareerOneStop U.S. Department of Labor. https://www.careeronestop.org/toolkit/careers/interest-assessment.aspx

Mind mapping your research topic (2020, Jan. 16). Hudlibrary [Video]. https://www.youtube.com/watch?v=WW-iO-SsId0

Skills matcher (n.d.). CareerOneStop U.S. Department of Labor. https://www.careeronestop.org/toolkit/Skills/skills-matcher.aspx

3

Determining Your Research Approach

Figure 3.0 Like this cow, researchers should establish a philosophical point of view to guide their research.

DOI: 10.4324/9781003214489-3

Ways We Acquire Knowledge

While there are different ways to acquire knowledge, not all of them are trustworthy. Relying on old traditions or your gut feelings isn't foolproof. Most social science researchers today use a model called the scientific method to understand the world around them (Kuhn, 1962; Meyers, 2014). The scientific method uses proscribed step-by-step processes, developed over centuries, to observe things we can experience with our senses. This method stresses objectivity, critical thinking, and logic. It also encourages a healthy dose of skepticism to question and retest our efforts. This chapter examines how researchers use the scientific method using different philosophical frameworks (Figure 3.1).

Your Research Framework

New researchers eager to collect and analyze data don't always spend time explaining *why* they chose a focus group instead of a survey – or some other data collection method. But thinking about your values, beliefs, and understanding about "the way things are" and the best way to produce knowledge are both important to explaining your research framework. As a new researcher, you should determine a research position based on how you make sense of the world and what you believe produces the most legitimate knowledge. These worldviews are called paradigms (Creswell, 2007; Guba & Lincoln, 1994, 2005; Punch, 2005).

How does this work for a communication researcher? In the field of human-based communication, people are sending and receiving information constantly. Our interactions with others create messages, even if we don't do anything (e.g., silence, inaction). Since there's a lot going on – multiple factors – understanding the meaning of communication behaviors and their messages can be complicated and messy. For example, context, the setting in which communication occurs, can change the meanings of the communication behavior and message. Beyond physical setting, things like age, gender, historical events, culture, economic status, and others can also affect communication.

Figure 3.1 Ways we acquire knowledge: intuition, authority, reason, and experience.

Communication frequently involves symbolism. Gestures and facial expressions change depending on the situation. Words, icons, and abstract symbols need a shared and agreed upon meaning to be useful. In geology, a rock is a rock; it has physical characteristics that can be measured and quantified. In communication, language can be difficult to measure, beyond just counting how many times a word is written or said. Observing and analyzing can tell a whole story. Scientists know what rocks and stones are, but people who tell each other, "You rock!" or "You're stoned!" are talking about something else altogether.

What Kind of Researcher Are You?

Social science researchers often move beyond physical properties (what we can see, touch, taste, and smell) to understand meanings that people assign to communication and other complicated social interactions. How well that can be done is debatable (especially for researchers!). As researchers, our personal assumptions are important for others to understand – to know where we're coming from. Let's have a look at some examples.

Four Common Research Paradigms – A research paradigm is your worldview concerning the research process that combines ontological, epistemological, axiological, and methodological beliefs (more about these below). A paradigm includes abstract beliefs and principles to guide researchers in conducting research effectively. Four common paradigms are: *positivism*, its close cousin post-positivism, constructivism-interpretivism, and critical theory (Guba & Lincoln, 1994).

Positivists think there is a single reality, external from the researcher, which can be discovered and measured by observation and experiment, and the researcher finds and measures that one objective truth. In this paradigm, a positivist researcher purposely limits interaction with the participant to maintain objectivity. Using the principles of the scientific method, positivists take a controlled and structured approach, and their research designs are fixed and often quantitative.

Post-positivists, like positivists, use observation and experiment to understand the physical and social world. Objectivity is valued but post-positivists also think it's not possible to totally ignore one's personal biases and experiences. This paradigm version is less structured and more flexible.

On the other end of the ontological spectrum, constructionist-interpretivist paradigms hold that "reality is constructed" by people (Hansen, 2004; Ponterotto, 2005, p. 129), and multiple realities can be experienced or constructed. This flexible, less-structured approach engages research participants to understand the meaning of something. A researcher's insights and interaction with research participants are part

of knowledge-making. Constructionist-interpretivists, for example, work collaboratively and flexibly with their research designs and believe that reality is contextual.

Another approach is the critical paradigm. Like constructionist-interpretivists, the researcher acknowledges that reality depends on whom you ask. In addition, critical theorists are interested in power structures and use their research for change. Critical research includes such schools of thought as feminism and neo-Marxism.

To arrive at the research paradigm best for you, let's examine what constitutes the real and knowable, how knowledge is produced, our values as researchers, our research frameworks, and our research methods. These issues are explored in ontology, epistemology, axiology, methodology, and method.

Step 1: Your Ontological View

What is true (or real) in the world? What is the nature of reality?

Ontology is a branch of philosophy concerned with the nature of reality – what exists (Figure 3.2).

Ontology asks what's real and knowable in the physical and social world – easy to understand when things have physical properties that provide sensory experience (see, hear, touch, taste, and smell), compared to human experiences that are perceptual and non-physical ("it seemed like she didn't understand").

A person's ontological stance in research deals with what can be researched effectively, if at all. Researchers who limit their investigations to things that exist independently from the researcher – things just lying around waiting to be observed like a sediment samples from a lake – will likely use more structured, quantitative techniques. Their approach to research

Ontology: What's Real, Knowable?

It's real. It's definitely a rock with rocky physical characteristics.

Cool! I agree it's real. (And it rocks!) I've noticed it has some unusual carvings on it too. Hmmmm....

I rock!

Rock on!

Figure 3.2 Ontology – what's real, knowable? For example, a rock.

is deductive, value-free, and generalizable. Those who think there are multiple realities depending on the context and whom you ask are likely to use more flexible, qualitative research techniques. Their approach may be more inductive, value-laden, or contextually unique.

Step 2: Your Epistemological View

How is knowledge produced and what methods can we use to create truthful knowledge?

Epistemology, another branch of philosophy, is the study of knowledge. And how we do research depends a lot on how knowledge is produced and what constitutes trustworthy knowledge (Figure 3.3).

Knowledge includes the notion of truth and confidence in our knowledge beliefs. (How do we know what we know?) Research should produce trustworthy knowledge based on reasoning, evidence and facts which are gathered through observation and experiment.

In the social sciences, the researcher's role in producing knowledge is particularly important. Some researchers maintain a neutral or objective stance in observations and experiments. There is an objective truth external to the researcher waiting to be discovered. Others think that knowledge creation is more complicated. Situation and historical context are important. The researcher's skills and insights are needed to interpret data's true meaning. Also, knowledge can be co-created with research participants to represent multiple truths.

A researcher's goal should be the production of trustworthy (truthful and accurate) knowledge.

Epistemology: How Do We Produce Knowledge?

Figure 3.3 Epistemology: How do we produce knowledge? For example, what can a rock tell us?

Figure 3.4 Axiology: What are our research ethics and values?

Step 3: Your Axiological View

What do you value as a researcher? How do your beliefs, values, and experiences affect the conduct of your research?

In research, axiology, another branch of philosophy, concerns the researcher's values and ethics when dealing with research participants. The power dynamic between a researcher and research subjects range from objective and distant, or a subjective, engaged one (Figure 3.4).

Whatever the approach, using human participants in research imposes ethical considerations such as respect for participants, informed consent, minimizing risks, beneficence, and proper researcher conduct. For example, researchers may consider the historical context of past interactions with informant groups to ensure ethical treatment of participants. Researchers who engage deeply with their research subjects should be transparent about how their experiences and perceptions can inform data collection and analysis.

Regardless of the researcher's personal values and views, researchers should protect research participants from harm and treat people with respect and dignity.

Step 4: Your Methodological View

What is the research framework or logical scheme to guide your research based on your ontological, epistemological, and axiological stances? (Figure 3.5)

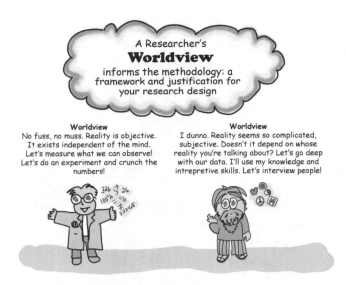

Worldview
No fuss, no muss. Reality is objective. It exists independent of the mind. Let's measure what we can observe! Let's do an experiment and crunch the numbers!

Worldview
I dunno. Reality seems so complicated, subjective. Doesn't it depend on whose reality you're talking about? Let's go deep with our data. I'll use my knowledge and intrepetive skills. Let's interview people!

Figure 3.5 Methodology: A researcher's worldview informs the methodology. This is a framework and justification for your research design.

Methodology is a framework, containing beliefs, values, processes, and procedures, that guides research strategy.

New researchers often think "methodology" means the data collection method. The two are connected – but distinctly different. Methodology is a rationale (a set of reasons) for research decisions, including justification for the research method (focus group, survey, etc.) you select. From your ontological, epistemological, and axiological assumptions, decisions about the research design become clearer. Some research strategies are comprehensive, providing guidance for research questions, sampling, data collection, and analysis procedures. Grounded theory, for example, is a complete methodology (Figure 3.6).

Step 5: Your Research Method

Which procedures can we use to acquire knowledge?

Methods are the tools for data collection. They're how researchers get their data. For example, researchers can gather information by observing or interviewing people (Figure 3.7).

The researcher's methodology (see above) guides the choice of research method. Some of the more common research methods examined in this text include observation, in-depth interview, focus group, case study, content analysis, survey, and experiment (Chapter 7).

How This Relates to Qualitative and Quantitative Research

It's worth noting that the research method selected usually determines the type of data you collect and analyze. There are two types of data: numeric and non-numeric. Quantitative data

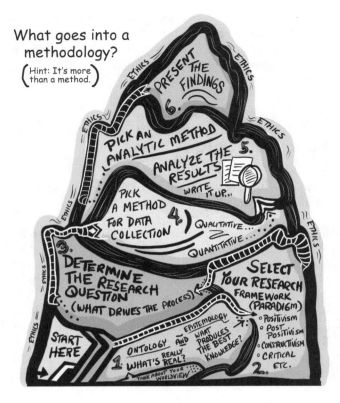

Figure 3.6 Methodology is more than a method of data collection.

is numeric data; it's all about the numbers. Researchers who collect numeric data are interested in establishing facts using measurement and quantities. Qualitative data is non-numeric. Researchers using non-numeric (textual, audio, and visual) data are interested in understanding the meaning of the data using observation and description (Sullivan & Sargeant, 2011). That doesn't mean that qualitative research is void of numbers, but the emphasis is on the qualities of the data.

Beyond the data collected, there are other characteristics associated with qualitative and quantitative research.

Method of Data Collection

Quantitative methods:
Surveys, experiments, etc.

Qualitative methods:
Observation, interviews, focus groups, case studies, etc.

Figure 3.7 Method of data collection.

Qualitative Methods:

- Acknowledge the influence of the researcher in the research process as knowledge interpreter or co-creator with participants
- Data is collected from participant observation and interviews often in naturalistic settings
- Data analysis involves pattern recognition
- Data is reported in word form

Quantitative Methods:

- Limit the influence of the researcher in data collection and analysis
- Research protocols are set before data is collected
- Data is the measurements of the phenomenon
- Data analysis relies on numerical and statistical measures
- Data is reported in numeric form

Some researchers use mixed methods, a combination of both approaches. For example, a research effort could include a focus group and an experiment.

Activities

What's Your Philosophical Research Stance?

Write a personal philosophical research statement. Explain:

1. How do you know what exists (is real)?

2. What is important in the development of legitimate, trustworthy knowledge?
3. How might your personal beliefs, values, status, and experiences affect your research?

Are You More Qualitative or Quantitative?

Based on your experience and skills:

1. Which type of research approach, qualitative or quantitative, do you feel most comfortable doing? Why?
2. What research methods interest you? Why?

Resources

- Complex Research Terminology Simplified: Paradigms, Ontology, Epistemology and Methodology
  https://www.youtube.com/watch?v=8xvpxBVCo0c
- Ontology and Epistemology, Positivism and Interpretivism
  https://www.youtube.com/watch?v=URWcOJWfSnI

References

Creswell, J. W. (2007). *Qualitative inquiry & research design: Choosing among five approaches* (2nd ed.). SAGE Publishing.

Denzin, N. K., & Lincoln, Y. S. (Eds.) (2000). *Handbook of qualitative research*. SAGE Publishing.

Gray, D. E. (2018). *Doing research in the real world*. SAGE Publishing.

Guba, E. G., & Lincoln, Y. S. (Eds.) (1989). What is this constructivist paradigm anyway? In *Fourth generation evaluation* (pp. 79–90). SAGE Publishing.

Guba, E. G., & Lincoln, Y. S. (1994). Competing paradigms in qualitative research. In N. K. Denzin, & Y. S. Lincoln (Eds.), *Handbook of qualitative research* (pp. 105–117). SAGE Publishing.

Guba, E. G., & Lincoln, Y. (Eds.) (2005). Paradigmatic controversies, contradictions & emerging confluences. In *The SAGE handbook of qualitative research* (3rd ed.) SAGE Publishing.

Hansen, J. T. (2004). Thoughts on knowing: Epistemic implications of counseling practice. *Journal of Counseling & Development*, 82, 131–138.

Kuhn, T. (1962). *The structure of scientific revolutions*. University of Chicago Press.

Meyers, R. G. (2014). *Understanding empiricism* (Ser. Understanding movements in modern thought). Routledge.

Ponterotto, J. G. (2005). Qualitative research in counseling psychology: A primer on research paradigms and philosophy of science. *Journal of Counseling Psychology*, 52(2), 126–136. doi: 10.1037/0022-0167.52.2.126.

Punch, K. (2005). *Introduction to social research: Quantitative and qualitative approaches*. SAGE Publishing.

Sullivan, G. M., & Sargeant, J. (2011). Qualities of qualitative research: Part I. *Journal of Graduate Medical Education*, 3(4), 449–452. https://doi.org/10.4300/JGME-D-11-00221.1 https://www.ncbi.nlm.nih.gov/pmc/articles/PMC3244304/

4

Thinking Ethically

Figure 4.0 It's easier than you think to cross the ethical line when doing research.

DOI: 10.4324/9781003214489-4

Ethical Research

Before starting any research project, you must understand and commit to ethical standards. Without ethics, you can get unreliable results, or worse: a project could hurt participants. First, let's take a look at ethical issues involving the researcher's role; second, we'll examine how to protect human subjects participating in research projects.

Researcher Misconduct

At every stage of research, things can go wrong, and a dishonest researcher might try to "fix things": throw out unfavorable observations, ignore important data features, misword or ask wrong questions, use biased samples, overgeneralize results, use misleading statistical procedures (such as flawed correlations and "data dredging") – even change or make up data. Researcher misconduct can be described in three ways: fabrication, falsification, and plagiarism (Figure 4.1). The U.S. department of Health and Human Services focuses on three key behaviors (Definition of Research Misconduct, n.d.; Steneck, 2007):

Fabrication – Pressure to discover exciting new findings can lead to scientific misconduct when the data recorded and/or the data findings are made up. As obvious as this may sound – don't make things up.

Falsification – Don't change the data collection process or the results of your data. This includes leaving out or distorting data to make the outcome look better or more interesting.

Plagiarism – Claiming someone else's work for your own is plagiarism. This type of dishonesty frequently happens in the literature review section when summarizing other people's research. Expressing another person's work or ideas as your own is a type of stealing. Make sure you give credit where credit is due (Figure 4.2).

While facts and common knowledge don't need to be cited ("Social media is popular today," or "Hollywood is the center of U.S. filmmaking"), uniquely expressed information should be restated in your own words, or directly quoted with an author in-text citation linked to the paper's reference section. For details on in-text citations and references see Chapter 10.

Figure 4.1 Transparency is foundational to academic research. Showing exactly how you conducted your research helps others assess the quality of your work and increase trust.

Figure 4.2 Stealing someone's ideas is "plagiarism." Always explain whose ideas, words, and expressions you're using with proper attribution.

Other Ethical Concerns for Researchers

Beyond avoiding outright misconduct, researchers must protect their work's integrity by addressing and eliminating unintentional, yet very real, ethical threats to the trustworthiness of the research.

Conflicts of Interest – A researcher's professional or personal connections to a research project can raise the possibility of a real or perceived conflict of interest. In this situation, the goals – the "interests" – of the research project and the thing it's researching are not just different, they're in "conflict."

For example, if you decide to research your karate club's communication efforts, the fact that you're a club member might be at odds with your research, particularly if your findings (results) show the club's communication is terrible and publishing that would embarrass the club. People might think you were influenced by your membership in the club. And even if you did everything right, it wouldn't look good. Solution? Research the communication of a karate club you aren't connected to.

Researchers should be transparent about their connections between competing interests and the research. Written statements describing those relationships should be included in the research report. The disclosure would spell out, for example, if a researcher's spouse works for the competing interest or the researcher owns stock in or serves on the board of the business.

Researchers who accept grants or other compensation from an organization to conduct research on behalf of the organization may feel – consciously or not – pressured to provide research results that the sponsoring organization wants. Always address this issue by declaring any personal or financial connections to the research topic up front and create safeguards to eliminate potential biases in how the research is conducted, reported, and peer reviewed (Romain, 2015). Researchers also should explain the degree of freedom given to conduct the research without interference from a competing interest.

Researcher Bias – Bias means prejudice for or against someone or something; you've already made up your mind, unfairly, before the research starts. Researchers are human,

Figure 4.3 Reflexivity is used by researchers to check their assumptions and reflect on both their past experiences, and anything else that might bear on a research effort that relies on their interpretive skills.

and bias can always be a challenge. The solution is to make the best possible choices in questions asked, sampling, data collection, and analysis. What motivates these decisions is important. Researcher bias is handled very differently by quantitative and qualitative researchers. Regardless of your approach, be up front about known and potential personal biases related to a research design and analysis. Of course, it's never acceptable to fabricate, distort or falsify information.

Research Bias and Quantitative Research – Quantitative researchers limit personal bias by guarding against their own unconscious feelings, values, or thoughts in their research. To eliminate bias, quantitative researchers often select random samples, limit interaction with subjects, ask objective questions, identify test variables before data collection, use empirically-based evidence, and, in one method, use multiple coders to cross check for consistent data collection.

Research Bias and Question Wording – Bias can show up in how research questions are worded. Loaded questions use false assumptions ("When did you last drive drunk?"), and leading questions can push those taking the survey toward a specific response ("Patriotic Americans buy U.S. produced products. What kind of vehicle do you plan to purchase?"). Bias can result in ignoring certain questions or using specific words, too. Use questions that are fair and value free (see patriotism in the example above). Beyond question wording, be sure to include questions that need to be asked. Ignoring certain questions can be a type of bias, too.

Research Bias and Qualitative Research – Qualitative researchers don't think objectivity is possible or even desirable. Instead they embrace their experiences, knowledge, and skills to interpret and/or co-create meaning with their research subjects. Qualitative research methods may emphasize a point

of view to create a framework of understanding. Still, both qualitative *and* research make claims anchored in data that comes from real experiences and/or observations.

Qualitative researchers use transparency and a process called reflexivity to maintain trustworthy results. Transparency measures are applied to each stage of research (Moravcsik, 2019). Examples of data transparency include excerpts or full transcripts from interviews or focus groups, or observation fieldnotes. Analytic transparency provides information about how the evidence was measured, interpreted, and analyzed by the researcher. And, production transparency refers to the research framework – its design, method, and theories that guided the research.

Reflexivity is a deliberate activity to situate the researcher's position relating to the research topic and recognize hidden assumptions and preconceptions based on personal experiences, values, beliefs, and attitudes (Figure 4.3). Reflexivity is used often in qualitative research and can include daily diary entries or memo writing to explore various research project elements. A researcher studying communication in a lower-income neighborhood, for example, should think about history and other factors about the neighborhood, what it means to be in a low-income neighborhood, and how the researcher's own socioeconomic background could reflect or distort the observations.

While your research approach can vary, misrepresenting data, whether intentional or not, is never acceptable. For example, let's say you are looking at a celebrity's Facebook posts. If you're a big fan of this person, you might be less willing to code a vulgar or racist comment for what it really is – vulgar or racist. Stick with the data. Research should always produce trustworthy results.

Figure 4.4 Safety always comes first in research involving people! Bubble wrap is optional.

Protecting Human Participants

Researchers assume the responsibility for developing trust-worthy information *and* protecting research participant safety, privacy, and other rights (Figure 4.4).

No human-based research data should be collected until you have approval from your college's research ethics committee. For example, if you want to do focus groups, your research proposal must undergo an ethics review before data collection begins. In the United States, higher education research project approval comes from a college or university's Institutional Review Board (IRB); IRBs are federally mandated and set standards for human research protections. Similar committees operate at educational institutions in many countries where they may be called research ethics committees or ethical review committees. Australia, for example, has the Human Research Ethics Committee (HREC).

These committees review research proposals carefully to ensure that design protocols adequately protect human subjects. Ethics committees can exempt or expedite projects that pose little risk to human subjects – such as focus groups and surveys using healthy adults – but others may require full board review, especially when vulnerable populations such as children are involved. Research classes may have blanket approval for teacher-supervised student research projects so students are free to collect data once the teacher approves the project. In all cases, work closely with your teacher to ensure that proper approvals are obtained before you interact with your research participants.

Ethical principles guiding college ethics committees are based on these key documents: the Nuremberg Code, the Declaration of Helsinki, and the Belmont Report. The U.S. government's *Belmont Report* (The Belmont Report, 1979), for example, has three key ethical principles: respect (informed consent), beneficence (maximizing benefit and minimizing risk), and justice (respect for subjects/human dignity), which it defines as follows:

- Respect – Individuals are autonomous beings and have rights to make their own decisions regarding research participation. Protecting one's innate rights is done through informed consent. Researchers should provide a statement that explains participation in research is voluntary, non-participation will not result in any harm, and the possible benefits or risks of participation.
- Beneficence – The welfare of research participants is a priority. Researchers should prevent or remove any potential harm to participants. In other words, do everything possible to protect the safety and wellbeing of your participants.
- Justice – Research benefits and risks should be fairly distributed throughout society. It {the research} should not exploit any specific group nor disproportionately advantage another.

Online Research Ethics

The internet poses unique ethical challenges about informed research consent, privacy, confidentiality, and anonymity. Researchers who use the internet as a tool to conduct research (online surveys, focus groups, ethnography, etc.) call this *internet-mediated research*. It can be reactive (a researcher gives people a survey to fill out) or nonreactive (a researcher collects data by observing online forum posts).

Technology and research practices are changing all the time. Most governments and ethics organizations can't keep up, so there is ongoing debate about ethical issues. To avoid any confusion, align your academic project with your college's ethics committee requirements. Next, "research your research" to figure out what kind of ethical protections are common, and then look for extra safeguards to protect your participants.

While governments have differing standards, areas of ethical concern are common. This section uses the U.S. Health and Human Services' Office of Human Research Protections (OHRP) Code of Federal Regulations (CFR) to examine these issues. Because technology is evolving quickly it's always a good idea to check for the latest information on internet research ethics guidance. The following are OHRP recommendations about internet research issues (OHRP):

Determining Private vs. Public Information – The internet is a vast information repository that's constantly creating new information on websites including online forums (Figure 4.5). OHRP considers a site private when users can "reasonably expect no observation or recording is taking place" {45 CFR 46.102(f)}. Public refers to activity performed in open spaces, such as speeches delivered in a park where anyone can stop by to listen. Private refers to activity performed generally in homes or invitation-only venues (Rosenberg, 2010).

Internet researchers need to be careful about collecting online data because some sites are more private than public. Check a site's policies and terms of service to see if its posts are considered private. Some information, such as medical records, are legally protected as private. Spaces that require membership registration, password, or other authorization to access are likely private, and the researcher should ask permission to collect data. Here's OHRP's general advice on private vs. public internet posts (Attachment B: Considerations and Recommendations, 2013):

> *If individuals intentionally post or otherwise provide information on the Internet, such information should be considered public unless existing law and the privacy policies and/or terms of service of the entity/entities receiving or hosting the information indicate that the information should be considered "private."*

Examples of online public behavior (texts, visuals, and audio recordings) include news site comment sections, blogs, YouTube videos, LinkedIn information, and Twitter posts.

Informed Consent for Internet Research – There's a lot of debate about informed consent (Bond et al., 2013).

That's because internet researchers can find it difficult to locate and contact individuals for informed consent because people use nicknames and/or don't respond to messages. This happens, for example, with comments posted to a news story or an online community forum. When risks to participants are low, you could get an IRB waiver. However, when research involves vulnerable populations such as minors, it will require consent.

OHRP guidance from its Common Rule says partial or total waivers may be granted when:

> *The research presents no more than minimal risk; the waiver will not adversely affect subjects' rights and welfare; the research could not practically be carried out without waiver; and, when appropriate, subjects will be provided with additional pertinent information after participation.*

Internet Surveys – Internet surveys are popular and easy to create and distribute. Ethical considerations include consent, identity verification, and comprehension. Low-risk research can include a simple check-off eligibility and comprehension statement such as "I am 18 years or older. I understand and agree," and hosting platforms such as SurveyMonkey can block repeat participants. Some online research studies include a short comprehension quiz. A website with additional information and research contact information can be established to improve understanding of the project. Riskier research should include more efforts to confirm eligibility criteria, comprehension, and gain necessary proper documentation.

Big Data Considerations – Internet research that mines publicly available Big Data sets is growing. Current regulations state that personal information that can't be "readily" identified and associated with the information is not considered human-based research, according to OHRP. That *sounds* good, but debate centers on the terms "readily" and "associated with the information," because Big Data is vulnerable to one's

Private vs. Public

Figure 4.5 Internet researchers should figure out whether the data they want is public or private. Site policies that say user data is public are not a green light for researchers, since (let's face it) most users agree to those policies without reading them. Ethically, you should get permission from a "members-only" password-protected site before using its data – even if you're a member!.

identity being re-identified (Howe III & Elenberg, 2020). That happens when some de-identified data sets are matched to other data points that may reveal a person's identity.

Beyond privacy considerations is the issue of consent. Because OHRP does not consider de-identified big data sets as human-based research, consent is not required (Howe III & Elenberg, 2020). Individuals are usually unaware that their personal information may be used beyond the original research purpose.

Content Analysis Considerations – Content analysis, a popular research method in communication research, focuses on messages, message characteristics, or cultural artifacts (books, films, speeches, news releases, art, lyrics, social media posts, websites, etc.) that contain messages accessible for data analysis. Most content analysis projects focus on publicly available communication. While such message items are not classified as human subject research, the data is created by humans – so there are issues to consider.

In particular, online forums and social media posts require ethical consideration since people probably aren't aware that they have provided consent for their information to be tracked and analyzed (Franz et al., 2019). Most users don't read lengthy terms and conditions before clicking "I agree," so that's not really informed consent. Online forum and social media users don't realize that their one click means that they've agreed their data can be accessed by third parties, including researchers.

Beyond problems with informed consent, online posts on Facebook, Twitter, and other platforms can be traced back to an individual even after identifying details have been removed. Those genuinely posting to online public forums, such as a group devoted to living with depression, don't realize that bad actors could be deceptively participating in the conversation. Published comments may expose those wishing to remain anonymous to reputational, criminal, and/or employment risks.

In reporting and presenting your research involving social media posts, you should avoid using any individual's communication *verbatim* – word for word – unless you have permission. You can also paraphrase quotes and remove all personally identifiable information, such as names and ages.

Protecting Coders – Not only are researchers supposed to protect research participants from harm, but in content analysis research the principle investigator has an ethical obligation to consider potential harm to content coders. Coders can be exposed to harmful media content including depictions of acts of extreme violence, such as torture and murder (Figure 4.6).

Coders' viewing experience is heightened by the higher level of attention and repeated viewings needed to code accurately compared to regular viewers (Signorielli, 2009). Coders should be screened for existing psychological conditions that could be worsened by viewing extreme content, informed about the nature of the research and its potential to change their attitudes, and debriefed at all stages of data collection (before,

Figure 4.6 Even coders may need protection, especially if the content being coded is disturbing.

during, and after) by the main investigator or supervising teacher (Linz, Donnerstein, and Penrod, 1984). Discussion should cover the injustice of the acts, the criminal or socially abhorrent nature, and how they are not acceptable.

Netnography Considerations – Researchers have adopted ethnography research practices for internet observations of cultures and communities called netnography (Kozinets, 1998). Popular in marketing and social science research, this method shares characteristics with content analysis. The ethical questions are similar, too. Should a researcher inform online communities of their presence (Anne-Marie et al, 2017)? Researchers can justify their decision based on how public and low risk the site is. How should participant anonymity be protected? Researchers can de-identify participants by removing names and other identifying information and paraphrasing quotes. Anne-Marie et al. (2017) found that most netnographic research studies did not mention ethics at all.

Academic Writing Examples

Example 1

Here's an example of a researcher's request on an internet forum, posted weekly, which resulted in negative comments and pushback from forum members. Ultimately, the researcher collected data from forums whose moderators did not object to the research, and terms and conditions allowed data collection (Sugiura et al., 2017):

My name is {researcher's name}. I am a PhD student of the Web Science Doctoral Training Centre, Faculty of Health Sciences, University of Southampton. I am currently conducting a research study titled "Understanding the purchase of medicine from the Web." I have joined this forum in order to obtain information about the purchase of medicines online. I will be looking at posts that are on this forum, so some information that you supply may be used for research purposes and included within the thesis and any accompanying publications. However, no identifying data will be obtained such as usernames, age, location, etc.; only the posts. These data will only be held on secure computers for the duration of the study, after which it will be permanently destroyed. I will be collecting data for the duration of eight weeks, commencing ... date ... and finishing ... date ...

For further information on how your information will be used, how the security of your information will be maintained and your rights to access your information, or if you are unhappy for your posts to be used within this research, please contact me: {researcher's name and email address}.

Example 2

Researchers Kelly-Hedrick, Grunberg, Brochu, and Zelkowitz (2018) explained their ethical reasoning for using a YouTube video sample for a study about infertility-related videos this way (Figure 4.7):

Figure 4.7 Researchers Kelly-Hedrick, Grunberg, Brochu, and Zelkowitz (2018) developed a rationale for using a YouTube public domain video sample.

Ethical Considerations

YouTube meets the criteria for a public online database as it is free, publicly accessible without requiring registration, and has a large membership size (Alexa, 2018; Eysenback & Till, 2001). Consistent with past research Eysenback & Till, 2001; Lewis, Heath, Sornberger & Arbuthnott, 2012), our institutional ethics board deemed ethics approval unnecessary as content relevant to this study was in the public domain. YouTube was accessed without a registered account to ensure accessed videos were publicly available and had no age restrictions.

Example 3

A study of public online forums providing peer support to young people with eating disorders created this ethics statement (Kendal et al., 2017):

Ethical Considerations

Online communities for young people are recognized as a valid focus for research (Montgomery and Gottlieb-Robles, 2006), and the forum was in the public domain. However, there is also a debate on the ethical issues around using publicly accessible online discussion for research (Bond et al., 2013; Kozinets, 2010). The identities of the forum users were unknown so we were not in a position to obtain individual consent from them. Instead, the charity gave us proxy consent to access and use the posts. To enhance transparency (Driver, 2006), we advertised and explained our research on the charity's website and Twitter feed before commencing the study. We protected the privacy of the forum users by removing terms and phrases that could identify them, including the name of the charity. We obtained ethical approval for this study in March 2012 from the UK NHS National Research Ethics Service and the University of Manchester Research Ethics Committee.

Activities

Crossing the (Ethical) Line

Using your research project topic determine any potential ethical issues.

1. Discuss how a researcher's actions could cause ethical issues. Remember, ethical issues can come up in any part of the research process.
2. Explain how transparency in the research process helps keep everyone honest.

Protecting Human Participants

There is an ongoing privacy debate about using people's message content from the internet.

Explain this debate using AoIR's Internet Research Ethics 3.0 guide or other resources. The AoIR guide is available at https://aoir.org/reports/ethics3.pdf (Franzke et al., 2020)

1. What's the difference between private and public internet spaces? What features indicate when a site is private?
2. How might using the exact wording of a person's writing on the internet lead to their identification even if you disguise or remove the person's name?

Resources

- Association of Internet Research
  https://aoir.org/reports/ethics3.pdf
- The Belmont Report
  https://www.hhs.gov/ohrp/regulations-and-policy/belmont-report/index.html
- Ethics Guidelines for Internet-Mediated Research
  https://www.bps.org.uk/sites/www.bps.org
- The European Convention on Human Rights
  https://www.echr.coe.int/documents/convention_eng.pdf
- The Nuremberg Code
  https://history.nih.gov/display/history/Nuremberg+Code
- Universal Declaration of Human Rights

https://www.un.org/sites/un2.un.org/files/udhr.pdf
- U.S. Health and Human Services: Electronic Code of Federal Regulations, Title 49, Part 11 (Protection of Human Subjects)
  https://www.govinfo.gov/app/details/CFR-2003-title49-vol1/CFR-2003-title49-vol1-part11.

Videos

- Ethical Approval: None Sought
  https://www.youtube.com/watch?v=7S5Uz7P7t5Y
- Ethical Online Interview Research
  https://www.youtube.com/watch?v=tucwOUFM-fz8&t=926s
- Internet Research Ethics
  https://www.youtube.com/watch?v=bjEmUz6NE4o
- MethodSpace Interview with Trena Paulus and Jessica Lester; Doing Qualitative Research in a Digital World
  https://www.youtube.com/watch?v=2tz4xfdTWRI&t=14s
- Online talk: Interview with Trena Paulus and Alyssa Wise
  https://www.youtube.com/watch?v=gsmPI5yFdS0&t=5s
- Part 3 – The Belmont Report: Basic Ethical Principles and their Application
  https://www.youtube.com/watch?v=M6AKIIhoFn4

References

Alexa. 2018. Youtube.com Traffic Statistics URL: https://www.alexa.com/siteinfo/youtube.com

Anne-Marie, T., Chau, N., & Kimppa Kai, K. (2017). Ethical questions related to using netnography as research method. *The Orbit Journal*, *1*(2), 1–11. https://doi.org/10.29297/orbit.v1i2.50

Attachment B: Considerations and recommendations concerning internet research and human subjects research regulations, with revisions (2013). Office for Human Research Protections, U.S. Department of Health and Human Services. https://www.hhs.gov/ohrp/sachrp-committee/recommendations/2013-may-20-letter-attachment-b/index.html

The Belmont Report (1979). Department of Health, Education, and Welfare. U.S. Department of Health and Human Services. https://www.hhs.gov/ohrp/regulations-and-policy/belmont-report/read-the-belmont-report/index.html

Bond, C., Ahmed, O., Hind, M., & Thomas, B. (2013). The conceptual and practical ethical dilemmas of using health discussion board posts as research data. *Journal of Medical Internet Research*, *15*, e112. https://doi.org/10.2196/jmir.2435

Definition of Research Misconduct (n.d.) Office of Research Integrity. https://ori.hhs.gov/definition-research-misconduct

Driver, M. (2006). Beyond the stalemate of economics versus ethics: Corporate social responsibility and the discourse of the organizational self. *Journal of business ethics*, *66*(4), 337–356. https://doi.org/10.1007/s10551-006-0012-7

Ethics guidelines for internet-mediated research (2017). British Psychological Society https://www.bps.org.uk/sites/www.bps.org.

Eysenbach, G., & Till, J. E. (2001). Ethical issues in qualitative research on internet communities. *BMJ*, *323*(7321), 1103–1105. https://doi.org/10.1136/bmj.323.7321.1103

Franz, D., Marsh, H. E., Chen, J. I., & Teo, A. R. (2019). Using Facebook for qualitative research: A brief primer. *Journal of Medical Internet Research*, *21*(8), e13544. doi: https://doi.org/10.2196/13544.

Franzke, A. S., Bechmann, A., Zimmer, M., & Ess, C. M. and the Association of Internet Researchers (2020). Internet research: Ethical guidelines 3.0. Association of Internet Researchers https://aoir.org/reports/ethics3.pdf

Howe, E. G. III, & Elenberg, F. (2020). Ethical challenges posed by big data. *Innovations in Clinical Neuroscience*, *17*(10–12), 24–30. https://www.ncbi.nlm.nih.gov/pmc/articles/PMC7819582/

Kelly-Hedrick, M., Grunberg, P. H., Brochu, F., & Zelkowitz, P. (2018). "It's totally okay to be sad, but never lose hope": content analysis of infertility-related videos on YouTube in relation to viewer preferences. *Journal of medical Internet research*, *20*(5), e10199. https://doi.org/10.2196/10199

Kendal, S., Kirk, S., Elvey, R., Catchpole, R., & Pryjmachuk, S. (2017). How a moderated online discussion forum facilitates support for young people with eating disorders. *Health Expectations: An International Journal of Public Participation in Health Care and Health Policy, 20*(1), 98–111. doi: https://doi.org/10.1111/hex.12439.

Kozinets, R. (1998). On netnography: Initial reflections on consumer research investigations of cyberculture. *Advances in Consumer Research, 26*, 366–371.

Kozinets, R. (2010). *Netnography: Doing ethnographic research online.* SAGE Publishing.

Lewis, S. P., Heath, N. L., Sornberger, M. J., & Arbuthnott, A. E. (2012). Helpful or harmful? An examination of viewers' responses to nonsuicidal self-injury videos on YouTube. *Journal of Adolescent Health, 51*(4), 380–385.

Linz, D., Donnerstein, E., & Penrod, S. (1984). The effects of multiple exposures to filmed violence against women. *Journal of Communication, 34*(3), 130–147.

Montgomery, K., & Gottlieb-Robles, B. (2006). Youth as e-citizens: The internet's contribution to civic engagement. In D. Buckingham, & R. Willett (Eds.), *Digital generations: Children, young people, and new media* (pp. 131–148). Lawrence Erlbaum Associates Publishers.

Moravcsik, A. (2019). Transparency in qualitative research. SAGE Research Methods, https://www.princeton.edu/~amoravcs/library/Transparencyin QualitativeResearch.pdf

The Nuremberg Code (1947). From Trials of War Criminals before the Nuremberg Military Tribunals under Control Council Law No. 10. Nuremberg, October 1946–April 1949. Washington, D.C. https://www.fhi360.org/sites/all/libraries/webpages/fhi-retc2/Resources/nuremburg_code.pdf

Romain, P. L. (2015). Conflicts of interest in research: Looking out for number one means keeping the primary interest front and center. *Current Reviews in Musculoskeletal Medicine, 8*(2), 122–127.

Rosenberg, A. (2010). Virtual world research ethics and the private-public distinction. *International Journal of Internet Research Ethics, 3*(12), 23–36. http://ijire.net/issue_3.1/3_rosenberg.pdf

Signorielli, N. (2009). Research ethics in content analysis. In A.B. Jordan, D. Kunkel, J. Manganello, & M. Fishbein (Eds.), *Media messages and public health: A decisions approach to content analysis* (88–96). New York, NY: Routledge.

Steneck, N. H. (2007). ORI introduction to the responsible conduct of research, U.S. Department of Health and Human Services. https://ori.hhs.gov/ori-introduction-responsible-conduct-research

Sugiura, L., Wiles, R., & Pope, C. (2017). Ethical challenges in online research: Public/private perceptions. *Research Ethics, 13*(3–4), 184–199. doi: https://doi.org/10.1177/1747016116650720.

Universal Declaration of Human Rights (1948). United Nations. https://www.un.org/sites/un2.un.org/files/udhr.pdf

5

Writing a Literature Review

Figure 5.0 Research librarians are there for you as you gain research skills.

DOI: 10.4324/9781003214489-5

Literature Review's Purpose

Once you choose a topic and a research question about it, the next step is the literature review, "a systematic and thorough search of all types of published literature in order to identify as many items as possible that are relevant to a particular topic" (Gash & Gash, 2000, p. 1). Already existing research studies, published and often available in library databases, are called "secondary research." This is different from "primary research." A researcher may decide that existing (secondary) research doesn't provide the needed information. To solve the problem, a researcher creates a research design and collects and analyzes new data. Essentially, primary research is new research containing fresh data insights (Figures 5.1 and 5.2).

A literature review provides readers with the current knowledge on a particular research topic based on what academic researchers and other experts have published on it. The secondary research and other existing data information are synthesized (combined and summarized) into a logical narrative (Henning, 2011). A good literature review presents a solid overview of the most authoritative, evidenced-based thinking, and it can also explain the topic's historical evolution, including controversies and competing theories.

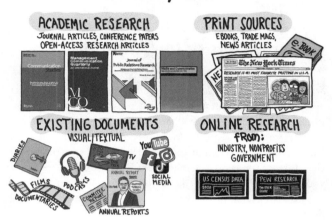

Figure 5.1 Existing sources contains primary data that has already been recorded, analyzed, or interpreted by someone else.

The literature review challenges many first-time researchers because it's time intensive and sometimes frustrating. However, if you have a topic that interests you, it's much easier (see Chapter 2). That interest and passion will inspire you

Figure 5.2 Primary data is generated by a researcher. It can be data directly observed, experienced, or recorded close to an event/source.

to learn more about the subject, easing the task of putting it all together. A well-done literature review will confirm that your research topic is worthy of further investigation.

This chapter is divided into five sections:

- Getting Ready to Commit
- Organizing It
- Finding Sources
- Judging Sources
- Writing It

Getting Ready to Commit

Stop and evaluate your topic now. If you skipped the last chapter and don't have a tentative research topic and question that interest you, take a look at Chapter 2, *Picking a Research Topic*, to help you find a topic that lines up with your interests. Remember, your research topic and question are still tentative. It's not too late to change. Ask: Do you really care about your topic? Will the topic keep you interested for a semester or two? An exciting topic will fuel you through the ups and downs of research.

Is Your Topic Doable and Worthwhile? – Assuming you have selected an interesting topic, determine if your proposed study is *doable* and *worthwhile*.

Doable should be easy to figure out: Do you have the time to do the project? Research takes time. A *lot* of time. To complete a study on time, most researchers limit the proposed research scope. After all, you can't research everything, and a research question helps set boundaries.

Judging a project's worthiness centers on the topic's importance. To put it another way, "Who cares?" Some researchers say any new knowledge is reason enough to do research, but new researchers should pick something that's not only personally interesting but significant, too. And, your project should meet class requirements. A marketing research class, for example, might require that projects focus on some marketing issue such as consumer behaviors related to loyalty programs or leisure time activities.

The question, "How do college students spend their spare time?" is better than, "What do college students do?" Narrowing the scope from *everything* college students do to just their "spare time" sounds more doable. Not only is it one population, *college students*, it's just one part of their daily activities, *spare time*.

A researcher might find that college students watch things on YouTube and Netflix, hang out with friends, and listen to music during their free time. Or a study might find college students don't *have* a lot of spare time because their schedules are filled by classes, study, work, and sleep. Either way, this research provides useful insights into a valuable resource – time. Other research questions could determine how leisure time affects health and the way people feel about ourselves.

Research on college students' spare time sounds not only doable but certainly worthwhile, and probably important to lots of academic folks. An interesting and worthwhile topic has probably been researched before, and it makes a literature review easier if there's plenty of published research to synthesize.

Rethinking Under-Researched Topics – Some research topics may appear undoable at first glance. Under-researched topics are more challenging when conducting a literature review. Sometimes it's not the topic, but its scope. Let's say you're interested in how college water polo players spend their spare time. It's possible that no research has been done on water polo players' spare time.

Very narrow database queries may yield no peer-reviewed studies about water polo players. So, broaden your scope. Consider other aspects of your topic rather than a specific population. In this case, the key component is "free time" (or leisure time). Search databases for leisure AND adults, or leisure AND athletes. It's more likely leisure time research studies exist when tied to broader populations – adults or college athletes.

Leisure as a concept has features that might be useful to include in a literature review. Look for scholarly articles about: 1) leisure trends; 2) leisure activity types; 3) Time spent in leisure pursuits; 4) the benefits of leisure and work-life balance; and 5) the history of leisure.

Emphasizing the broader concept of leisure time rather than just water polo players should provide enough articles for a literature review. And, since you have identified a research "gap" – no college water polo leisure time studies – your research will help fill that gap. Way to go!

Organizing It: A Literature Review's Structure

A literature review is a big part of a college research paper. Take the time to do it right. A simple outline can organize your work and guide your database searching:

- Introducing the topic, concepts, and key terms
- Establishing the topic's importance (impact on society, history, current trends)
- Selecting peer-reviewed studies and theories
- Identifying areas of agreement, disagreement, and gaps about the topic

Breaking down a literature review into sections with headings helps create a cohesive look at a topic. It also more manageable. Continuing the example of leisure, here are some suggestions:

Introduction – Start with definitions of key concepts, such as leisure. Since leisure means different things to different people, there's probably more than one definition. Find definitions in past research studies and use them or modify them as needed.

Importance – After you have defined leisure, explain its importance today. This section should justify the need to examine the phenomenon. How big is the industry? Offer examples of what we mean by leisure today. Include statistics about the size, economic impact, and time people devote to leisure activity. What does it involve? What are the current trends? How do people value it? Are there cultural differences? How does leisure affect wellbeing and self-worth? Next, discuss how the concept of leisure has changed over time, especially key events/people or ideas. It wasn't that long ago that leisure was something for just the very rich.

Peer-Reviewed Studies – The body of your literature review should contain relevant research studies and theories about leisure as they relate to your research question. Include scholarly books if available.

The "Writing It" section of this chapter will cover how to incorporate multiple sources into a compact and integrated whole. Keep in mind that summarizing isn't enough, you need to synthesize research studies. Synthesizing means concisely combining similar things together into a logical whole. If you have three studies that found college athletes enjoy watching televised sports and playing sports-oriented computer games then they could be combined (synthesized) into a compact statement with in-text citations linked to the three studies. A helpful synthesizing tool, a literature review matrix, is provided in the Resources at the end of this chapter.

Theoretical Framework – As you synthesize peer-reviewed articles, include a theory or theories related to your topic. Theory offers valuable explanations and predictions about *phenomena* (observable facts or events). A theory explains and predicts how things work. A relevant theory for your topic can do two important things: 1) Guide the design of a good research question, and 2) Provide a theoretical framework, a "lens" for your work.

A theoretical framework is "a structure that guides research… constructed by using an established explanation of certain phenomena and relationships" (Eisenhart, 1991, p. 205). A theory (or theories) selected for your theoretical framework should reflect your thinking about how your phenomenon functions in the real world. For example, media uses and gratification theory (Blumler & Katz, 1974) suggests that people use the media for specific uses (such as finding shopping deals

Figure 5.3 Media uses-gratification theory explain why we use or pay attention to certain media.

or information on political candidates) and entertainment (Figure 5.3).

Select a theory that you think explains that specific phenomenon. Your research data will attempt to confirm, expand or challenge the theory.

Theoretical Counterpoints – A theory is not final proof of something, but it does have supporting evidence. And any research studies that refute the theory can be included in your literature review. A theoretical debate helps researchers remain alert for any potential outcome of their study.

Theoretical Gaps – Finally, mention any gaps in our understanding of the topic. These gaps may provide you with even better ideas for research. As noted earlier, studies about water polo players and leisure time may be a first – filling a knowledge gap.

Finding Solid Sources

As mentioned, a good literature review is important and covers a lot of ground. A complete picture of your topic from reliable sources requires certain skills, diligence, and time.

Resist the Urge to Rush – It's hard to overstate the importance of the literature review for academic research. Some first-time researchers want to do it fast so they can collect and analyze data – but remember, a literature review that's done right offers many benefits for your research design. And the old saying "Don't reinvent the wheel" is especially true in research, because research builds on other efforts – and you don't want to find yourself reinventing someone else's wheel! But published studies often contain things you can reuse or modify in your own research. Specifically, a careful scan of the existing literature can:

- Justify the topic's importance, history, and current trends
- Identify peer-reviewed studies you may have missed
- Identify theories for your research
- Identify research design options (sampling, data collection methods, and data analysis techniques)
- Identify ethical concerns
- Define key concepts and variables
- Identify existing knowledge gaps (that you might want to fill)

Authoritative Sources – Authoritative sources are trusted because they are accurate and true. Research is authoritative because it relies on evidence that produces accurate and truthful information. Sources without proof are just opinions. Credible, or believable, information includes scientific research, trained experts, primary (original) documents/sources, and first-person accounts.

Peer-reviewed research is considered the "gold standard" of evidence because of its rigorous review process. It is vetted by experts knowledgeable about the topic. Research that makes it through the peer-review process is often published in academic journals.

For this reason, rely on peer-reviewed studies for most of your literature review. Always check with your instructor, who may require a minimum number of peer-reviewed research articles for your literature review.

Beyond peer-reviewed studies there are other trustworthy informational sources. Experts, whose research, experience and/or educational credentials, are highly regarded by others in the field; news organizations whose work is subject to rigorous fact-checking, and industry, nonprofits, and governmental agencies that produce evidence-based information.

All authoritative sources have this in common: facts or other evidence. Of course, hidden agendas exist, and in an era of increasing misinformation and data manipulation make sure you assess sources carefully. More on this subject in the "Judging Source Quality" section of this chapter.

Evaluating Source Quality – There two widely used source evaluation criteria methods – CRAAP (Blakeslee, 2004) and its close relative, TRAAP. These acronyms provide handy ways to check a source's usefulness for a literature review. CRAAP criteria are currency (timeliness); relevance, authority, accuracy, and purpose. TRAPP stands for timeliness, relevance, authority, accuracy, and purpose.

Peer Review – In the research world, the most trusted information includes *peer-reviewed* articles. Research articles undergoing peer review are examined by respected experts in the field who can approve or reject research papers for publication based on a number of quality standards. Peer review is thorough – "rigorous," as academics like to say – and it's THE trusted standard for academic publishing. Peer review is "blind," which means the identity of the study's author is not revealed to reviewers (Figure 5.4).

Blind Peer Review

Figure 5.4 We (your academic peers) will read your (whoever you are) research paper and judge its worthiness for publication.

Still, just because a study is peer-reviewed doesn't mean it's perfect. Journals are run by humans and humans make mistakes – sometimes they might be biased. As Thacker and Tennant (2019) pointed out, peer review has failed to point out dubious funding sources, ghostwriting, poorly performed research, and has kept certain types of legitimate research from being published. Some of those potential problems were caught and addressed; a website called Retraction Watch reports on published peer-reviewed studies that have been called out and withdrawn for various ethical or professional failings.

Despite these problems, peer review is the best way to ensure publication of the highest quality research. And that's why you should use peer-reviewed content for your research project's literature review.

How to Find Peer-Reviewed Sources – Accepted peer-reviewed research appears in research journals. Your literature review should include many peer-reviewed research articles. Use your library's academic databases and "peer review" filter to select only peer-reviewed articles. This will weed out popular publications such as newspapers, magazines, blogs, and books that don't undergo academic peer review.

Here's another way: Check the first few pages of an academic publication to see if it lists editorial board members with doctoral degrees who work for academic institutions or other well-respected organizations. Next, look at the articles. They should resemble the organization of your own research project – title, abstract, introduction, literature review, method, results (findings), discussion, conclusion, and references. If a publication has an editorial review board with articles

constructed in the scholarly mode, the content is likely peer-reviewed.

Journal Terminology Confusion – Don't let the term "journal" confuse you. Just because a publication has "journal" in its title doesn't mean it's scholarly or contains peer-reviewed content. *The Wall Street Journal* is not a scholarly publication. It's a newspaper, and its articles aren't peer reviewed. "Journal" articles that don't look like research articles should be checked.

Free Access Scholarly Journals – The *open science movement* – intended to free research from for-profit publishers – is growing rapidly. It's not perfect; critics say some not-so-great work gets published this way. You can check a journal's rank (see Research Journal Rankings above) to determine its overall quality. Your library's electronic database searches include open-access research publications and will filter for peer-reviewed journal articles. You can also do internet search "open-access journals" plus a specific domain field to see what's available (open-access journals – marketing) (Figure 5.5).

CORE: Open Access Scholarly Data Aggregator – CORE (https://core.ac.uk/) claims to be the "world's largest collection of open access research papers," which may or may not be peer-reviewed. It's easy to access and use; just type search terms into its search bar. It provides tools for discovering related articles and data management.

Google Scholar – Google Scholar's repository includes peer-reviewed and non-peer-reviewed research. If your college has the Google Scholar database then its articles are free. If

Figure 5.5 "Unlocking" published research gives you all kinds of help for research project design. Peer-reviewed studies provide theory and conceptual definitions, study protocols, other literature sources – and more!

you access it from the internet, you may encounter a paywall for some articles. If that happens, copy the paper's citation and check other library databases or request it through interlibrary loan. For search tips using Google Scholar, go to: https://scholar.google.com/intl/en/scholar/help.html.

Other Online Repositories – While not peer-reviewed, primary (original) texts such as diaries, photographs, videos, interview transcripts, handwritten lyrics, advertisements, and emails, are valuable sources for researchers. Online repositories, archives, or special collections can provide treasure troves of interesting items. Reputable repositories offer primary documents or other scholarly materials. Many museums, libraries, and government agencies provide online access to primary documents. It's always worth doing an internet search for online or digital archives related to your topic. Some examples include:

- National Archive for Data on Arts & Culture – https://www.icpsr.umich.edu/web/pages/NADAC/index.html
- Public Library of Science (PLOS) – https://pubmed.ncbi.nlm.nih.gov/
- National Library of Medicine's PubMed – https://pubmed.ncbi.nlm.nih.gov/
- The Library of Congress' catalog – https://catalog.loc.gov/
- The National Archives – https://www.archives.gov/research/catalog
- The Living Room Candidate – http://www.livingroomcandidate.org/
- GovInfo – https://www.govinfo.gov/

Internet Archive – This archive deserves attention because of its diverse and accessible collections of primary materials. Of particular interest is its Wayback Machine archive of 475 billion web pages (About the Internet Archive, n.d.) It also offers free access to books, audio recordings, videos, images and software programs. Here are links to its archives:

- Internet Archive's main search bar – https://archive.org/
- Wayback Machine (web pages) – https://archive.org/web/
- eBook and Texts – https://archive.org/details/texts
- Open Library – https://openlibrary.org/
- Audio Archive – https://archive.org/details/audio
- Software Collection – https://archive.org/details/software
- Internet Arcade – https://archive.org/details/internetarcade
- Moving Images Collection – https://archive.org/details/movies
- Internet Archive TV News (including 9/11 terrorists attacks) – https://archive.org/details/tv
- Image – https://archive.org/details/image

Books – While printed books and eBooks are not considered peer-reviewed, many are considered authoritative. Books published by university presses and other respected academic publishers or trade publishers are subjected to some kind of editorial review. Seminal works by scholars within academic disciplines are frequently referenced in scholarly works. Look for books written by scholars with a strong peer-reviewed

publication record. An extensive bibliography and/or footnotes usually demonstrates that a publication has been thoroughly researched.

Academic Conference Papers – Academic conferences present research papers, often selected through a rigorous peer-review process. These big meetings give researchers an opportunity to present their work for feedback. Researchers then revise and submit their research to a journal for yet another peer review and, hopefully, publication. Access to conference papers may require membership in conference-related organizations, but some papers can be found free online. Ask your instructor if conference papers are acceptable for your research project.

Dissertations and Theses – Library databases such as ProQuest Dissertations & Theses Global database are additional sources of academic research produced by master's and doctoral students. Ask your instructor if these sources are acceptable for your research project.

Research Librarians are Your Secret Weapons! – If someone offered free help so you could succeed, would you say yes? There's a powerful (almost magical!) free resource that can help you create a successful literature review.

It's actually a person, or persons. Reference librarians can track down academic resources; it's what they do – what they studied in school! They are experts in finding stuff; they know the library's databases backward and forward. And you'll need an expert, because each database has unique features that a less experienced user might not know about.

Reference librarians can suggest the best databases for your topic, help you submit interlibrary loan requests for items outside your library, and – most important – help refine your search results. Databases require words and phrases to get started. Search terms may flood you with results or leave you high and dry. Finding the right search terms that give you useful results is challenging. Specific database tools, filters and limiters, can narrow searches and produce better quality results. But what words, phrases, and terms will work best? This text offers several approaches, but asking a reference librarian for help by phone, chat, email, or face-to-face by appointment is always an option. Many libraries have great website research resources, too. Connect with a reference librarian so no stone is left unturned when you're looking for literature review articles.

Academic Databases – You can locate authoritative information quickly and free of charge using your library's databases. It's important to directly log into your college's library's databases rather than going to the database's commercial website, which will charge download fees. Never pay for research; if you find something that's unavailable from your library, copy the citation details and request an interlibrary loan, which is generally easy, fast, and always free for students.

If your database search turns up abstracts of articles but not the full text, try another database. Always search multiple databases when building your literature review. If no full-text article is available, request a copy through interlibrary loan, usually by filling out a form on the college library website. It's easy and fast; most college libraries will email you links to PDF file copies of the requested articles within days.

WorldCat's Global Network – Start your database search with WorldCat. This database networks your college's library holdings to about 7,000 other libraries and institutions, connecting to you 57 million content records! (Inside WorldCat, n.d.) It provides access to research articles, books, music, videos, audiobooks, historical documents and photos, and some specialized reference databases. WorldCat items outside your library's holdings can be requested through interlibrary loan.

Use Multiple Databases – It's always a good idea to check multiple databases. Some colleges offer more than 100 databases for informational searches. Each differs in offerings and operation. Check your library's website for database descriptions or guides. Some databases are discipline specific, but others are multidisciplinary. And, as always, check with a reference librarian for help. For example, the "Communication & Mass Media Complete" database is important for mass media research, but there are plenty of others that offer communication and mass media sources because communication research is often multidisciplinary:

- ABI/INFORM Collection (ProQuest)
- Academic Search Premier (EBSCO)
- Business Source Premier (EBSCO)
- Business Source Ultimate (EBSCO)
- Communication Abstracts (EBSCO)
- Communication & Mass Media Complete (EBSCO)
- Film & Television Literature Index (EBSCO)
- JSTOR
- LexisNexis
- Newspaper Source Plus (EBSCO)
- Project MUSE
- ProQuest
- PsycINFO (via ProQuest)
- Scopus (Elsevier)

Keyword, Phrase, and Subject Searches

Keyword Searches – Keyword searches use exact words to search information. To do a keyword search, list any word or phrase that relates to your research question. To expand your search, consult a thesaurus for synonyms, words or phrases with similar meanings. Keyword searches only use the words you provide, so synonyms can help uncover additional information that your first keyword choices might miss. Researchers who work in the realm of leisure-time activities, for example,

may use "play," "hobby," "recreation," "amusement," "R and R" (rest and relaxation), "vacation," or other terms besides "leisure."

Phrase Searches – Phrase searches link two or more keywords together with quotation marks. The phrase "public relations" in quotations will return results with that exact phrase only. Without quotation marks, the search will retrieve mostly irrelevant information since the words "public" and "relations" can be situated separately anywhere in a document.

Keyword and phrase search tips:

- Make a list of words and phrases that describe your research concepts. Use synonyms.
- Keep phrases together with quotation marks
- Abbreviations and full words do matter – try both.
- Figures and dates can be numbers or words – try both.

Subject Searches – If keyword searches offer a lot of irrelevant articles, try a subject search. Subject searches use predefined terms *about* a topic whereas keyword searches use specific words you choose (Figure 5.6).

Subject searches produce highly relevant information related to your topic. To set up a subject search, select the "subject" filter option. It's often found in a pull-down menu containing other search options, (author, abstract, title, etc.) and you will need to use Library of Congress subject terms (see below).

Subject terms are found in the online catalog entry. Sometimes you may need to click on "more details" to see them. Subject terms may also be provided in the database's thesaurus. If you don't know what subject terms are best for your topic, start with a general search. Once you have an article/book relevant to your research topic, look at the subject terms in its online entry.

Figure 5.6 A thesaurus can expand your search by finding terms similar to key topic words and phrases.

Subject searches generally return fewer but more relevant items. Here are some tips:

- Start with a general search and check relevant article/book online catalog entries to see what subject terms were used.
- Subject terms can be found in the online database catalog entry or its thesaurus.
- Use SearchFAST for subject terms at https://fast.oclc.org/searchfast/.
- Use the Library of Congress for subject terms at https://id.loc.gov/authorities/subjects.html.

Search Aids

Boolean Operators for Searches – Keyword, phrase, or subject searches can be improved by using Boolean operators. Use two or more of your keywords, including synonyms for certain terms, and use one or more of the three Boolean operators – AND, OR, or NOT – to focus your search. Two to four unique or specific keywords works best (Figure 5.7). Here's how it works:

- Podcast AND promotion (to limit your search to things that involve both items)
- Podcast OR webcast (to expand your search)
- Podcast NOT videocast (to limit your search)

Always consider alternative search terms. Academic researchers may use alternate or specialized words. For example, when looking for articles about sports fans, you might see the term "spectator." The word "promotion" in the first example above (Podcast AND promotion) could have alternative keywords to consider for additional searches. Consider expanding promotion by using promotion-related terms with the Boolean operator "or." Example: podcast AND promotion OR marketing OR publicity.

Truncation, Stemming – Truncation, making something shorter, is a good way to broaden your search so you'll get results with different word endings. (Truncation is also called stemming.) It works differently from database to database, but usually you enter most of a word and finish it with one of the following symbols: *, ?, #, or !, depending on the database you're using. A research librarian can help you pick the right symbol and truncating/stemming strategy for your search term.

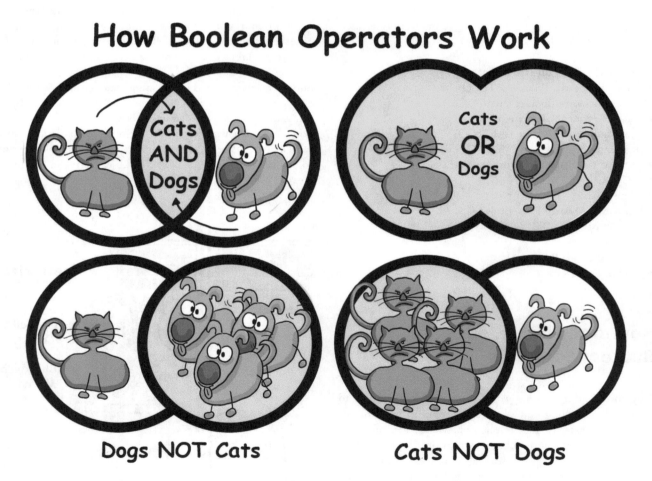

Figure 5.7 Boolean operators use the words "and," "or," "not," and "and not" to expand or limit database keyword searches.

- The asterisk is a common stemming symbol. Here are examples:
- Engag* search will give you results with engage, engaged, engaging, and engagement
- Educat* results will include educate, education, educating, and educated
- Child* will yield child, childs, children, childrens, and childhood

Don't truncate too much or you'll get things you don't want in your search. For example: stemming *com* could result in very different results such as communicate, communist, computer, commercial, comb, etc.

Parentheses – You can use parentheses to expand and prioritize your search. The search engine reads and acts on words inside parentheses first, then any info outside the parentheses. Here's an example:

(podcast OR netcast) AND promot*
(United States AND football) OR NFL

In the first example, the search results may or may not contain *podcast* or *netcast* but will contain all forms of *promot**. In the second example, all results would be items with the words *United States* and *football* together – and items with *NFL* by itself. Using *United States* AND *football* avoids lots of soccer results, since soccer is called "football" almost everywhere in the world except the USA.

Field Filters – Databases provide many ways to focus your search by using field filters.

Author Searching – Let's say you find a perfect article about your topic. Some researcher-authors spend their careers focused on a particular topic, so an author search might lead to many relevant articles. Author searches, like keyword and subject searches, are good ways to filter your results.

In addition to "author" and "subject" searching, common field filters include:

- All text
- Title
- Geographic terms
- People
- Company ticker symbol

Using Search Limiters/Filters – To keep your search manageable, consider these filters available in most databases:

- Full text
- Peer reviewed
- Publication date
- Publication/source type
- Language

Searching within a Single Publication – You can limit a search to one publication, such as a particular academic journal. Top-rated journals offer quality articles on specific topics. For example, the *Journal of Public Relations Research* is considered the premier academic journal for public relations research. Searching this publication's past issues can ensure high quality and respected public relations-related research results.

Reference List – Sometimes one good article can make all the difference. When you find one that closely matches your topic, look at its reference section for additional articles on your topic – and then check out *those* articles' reference sections for *more* relevant articles, and so on.

10 Tips for Getting Great Search Results

1. Search in more than one database.
2. Look for and use the "peer-reviewed" filter option.
3. Think of all the possible ways to express your topic, then think some more!
4. Subject searching may work better than keyword searching.
5. Use "AND" to combine keywords and phrases. Example: "social media" and "youth."
6. Use "OR" to get similar meaning words. Example: "car" or "automobile."
7. Use "NOT" when you're getting too many unusable results. Example: "mass media" not "radio."
8. Use an asterisk (*) to get all a search term's forms, like this: communicat* for results including communicate, communicated, communication, communicating, and communicator.
9. Don't be afraid to use interlibrary loan. It's fast, easy, and free.
10. Ask your research librarian for help and suggestions.

Helpful Database Management Tools – Each database has useful tools to help you search efficiently. Here are a few functions commonly available in database searches:

- **Cite** – This creates a reference citation style (e.g., APA, MLA, Chicago, etc.) for your source. While you must be careful when using these resources, they give you a nice starting place for citations.
- **Save** – Allows you to quickly save your articles into a folder for viewing later, and it usually requires an account. A folder will display your articles.
- **Sort** – Most searches default to either *relevance* or *date*; start with the *relevance* setting.

Writing It

You're halfway there if you have gathered good authoritative literature on your topic. Next, write a short and critical look at what's known about your topic – hard work but worth it!

You will better understand the topic and other researchers' approaches to it. And both of those outcomes will help you do a stronger project. As noted at the beginning of this chapter, resist the urge to rush this task. Here are helpful suggestions to make it a little easier:

Highlight/Take Notes – As you find articles, start reading them. Highlight main ideas. Multiple colors can help you keep track of themes/ideas. Or take notes on significant elements related to your topic.

Literature Review Matrix – As you take notes, use a Literature Review Matrix to organize article information for a literature review (Ingram et al., 2006). Put key information into your matrix, such as research questions, method, and results. A video about this concept is located in chapter Resources section.

Organize by Themes – "Bucket organizing" quickly brings order to chaos. Putting similar things into buckets will organize articles by common themes, the main ideas or topics that show up over and over again in articles.

Organizing by themes, rather than individual authors/works, keeps the focus on key elements (themes) of scholarly works. Within themes, conflicting ideas may show up, so make sure you present both/all sides. Combining sources by common themes is the first step in synthesizing information. It will keep you from creating small summaries of individual articles, an annotated bibliography.

Synthesize, Don't Summarize – As you write, your goal is to synthesize the information. Synthesizing is different from summarizing information. Summarizing condenses a single author's information as a recap of key points. Synthesizing means condensing and combining multiple items into a coherent whole (Figure 5.8).

A researcher synthesizes information by finding and describing the relationships between or among the sources. Often, this includes isolating commonalities (repetitions) and contradictions presented by multiple authors about a topic/research question. For instance, you may discuss how multiple authors have debated the ethics of online research. This could be organized by consent, privacy, and risk concerns. Synthesizing takes more time because you are critically evaluating what's being said about a topic and organizing those results. Structure your paragraph this way: "a main idea, evidence from multiple sources, and analysis of those multiple sources together" (Synthesizing Your Sources, n.d.).

Avoid Your Opinions – Although experts may offer opinions about a topic, the literature review is not the place for *your* opinions. Your opinion is provided at the end of the paper in the discussion section. Your literature review should contain and synthesize only findings from authoritative sources about your research topic.

Avoid Direct Quotes – Rephrasing others' information into your own words is difficult but necessary to avoid *plagiarism*,

Figure 5.8 Synthesizing is different from summarizing. Synthesizing combines information together to create a cohesive new idea.

using people's work without credit. To make this more challenging, literature reviews discourage heavy use of direct quotes, so you have to consolidate and blend multiple sources rather than separately describing each source's key information. Doing this well shows that you truly understand the information.

Paraphrasing starts with reading, rereading, and understanding. Take notes on the significant elements. Next, restate the key idea without looking at the original material. If you notice that you have reused some of the original language, use your word processor's synonym function. (Using Microsoft Word's PC version, for example, right click on a word in your document, find "synonyms" and click to get options for the word.)

Citing Sources – Even paraphrased information needs to credit the originator. There are two ways researchers acknowledge other people's work: in-text citations and references.

In-text citations are the abbreviated references that appear within your research writing. When you are directly quoting or paraphrasing material from other people's work, you must have an in-text citation. Citations refer readers to entries in your full reference section at the end of your paper. Research teachers take proper attribution of people's material seriously, and you should too.

It's not uncommon to see multiple papers and their authors referenced together in a single in-text citation. That's because when you synthesize information, you are often combining several articles that have similar conclusions or statements. Instructors will take this as a good sign that you are synthesizing, not just summarizing.

References, while not a part of the literature review, directly correspond to any in-text citation. A reference list contains the full citation of all in-text citations. This list is a standalone section at the end of your research report.

This book uses the American Psychological Association (APA) citation style; examples cited follow APA. Other frequently used citation styles are Modern Language Association (MLA) and Chicago Manual of Style (CMS). Your teacher will determine which citation style you should use.

The basic APA format for an in-text citation is: (last name, publication year), but, of course, specific rules cover multiple authors, direct quotes, missing page numbers, and no authors.

More about In-Text Citations – Many research teachers and students like the convenience of online resources. My favorite site for APA help is the well-known Purdue Online Writing Lab (OWL), https://owl.purdue.edu/owl/purdue_owl.html. It has a wealth of APA resources and examples and also provides help with basic academic writing and research. Be sure to check out their vidcasts, videos about academic writing, citation styles, and other topics.

APA has its own website resources, but most require a subscription fee. Its free resources are located in APA's frequently asked questions and blog at https://apastyle.apa.org/learn/faqs and https://blog.apastyle.org/apastyle/.

Use Transitions – Good writing requires good *transitions*, the linking words, phrases or sentences that tell the reader you are moving into new or different information. Transitions can link sentences in or between paragraphs, and they can help join sections of your paper. When you want to add information, for example, transitional words could be "additionally" and "furthermore." To show an example, use phrases such as "for example," "for instance," or "to illustrate." To move to a new section, use a phrase like "the next section will explore..."

Use Headings – A great way to organize similar material is with headings. Signal to your reader when you change topics/themes with headings. Headings organize large text segments and help readers locate information quickly. The American Psychological Association (APA) style provides guidance for using headings. Most student papers will use APA levels 1 and 2 headings but it is possible to use up to five different level headings. More general guidance is provided in Chapter 10.

How to Demystify Impenetrable Research Articles – Some academic research writing can be, well, a bit thick. Strange terminology, unfamiliar theories, complicated statistical procedures, and dense writing can mystify even academics.

So, what should you do when you have a research article that looks like it's a good fit – but the study's results section is hard to understand? Here are some suggestions:

- Read the abstract. It should contain the basic elements of the research, including its key findings (results) in plain English. But don't stop there.
- Read the introduction, discussion, and conclusion sections. The discussion section should repeat the key findings and explain what they mean. The conclusion section may also provide you more clues about the researcher's discovery.
- Just because you don't understand some of the words or the math shouldn't keep you from figuring out the article's key conclusions.

Academic Writing Examples

Example 1

Factors influencing healthy food choices in college students was the topic of Amore et al.'s (2019) focus group study (Figure 5.9). Here's the study's literature review:

College students have poor nutritional habits, with fruit and vegetable consumption below the recommended five servings a day and frequent fast food or fried food consumption (Racette et al., 2005; American College Health Association, 2016). The college environment has been termed an "obesogenic environment" due to high access to low nutrient, energy dense foods and the high-calorie environment of the university dorm (Nelson & Story, 2009). College students may not immediately realize the impact of their poor nutritional habits because college students have high energy metabolism as they reach peak lean body mass (a significant contributor to resting energy expenditure) around the time of college years (Boot et al., 2010). With high energy expenditure, calories consumed in the college years are greater than at other points in life.

Eating behaviors of college students may carry over to later life, as the college years are a critical period in habit formation (Nelson et al., 2008). For this reason, the college years are also a potential period

Figure 5.9 Amore et al.'s (2019) focus group study focused on factors influencing health food choices in college students..

of intervention. The college years present an opportunity to acquire healthy habits as students enter emerging adulthood, in which change occurs more frequently than at any other point in life (Arnett, 2007). While the college years are a potential period of intervention, recent research points to the lack of nutrition education for college students, particularly in healthy weight management (Schwartz & Richardson, 2015).

To design effective nutrition education interventions for college students, research is needed to determine the factors influencing college students' food choices. Previous research studies using focus groups have identified several determinants of eating behaviors in college students, such as taste preference, availability and accessibility of foods, cost, and other college life factors such as the characteristics of the university, student societies, and exams (Ashton et al., 2015; Deliens et al., 2014; Hartman et al., 2013 and LaCaille et al., 2011). Several of these studies have referenced the socio-ecological model, which identifies influences at the individual, social environmental, physical environmental, and macrosystem levels and is used in health promotion to better understand not only the individual but the unique environment in which he/she lives (Stokols, 1996). Previous studies examining the barriers and enablers to healthy eating in college students have been conducted in the continental US, Europe, Australia, and New Zealand, but there have been no such studies performed in Hawai'i. To address the needs of this population, the objective of this study was to identify barriers and enablers of healthy eating in college students in Hawai'i.

Example 2

Torrance et al.'s (2020) examination of gambling advertising included describing the economic significance of the gambling industry, gambling's links to public health, and an overview of its gambling advertising including content that might be misleading. Here's the literature review section:

The complexity and availability of gambling continues to grow on an international scale (Lawn et al., 2020; Winters & Smith, 2019). In recent years, there has also been a corresponding increase in the prevalence, diversity and intensity of gambling advertising (Browne et al., 2019; Newall, 2017). This expansion is facilitated by significant industry expenditure; especially within jurisdictions that have previously liberalised gambling such as the United Kingdom (UK) and Australia. Estimates indicate that Australian gambling industry spending on marketing and promotion has increased by 33% per year since 2011 to $273 million in 2018 (Gambling advertising, n.d.). UK industry spending grew over 17% per year from 2014 to 2018, reaching an estimated total of £1.5 billion (GambleAware, 2018). This advertising expenditure represents 10.34% of the £14.5 billion gross yield of the UK gambling industry in 2018 (Gambling Commission, 2016). Such funding has led to the development of sophisticated advertising campaigns that are disseminated across traditional media such as television (Håkansson & Widinghoff, 2019) and via sports sponsorship (Newell, 2017). In addition, these campaigns have resourcefully adapted to the digital sphere via online and social media marketing (Thomas, 2018; Houghton et al., 2020). This shift towards the online environment has granted gambling operators uninterrupted advertising space; especially during the Covid-19 pandemic. Therefore, attempts to curtail TV gambling advertising (as seen within the UK) during periods of lockdown may have little effect on reducing overall exposure amongst young or vulnerable audiences (Rossi et al., 2021).

Emerging literature has highlighted gambling as a compounding issue of public health (David et al., 2020; John et al., 2020). The harmful effects of gambling and associated advertising have been suggested to extend beyond populations of disordered gamblers and are apparent across the entire harm-spectrum; including children and young people (Browne et al., 2019; Clark et al., 2020; Muggleton et al., 2021). Comparable to previously conducted reviews of alcohol and tobacco (Anderson et al., 2009; Paynter & Edwards, 2009), two recently published systematic reviews (Bouguettaya et al., 2020; Newall et al., 2019) and one narrative review (Sulkunen et al., 2019) have indicated that gambling advertising is facilitative of induced gambling intentions or cravings, increased participation and riskier (more impulsive) betting. However, these reviews also identify many of the methodological gaps within the existing gambling advertising research. Within the literature there is an emphasis placed upon the self-reported effects of gambling advertising exposure, especially amongst disordered gamblers. An empirical concentration upon disordered gamblers may pathologize the issue of gambling-harm induced by advertising. This may draw attention away from advertising-induced harm experienced by low-moderate risk gamblers (Bouguettaya et al., 2020). Furthermore, the self-reported effects of gambling advertising are often hindered by recall and self-report bias. This may be due (in-part) to the Third Person Effect (Davidson, 1983; Torrance et al., 2020) in which individuals are more likely to perceive the impacts of marketing amongst others rather than themselves. In contrast, there is a paucity of research that focuses upon the specific characteristics and mechanisms that underpin emergent gambling advertisements.

There is a growing academic consensus that gambling advertising may incorporate content that is deemed misleading, utilises demographic targeting and uses embedded promotion (McGee, 2020; Roderique-Davies et al., 2020; Torrance et al., 2020). However, to date, no review has aimed to provide a taxonomy of gambling advertising characteristics. As observed in the movement towards increased control of tobacco advertising (Hastings & MacFadyen, 2000; Pollay, 1995; World Health Organization, 2013), studies that aim to investigate the specific marketing methods utilised by the industry offer an insightful contribution in the shift towards regulatory reform and industry marketing that is more ethical and transparent. Therefore, the current review of gambling advertising characteristics seeks to complement the existing reviews of advertising effect as well as the future literature. This contribution is also warranted in order to appropriately inform the decisions of policymakers and researchers regarding effective harm-reduction strategies.

Due to the fluctuating methods of gambling advertising that largely remain free from effective regulation (Hörnle et al., 2019), this review aimed to examine the empirical evidence concerning the nature and characteristics of emerging (2015–2020) gambling advertisements. Specifically, this review aimed to investigate:

- The content and narratives incorporated within gambling advertising.
- The methods of gambling advertising delivery and placement.
- The mechanics and structural features of gambling advertising, for example, design, usability and complexity.

Activities

Get to Know Your Reference Librarian

Make an individual appointment with a reference librarian. Ask about:

1. An overall strategy for using library resources
2. Databases that focus on your topic
3. How to use database search tools to help your search process
4. How to access research librarians for specific help
5. Interlibrary loan process; how does it work, how easy is it?
6. Briefly describe the results of your interaction with the librarian. What did you learn specifically that will aid you in building your literature review?

Finding Authoritative News Sources

To start your literature review, start with search terms to find news articles about your topic.

1. Using your university's library databases, locate five news articles about your research topic.
2. Use nationally known news sources such as *The New York Times, The Washington Post, The Wall Street Journal, USA Today, CNN, NBC, CBS, ABC*, etc. If you are unfamiliar with a news source, assess the information outlined in the section "Finding Solid Sources" in this chapter.
3. Keep track of your search terms. Use variations of the search terms by using a thesaurus, if necessary, to find more synonyms for your search terms. Look at how researchers use the terminology to describe your topic. Look at the research article's reference section for potential additional sources.

Using a Literature Review Matrix

- Using the literature review matrix (see a video in the Resources), find 10 peer-reviewed articles about your research topic.
- For each study, record various details such as foundational theories, conclusions, and research design approach. Include the APA citation for insertion in your document.
- Note common themes or other similarities that could be combined (synthesized) within a literature review.

Resources

- How Can You Assess if a Source is Legitimate? (The CRAAP/TRAAP Tests)
  https://libguides.anu.edu.au/c.php?g=906019&p=6594267
- Evaluating Information – Applying the CRAAP Test
  https://library.csuchico.edu/sites/default/files/craap-test.pdf
- Evaluating Sources
  https://guides.library.jhu.edu/evaluate
- The TRAPP Method: Evaluate Your Sources
  https://guides.library.jhu.edu/evaluate
- Basics of Literature Reviews
  https://academicguides.waldenu.edu/writingcenter/assignments/literaturereview
- How to Develop a Literature Review Matrix?
  https://www.youtube.com/watch?v=d5dUOnyJj68
- What is Paraphrasing?
  https://www.youtube.com/watch?v=UCjMSpr52Zk
- Research Synthesis
  https://www.youtube.com/watch?v=ObK6J7vGnw8

References

American College Health Association. *Fall 2016 group reference executive summary* (2016). National College Health Assessment II. https://www.acha.org/documents/ncha/NCHA-II_FALL_2016_REFERENCE_GROUP_EXECUTIVE_SUMMARY.pdf

Amore, L., Buchthal, O. V., & Banna, J. C. (2019). Identifying perceived barriers and enablers of healthy eating in college students in Hawai'i: A qualitative study using focus groups. *BMC Nutrition*, 5(1), 1–11.

Anderson, P., De Bruijn, A., Angus, K., Gordon, R., & Hastings, G. (2009). Impact of alcohol advertising and media exposure on adolescent alcohol use: A systematic review of longitudinal studies. *Alcohol Alcoholism*, 44(3), 229–243. doi: https://doi.org/10.1093/alcalc/agn115.

Arnett, J. J. (2007). Emerging adulthood: What is it, and what is it good for? *Child Development Perspectives*, 1(2), 68–73. doi: https://doi.org/10.1111/j.1750-8606.2007.00016.x.

Ashton, L. M., Hutchesson, M. J., Rollo, M. E., Morgan, P. J., Thompson, D. I., & Collins, C. E. (2015). Young adult males' motivators and perceived barriers towards eating healthily and being active: A qualitative study. *International Journal of Behavioral Nutrition and Physical Activity*, 12(1), 93. doi: https://doi.org/10.1186/s12966-015-0257-6.

Blakeslee, S. (2004). The CRAAP Test. *LOEX Quarterly*, 31(3), 6–7. https://commons.emich.edu/loexquarterly/vol31/iss3/4

Blumler, J. G., & Katz, E. (1974). *The uses of mass communications: Current perspectives on gratifications research*. SAGE Publishing.

Boot, A. M., de Ridder, M. A. J., van der Sluis, I. M., van Slobbe, I., Krenning, E. P., Keizer-Schrama, de Muinck, & Sabine, M. P. F. (2010). Peak bone mineral density, lean body mass and fractures. *Bone*, 46(2), 336–341. doi: https://doi.org/10.1016/j.bone.2009.10.003.

Bouguettaya, A., Lynott, D., Carter, A., Zerhouni, O., Meyer, S., Ladegaard, I., Gardner, J., & O'Brien, K. S. (2020). The relationship between gambling advertising and gambling attitudes, intentions and behaviours: A critical and meta-analytic review. *Current Opinion in Behavioral Sciences*, 31, 89–101. https://doi.org/10.1016/j.cobeha.2020.02.010

Browne, M., Hing, N., Russell, A. M., Thomas, A., & Jenkinson, R. (2019). The impact of exposure to wagering advertisements and inducements on intended and actual betting expenditure: An ecological momentary assessment study. *Journal of Behavioral Addiction*, 8(1), 146–156. doi: https://doi.org/10.1556/2006.8.2019.10.

Clark, H., Coll-Seck, A. M., Banerjee, A., Peterson, S., Dalglish, S. L., Ameratunga, S., Balabanova, D., Bhan, M. K., Bhutta, Z. A., Borrazzo, J., Claeson, M., Doherty, T., El-Jardali, F., George, A. S., Gichaga, A., Gram, L., Hipgrave, D. B., Kwamie, A., Meng, Q., & Costello, A. (2020). A future for the world's children? A WHO-UNICEF-Lancet Commission. *Lancet (London, England)*, 395(10224), 605–658. doi: https://doi.org/10.1016/S0140-6736(19)32540-1.

David, J. L., Thomas, S. L., Randle, M., & Daube, M. (2020). A public health advocacy approach for preventing and reducing gambling related harm. *Australian and New Zealand Journal of Public Health*, 44(1), 14–19. doi: https://doi.org/10.1111/1753-6405.12949.

Davison, W. P. (1983). The third-person effect in communication. *Public opinion quarterly*, 47(1), 1–15. https://doi.org/10.1086/268763

Deliens, T., Clarys, P., De Bourdeaudhuij, I., & Deforche, B. (2014). Determinants of eating behaviour in university students: A qualitative study using focus group discussions. *BMC Public Health*, 14(1), 1–22. doi: https://doi.org/10.1186/1471-2458-14-53.

Eisenhart, M. (1991). Conceptual frameworks for research circa 1991: Ideas from a cultural anthropologist; implications for mathematics education researchers (Conference proceedings). North American Chapter of the International Group for the Psychology of Mathematics Education, 1991, 202–2019. Blacksburg, VA.

GambleAware. Press Release. 2018. Gambling companies spend £1.2 billion marketing online, five times more than on television ads. https://www.begambleaware.org/sites/default/files/2020-12/2018-11-24-gambling-marketing-online-five-times-tv-ad-spend.pdf

Gambling Commission. *Industry statistics - April 2016 to March 2018*. Clifton Davies Consultancy. https://cliftondavies.com/wp-content/uploads/2019/05/GC-Gambling-industry-statistics-report-May-2019.pdf

Gash, S. (2000). *Effective literature searching for research*. Gower.

Håkansson, A., & Widinghoff, C. (2019). Television gambling advertisements: Extent and content of gambling advertisements with a focus on potential high-risk commercial messages. *Addictive Behaviors Report*, 9,100182. https://doi.org/10.1016/j.abrep.2019.100182

Hartman, H., Wadsworth, D. P., Penny, S., van Assema, P., & Page, R. (2013). Psychosocial determinants of fruit and vegetable consumption among students in a New Zealand university: Results of focus group interviews. *Appetite*, 65, 35–42. https://doi.org/10.1016/j.appet.2013.02.005

Hastings, G., & MacFadyen, L. (2000). A day in the life of an advertising man: Review of internal documents from the UK tobacco industry's principal advertising agencies. *BMJ: British Medical Journal*, *321*(7257), 366–371. doi: https://doi.org/10.1136/bmj.321.7257.366.

Henning, T. B. (2011). Literature review: Synthesizing multiple sources. Indiana University, University Writing Center. https://guides.library.jhu.edu/ld.php?content_id=16149115

Houghton, S., Moss, M., & Casey, E. (2020). Affiliate marketing of sports betting–a cause for concern? *International Gambling Studies*, *20*(2), 240–245. doi: https://doi.org/10.1080/14459795.2020.1718737.

Ingram, L., Hussey, J., Tigani, M., Hemmelgarn, M., & Huneycutt, S. (2006). *Writing a literature review and using a synthesis matrix*. NC State University Writing and Speaking Tutorial Service. https://guides.library.jhu.edu/ld.php?content_id=16149009

John, B., Holloway, K., Davies, N., May, T., Buhociu, M., Cousins, A. L., Thomas, S., & Roderique-Davies, G. (2020). Gambling harm as a global public health concern: A mixed method investigation of trends in Wales. *Frontiers in Public Health*, 8. https://doi.org/10.3389/fpubh.2020.00320

LaCaille, L. J., Dauner, K. N., Krambeer, R. J., & Pedersen, J. (2011). Psychosocial and environmental determinants of eating behaviors, physical activity, and weight change among college students: A qualitative analysis. *Journal of American College Health*, *59*(6), 531–538. doi: https://doi.org/10.1080/07448481.2010.523855.

Lawn, S., Oster, C., Riley, B., Smith, D., Baigent, M., & Rahamathulla, M. (2020). A literature review and gap analysis of emerging technologies and new trends in gambling. *International Journal of Environmental Research Public Health*, *17*(3), 744. doi: https://doi.org/10.3390/ijerph17030744.

McGee, D. (2020). On the normalisation of online sports gambling among young adult men in the UK: A public health perspective. *Public Health*, *184*, 89–94. https://doi.org/10.1016/j.puhe.2020.04.018

Muggleton, N., Parpart, P., Newall, P., Leake, D., Gathergood, J., & Stewart, N. (2021). The association between gambling and financial, social and health outcomes in big financial data. *Natural Human Behavior*, *5*(3), 319–326. doi: https://doi.org/10.1038/s41562-020-01045-w.

Nelson, M. C., & Story, M. (2009). Food environments in university dorms: 20,000 calories per dorm room and counting. *American Journal Preventive Medicine*, *36*(6), 523–526. doi: https://doi.org/10.1016/j.amepre.2009.01.030.

Nelson, M. C., Story, M., Larson, N. I., Neumark-Sztainer, D., & Lytle, L. A. (2008). Emerging adulthood and college-aged youth: An overlooked age for weight-related behavior change. *Obesity*, *16*(10), 2205–2211. doi: https://doi.org/10.1038/oby.

Newall, P. W. (2017). Behavioral complexity of British gambling advertising. *Addictive Research and Theory*, *25*(6), 505–511. doi: https://doi.org/10.1080/16066359.2017.1287901.

Newall, P. W., Moodie, C., Reith, G., Stead, M., Critchlow, N., Morgan, A., & Dobbie, F. (2019). Gambling marketing from 2014 to 2018: A literature review. *Current Addiction Reports*, *6*(2), 49–56. doi: https://doi.org/10.1007/s40429-019-00239-1.

Paynter, J., & Edwards, R. (2009). The impact of tobacco promotion at the point of sale: A systematic review. *Nicotine Tobacco Research*, *11*(1), 25–35. doi: https://doi.org/10.1093/ntr/ntn002.

Pollay, R. W. (1995). Targeting tactics in selling smoke: Youthful aspects of 20th century cigarette advertising. *Journal of Marketing Theory and Practice*, *3*(1), 1–22. doi: https://doi.org/10.1080/10696679.1995.11501675.

Racette, S. B., Deusinger, S., Strube, M. J., Highstein, G. R., & Deusinger, R. H. (2005). Weight changes, exercise, and dietary patterns during freshman and sophomore years of college. *Journal of American College Health*, *53*(6), 245–251. https://doi.org/10.3200/JACH.53.6.245-251

Roderique-Davies, G., Torrance, J., Bhairon, T., Cousins, A., & John, B. (2020). Embedded gambling promotion in football: An explorative study of cue-exposure and urge to gamble. *Journal of Gambling Studies*, *36*(3), 1013–1025. doi: https://doi.org/10.1007/s10899-020-09949-y.

Rossi, R., Nairn, A., Smith, J., & Inskip, C. (2021). Express: "Get a £10 free bet every week!"– Gambling advertising on Twitter: Volume, content, followers, engagement and regulatory compliance. *Journal of Public Policy Marketing*, *40*(4), 487–504. doi: https://doi.org/10.1177/0743915621999674.

Schwartz, J., & Richardson, C. G. (2015). Exploring the potential for internet-based interventions for treatment of overweight and obesity in college students. *Global Health Promotions*, *22*(4), 20–28. doi: https://doi.org/10.1177/1757975914547546.

Stokols, D. (1996). Translating social ecological theory into guidelines for community health promotion. *American journal of health promotion*, *10*(4), 282–298. https://doi.org/10.4278/0890-1171-10.4.282

Sulkunen, P., Babor, T. F., Cisneros Örnberg, J., Egerer, M., Hellman, M., Livingstone, C., Marionneau, V., Nikkinen, J., Orford, J., Room, R., & Rossow, I. (2019). Setting limits: Gambling, science and public policy. In *Industry strategies and their regulation: Marketing, game features, and venue characteristics*. Oxford University Press. https://doi.org/10.1093/oso/9780198817321.003.0008

Thacker, P. D., & Tennant, J. (2019, Aug. 1). Why we shouldn't take peer review as the 'gold standard.' *The Washington Post*. https://www.washingtonpost.com/outlook/why-we-shouldnt-take-peer-review-as-the-gold-standard/2019/08/01/fd90749a-b229-11e9-8949-5f36ff92706e_story.html

Torrance, J., John, B., Greville, J., O'Hanrahan, M., Davies, N., & Roderique-Davies, G. (2021). Emergent gambling advertising; A rapid review of marketing content, delivery and structural features. *BMC Public Health*, *21*(1), 1–13. https://bmcpublichealth.biomedcentral.com/articles/10.1186/s12889-021-10805-w

Walden University (n.d.). *Synthesizing your sources*. Walden University Writing Center. https://academicguides.waldenu.edu/writingcenter/assignments/literaturereview/synthesizing#s-lg-box-2873682

Winters, K. C., & Smith, N. D. (2019). Gambling expansion and its association with disordered gambling trends. In Shaffer, H. J., Blaszczynski, A., Ladouceur, R., Fong, D., & Collins, P. (Eds.), *Responsible Gambling: Primary Stakeholder Perspectives*, 85. https://doi.org/10.1093/med-psych/9780190074562.003.0004

World Health Organization (2013). *WHO report on the global tobacco epidemic 2013*. https://apps.who.int/iris/bitstream/handle/10665/85380/9789241505871_eng.pdf

Writing a Research Question and Hypothesis

Why do we dream?
Why is time so slow?
Why is the grass green?
Why do my feet stink?
When Fluffy dies where does h
Can I hav   or lunch?

Figure 6.0 A good question is at the heart of good research.

DOI: 10.4324/9781003214489-6

Research Questions and Hypotheses

Research design can be done in three ways: exploratory, descriptive, and explanatory. The first two use research questions; explanatory designs use hypotheses and research questions.

Research topics that are not well understood usually call for exploratory or descriptive research designs. Exploratory research seeks to deeply understand something; descriptive research, to describe and define it. These approaches often use observation, interview/focus group, content analysis, survey, and case study designs.

When a phenomenon is better understood, an explanatory design can test relationships between variables that might explain an important aspect about the phenomenon. The variables are usually identified from previous exploratory or descriptive research. In explanatory research, a statement (hypothesis) is used to predict what will happen between variables. The results can prove or disprove a cause/effect relationship between variables. Experimental designs are used for explanatory research (Figure 6.1).

Writing a Research Question

Because they occupy just a few lines or so, research questions often don't get a lot of attention from new student researchers. They may be short, but research questions are really important because they're the heart of your research project. Everything you do in the project is directed toward answering them.

Figure 6.1 Every research project should answer a key question and/or support of disprove a hypothesis. Research questions and hypotheses keep you focused on what matters.

A good research question will keep your research focused and manageable (Denscombe, 2014). When a chosen topic does not have a firm theoretical framework, research questions are the starting point.

Aim for 2–4 research questions for a simple, first research project. Questions should effectively narrow the scope of your research, but not so much that the project doesn't provide useful and/or interesting information.

Questions should be important enough to justify the time and expense it takes to do the research. For example, VOX-Pol, a European research group, (Berger, 2018) wanted to know: "What was the most popular website extreme alt-right Twitter users included in their posts?" The answer was YouTube, which had been criticized for algorithms that funneled some users to increasingly extreme content. A simple but important question on what alt-right followers were using to promote similar views, helped this research make an original contribution to understanding how such views were spreading.

How to Develop a Research Question – In Chapter 2 you developed your research topic and some questions about it, a starting point that informs how the research questions are formed. Questions need to be clear, specific, and include a population and a variable. Looking at research questions presented in published research about your topic can help, since you can replicate or modify research question wording using the same or a different context or population.

Elements of a Good Research Question – Your research question(s) should be:

- Focused on your research topic
- Address "how," "what," "why," "where," and/or "when"
- Easy to understand
- Interesting and important enough to justify your efforts (time and money)
- Answerable using available information
- Manageable in scope, but not too narrow
- Related to your theoretical framework
- Supportive or contradictory about theory

Research Questions in Quantitative Research – Quantitative researchers use descriptive, comparative, and explanatory questions, often with "what" or "why" as the first word, and the questions are tied to a theoretical framework. Descriptive and comparative questions can have one or more variables, although you quantify just one variable at a time. Explanatory questions contain two variables (a dependent and an independent variable) that seek to determine the relationship among the two. Questions should be specific and clearly stated.

Research Questions in Qualitative Research – In qualitative research, the researcher is interested in exploring and describing how people experience the world. Researchers use "how" and "what" questions to understand those experiences.

Questions may be somewhat broad so the topic can be broadly explored. And as researchers analyze and understand early answers, they can change questions; clarifying, expanding, or removing parts of them.

Writing a Hypothesis

A *hypothesis* is an educated guess that predicts what will happen in a relationship between variables. Often, hypotheses come from theories. A variable is something (person, place, or thing) that varies and is measurable. A hypothesis needs an independent and dependent variable. An independent variable is the cause and the dependent variable is the effect – what gets measured. A hypothesis is a statement (not a question) that can be either proven or disproven, often an "if/then this" statement. "If _____ (this happens – independent variable), then _____ (this – dependent variable) will happen" (Figure 6.2).

An example of a variable could be the appearance of the phrase "climate change" in news media coverage. The phrase "climate change" is the variable that varies by how many times it appears (from zero to XX number of times) in the news.

A hypothesis about the appearance of the phrase "climate change" could be tested between liberal and conservative news media: "Media outlets that publish mostly liberal views will use the term 'climate change' more frequently than media

Figure 6.2 Student grades are a dependent variable that can be observed and measured. Amount of time spent studying – reading the textbook, and so on – that's the independent variable to manipulate. Did a student study a lot, some, or not at all? And whose GPA is higher?

outlets that take mostly conservative positions." Another simple hypothesis might be "If an Instagram post contains a cute dog or cat photo, then it will get more likes than a post with a picture of nature without animals."

Writing a Hypothesis – A good hypothesis will have these characteristics:

• Clearly written statement, not a question
• Makes a prediction (If _____ happens, then _____ will happen.)
• Testable (proved or disproved)
• Identifies the independent and dependent variables; the independent variable is what you predict will have an effect on the dependent variable, and the dependent variable is the thing you expect to be affected.

Hypotheses in Qualitative Research – In qualitative research, there is debate about using the terms hypothesis and variable. Many publications about qualitative research design don't use those terms. Instead, some advocate using somewhat open-ended research questions and focusing on "routine processes of daily life" (Lareau, 2012, p. 672) and how those processes are situated "in a specific social context" (p. 673). Instead of an emphasis on event frequencies, these qualitative researchers "want to understand how individuals interpret and understand an event" (p. 673).

While quantitative researchers like to stick to their advance design protocols, qualitative researchers embrace a more flexible design approach that keeps the researcher open to, and free to follow, unexpected things they find out from subject interviews. This can lead to discarded and added research questions during data collection.

Still, some qualitative researchers do use hypotheses and variables. They maintain a commitment to flexible inquiry with a tentative hypothesis developed after some data is collected and a researcher deeply engages with that data. In this approach, qualitative researchers can "test" hypotheses by "refuting, proving, confirming or verifying" with available data (Chigbu, 2019, p. 18).

Placement of the Hypothesis and Research Question – A hypothesis and research question is placed at the end of your literature review.

Academic Writing Examples

Example 1

A study that examined the persuasive message design features of a Centers for Disease Control and Prevention smoking campaign (Skubisz et al., 2017, p. 16) was descriptive, with nine research questions and no hypothesis.

This project is a content analysis of the CDC's TIPS campaign, based on the aforementioned variables. The presence or absence of content variables will be used to identify which message strategies may be attributed to the success of the campaign. The following research questions will guide this project. In the TIPS campaign:

RQ1: What types of emotional appeals are present?
RQ2: Do messages communicate efficacy (self and response)?
RQ3: What types of evidence are present?
RQ4: How are the arguments communicated (one-sided or two-sided)?
RQ5: Are visual or language cues present?
RQ6: Are injunctive or descriptive norms mentioned?
RQ7: What attitude functions are communicated?
RQ8: How are the arguments framed?
RQ9: What source cues are present?

Example 2

In a study that looked at how businesses were making environmental claims about their products (e.g., general environmental benefits, composability, recycled content, ozone-friendliness, etc.) the researchers used no hypothesis, and four research questions (Carlson et al., 1993, p. 29) (Figure 6.3):

1. *What types of environmental claims are being used by firms to promote their green concern?*
2. *How frequently does each type of claim appear among environmental advertisements?*
3. *Is there a high incidence of misleading or deceptive claims among environmental ads?*
4. *Are some types of environmental claims more likely to be deemed misleading or deceptive?*

Example 3

Researchers Hassan et al. (2021) looked at beauty industry social media influencers' ("beauty gurus") overall credibility in influencing female millennials' choice of cosmetic brands. The credibility traits examined in this study included: SMI's knowledge/ expert use of cosmetic products, relatability (via characteristics of accessibility, authenticity, believability, imitability, and intimacy) and helpfulness, self-confidence, articulation, and trust factors (benevolence and integrity). Here's how they worded their hypotheses:

H1: Knowledge of the SMI has a positive effect on their followers' trust.
H2: Relatability of the SMI has a positive effect on trust.
H3: Helpfulness of the SMI has a positive effect on trust.
H4: Self-confidence of the SMI has a positive effect on trust.
H5: Articulation of the SMI has a positive effect on trust.
H6: Trust in the SMI has a positive effect on the purchase of cosmetics products.

Figure 6.3 Carlson et al. (1993) examined environmental advertising claims. One research question they asked: What types of environmental claims are being used by firms to promote their green concern?

Activities

Writing Research Questions

Develop two potential research questions for your research topic.

1. Ask questions that are important enough to research.
2. Make your questions clear, short and focused.
3. Make sure your questions can be answered with data you collect.

Writing Hypotheses

Develop two potential hypotheses for your research topic.

1. Select a theory that you want to explore in relation to your topic.
2. The hypothesis is a predicted cause-and-effect relationship. If Thing A happens, then Thing B will result; for example, if you study more, your grades will improve.

3. Identify the independent variable, the thing the researcher controls (if Thing A happens).
4. Identify the dependent variable. The dependent variable is the result of the independent variable's manipulation (Thing B will result).

Resources

- How Do I Turn a Topic into a Research Question? https://www.youtube.com/channel/UCXCfuP-6UOBQxOtzR6_N5Gw
- How to Develop a Good Research Hypothesis https://www.enago.com/academy/how-to-develop-a-good-research-hypothesis/
- Using the 5Ws to develop a research question https://www.youtube.com/channel/UCXCfuP-6UOBQxOtzR6_N5Gw

References

Berger, J. M. (2018). The alt-right Twitter census: Defining and describing the audience for alt-right content on Twitter. VOX-Pol Network of Excellence. https://www.voxpol.eu/download/vox-pol_publication/AltRightTwitterCensus.pdf

Carlson, L., Grove, S. J., & Kangun, N. (1993). A content analysis of environmental advertising claims: A matrix method approach. *Journal of Advertising*, 22(3), 27. https://www.jstor.org/stable/4188888

Chigbu, U. E. (2019). Visually hypothesizing in scientific paper writing: Confirming and refuting qualitative research hypotheses using diagrams, Publications, 7(1). doi:10.3390/publications7010022

Denscombe, M. (2014). *The good research guide: For small-scale research projects* (Series: Open up study skills). Open University Press.

Hassan, S. H., Teo, S. Z., Ramayah, T., & Al-Kumaim, N. H. (2021). The credibility of social media beauty gurus in young millennials' cosmetic product choice. *PLoS One*, *16*(3), e0249286. doi: https://doi.org/10.1371/journal.pone.0249286.

Lareau, A. (2012). Using the terms "hypothesis" and "variable" for qualitative work: A critical reflection. *Journal of Marriage and Family*, 74(4), 671–677. http://www.jstor.org/stable/41678748

Skubisz, C., Miller, A., Hinsberg, L., Kaur, S., & Miller, G. A. (2016). Tips from former smokers: a content analysis of persuasive message features. *International Quarterly of Community Health Education*, 37(1), 13–20.

7

Choosing a Research Method

Figure 7.0 A research design explains in detail how the research was carried out.

DOI: 10.4324/9781003214489-7

The Method Section

New researchers starting to form a research project think first: "I'm going to do a..." (survey, a focus group, or an experiment). This is understandable since surveys, focus groups, and experiments are well-known methods of data collection. They are superstar methods that pop up in public discussions about research. It's only natural to think of your project initially in terms of your data collection method.

Jumping to a data collection method, however, shouldn't happen until you have considered a few other things. But, you say, "I know I'm going to do a survey! What's there to consider?" Just saying you want to do a survey isn't good enough in research. The method you select needs to be appropriate for the research goal. To select the most appropriate research method(s), consider the following:

> **Your Research Paradigm** – There are different viewpoints on what produces the most trustworthy research. Chapter 3 "Determining Your Research Approach" discusses researcher paradigms, which are the beliefs and organizing frameworks that researchers use to approach their research work. A researcher should select a paradigm that fits their worldview. This research paradigm guides the research design.

A researcher who embraces a positivist paradigm believes a researcher should limit his observation to what could be objectively observed with our senses. He also would distance himself as much as possible from his personal values and limit his interaction with research subjects when conducting a study. This research view is more suited to experiments or other quantitative methods.

Other research paradigms see reality and the researcher's role quite differently. A constructivist paradigm, for example, views reality as subjective, possibly representing multiple realities. The researcher interacts with study participants and takes a central role in the data interpretation. This paradigm is more suited to qualitative research methods, such as observation and interview methods.

Your Research Goal – A research goal guides your selection of a data collection method. Your research question and/or hypothesis focuses on your research goal. Do you need to find a definitive (casual) link between variables? Or do you want to investigate something that's new or not well understood?

Exploratory and descriptive research methods are better suited for this research that explores or describes something. True experiments are best for determining cause and effect between variables. Chapter 6 "Writing a Research Question and Hypothesis" provides further guidance.

Your Research Strengths – If you are comfortable working with numbers and statistics, you might be more suited to quantitative methods, such as experiment or survey. If you like the idea of watching people's behaviors or interviewing people, then you might be better suited to qualitative methods. Qualitative researchers are good at finding meaningful patterns within observed or textual data. Often, they have good interviewing subjects.

What Data is Available? – Research projects depend on available data sources. These data sources must represent the population characteristics you are trying to study. Some types of data collection methods require as few as one to many hundreds of participants. Surveys, for example, often need above 100 responses to generate reliable information. You would need access to a large enough sample to conduct the survey. A case study, however, can be done with just one representative member of a population. This data collection approach could, for example, study just one nonprofit organization's marketing strategy for a research study.

Popular Research Methods

In mass communication research, there are seven popular research methods for data collection, which are described in this chapter:

- Observation
- In-Depth Interview
- Focus Group
- Case Study
- Content Analysis
- Survey
- Experiment

There are variations of these methods beyond what this book provides. There are also other methods of data collection and you can also use a mixed method approach. Mixed methods refers to collecting the data using two or more different research methods. For example, you could conduct a research project that used in-depth interviews and a survey.

What Goes in a Method Section?

The research report's method section includes more than a descriptive statement about the appropriateness of your data collection method. It should clearly explain the sampling and protocols established to gather your data, too. Address the following items in your method section:

Research Approach – Researchers should mention the research paradigm that guides their research approach. Popular research paradigms are positivism, post-positivism, critical theory, and constructionism.

Research Questions – Provide your key research question(s) and/or hypotheses. These should relate specifically to your topic.

Define the Key Concepts – Your research readers should know what you mean by important concepts or terms you're using. This is particularly true for deductive research. Provide well-thought-out definitions for your study's major concepts. For example, if your research topic is social media influencers you should define what "social media influencer" means in the context of your study. Seek definitions created by researchers or other experts. If you know your study's variables (things you observe and/or manipulate), provide short definitions of them.

Method – Briefly explain why your data collection method (focus group, survey, etc.) was used and why it was selected to answer your research question. Seven research methods are described in this chapter. Explain the key advantages of the method you're using over other methods.

Ethical Considerations – Let's assume all social science research involves ethical considerations for the protection of study participants and their personal data. Discuss how you protected people's right to know (informed consent), safety, privacy, and dignity. Refer to Chapter 4 "Thinking Ethically" for more information.

Procedures – Briefly describe the data collection protocol (system of rules) you followed for data collection and analysis. Your protocols ensure that the data collected and analyzed were treated uniformly and that it was clear to everyone involved what needed to be done, and in the what order. It's prudent to run your data collection protocols and any data collection instrument by someone with more experience than you for critical feedback.

Pretesting – If you used a formal way of collecting your data – such as an interview guide or a survey – these data collection "instruments" need to be tested first before they are used. This can be done with a small group that represents the characteristics of your target population. Describe how you pretested your data collection instrument and any changes you made as a result of the test.

Sampling and Sampling Options – Describe the population characteristics for your study. Explain how many people or things were included in the sample and the sampling technique used to obtain them. Probability samples rely on the random selection principle, in which each member of a population has equal chance of selection. Random sampling is valued because it accurately represents (can be generalized to) the larger population (Figure 7.1). A sampling frame containing the complete list of your population is needed for probability sampling (Figure 7.2). Frequently used probability samples are:

- **Simple Random Sampling** – Easy and popular, similar to pulling names out of a hat. Each name on a piece of paper item has an equal chance of being selected.
- **Systematic Random Sampling** – Good for selecting subjects from a list using a random starting point and using a fixed, periodic interval for selection.

Generalizability

Figure 7.1 Generalizability means that the results from random population samples are representative of the total population.

Sampling Frame

Figure 7.2 A sampling frame is a list of the entire population eligible to be included within the specific framework of a research study.

- **Stratified Random Sampling** – Useful for looking at subpopulations with shared characteristics; random selection is conducted from the subgroups.
- **Cluster Sampling** – This often is used when you want to sample large, dispersed populations. This type of sampling accommodates geographic grouping, such as, randomly selecting two cities within a geographic region to test a new advertising campaign.

Nonprobability samples are less reliable than probability samples, and that means you won't be able to generalize your findings to the total population. Still, a nonprobability sample can provide good insights into the total population. Frequently used nonprobability samples are:

- **Convenience Sampling** – Samples whatever's easily available
- **Judgmental (Purposeful) Sampling** – Good for the researcher identifying and selecting messages especially relevant to the study questions based on specific characteristics.
- **Snowball Sampling** – This method gets its name based on how a snowball grows in size as it rolls down a hill (Figure 7.3). Similarly, a researcher trying to locate hard-to-find populations (such as hard-core shoppers or players of a specific video game) a snowball sample grows as members are asked to help identify other people with similar characteristics.
- **Quota Sampling** – Good for proportionally reflecting some characteristics of an entire population. Samples are subdivided into groups that reflect certain features.

Figure 7.3 A snowball sample grows in size as individuals identify others with certain key characteristics.

OBSERVATION

Figure 7.4 Observation research is everywhere!

What Is Observational Research?

Observation researchers essentially watch or listen to participants' physical or communication behaviors and interactions. They observe how people act in certain settings. Unlike what we do when we just watch things, observation research follows certain protocols. This method can't determine what people are thinking, but it carefully records who, what, where, when, and how people are doing things (Harvey, 2018). Observation is popular in program evaluation, classroom evaluations, and in understanding user/customer experience.

Observation research's three basic choices are: controlled, naturalistic, and participant. Each technique requires recording observations, usually with field notes (Figure 7.5).

Controlled Observation – Controlled observations are carried out in artificial settings such as a lab kitchen, play area, etc. Variables are controlled.

Naturalistic Observations – Naturalistic observations are carried out where behaviors naturally occur, such as in a participant's kitchen or workplace. Informed consent is obtained unless the observation takes place in a public space. Researchers try to be unobtrusive and not interrupt behaviors. Observations can include recorded observations, again, with permission. Discreetly placed video cameras are best.

In disguised (sometimes called covert) observation people are observed without their knowledge or consent. Researchers who use disguised observation have justified its use because the observed activity is important but so socially shunned or illegal that people would rarely participate knowingly. This text does not recommend disguised observation for new researchers because of the obvious ethical and safety issues involved. If the only way to observe authentic behaviors is covertly, and the potential benefit is large and the risk is low, your college's ethics committee may permit covert observation. An opt-out option should be available to allow participants an opportunity to have their data removed from the research once they are informed of the project.

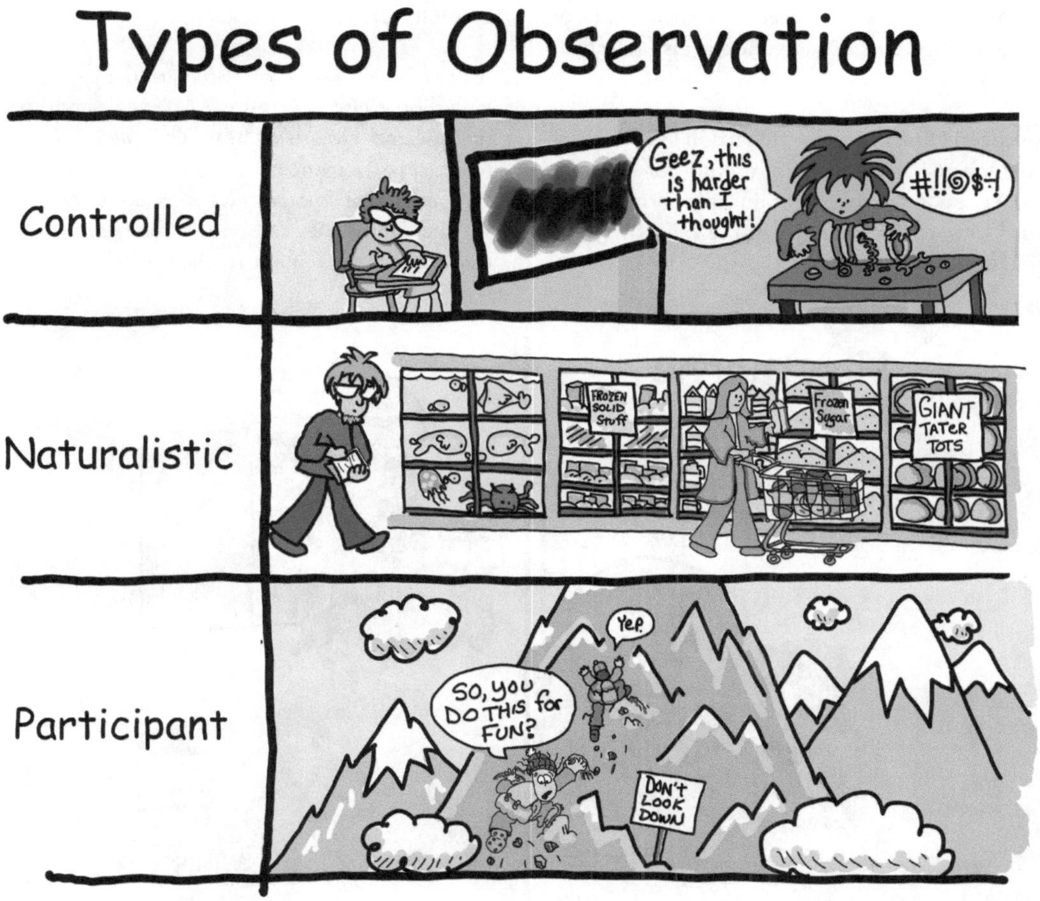

Figure 7.5 A controlled observation often happens in a lab setting where everything (the variables) is controlled. Naturalistic observation occurs in a real-world place where behaviors occur naturally. In participatory observation the researcher joins the activity with the subject.

Netnography – A new type of naturalistic observation, *netnography* focuses on the behaviors and interactions with others in social media and other online settings. Discussion groups, Facebook group pages, and other public online communities can be observed using this data collection method.

Participate (Participatory) Observation – Some researchers go beyond a silent bystander role to engage fully in the participant experience, like tagging along with those under observation when they go to the mall or a social club meeting. This method can include depth interviews, too. An immersive experience can build stronger researcher-participant relationships and insights.

Why Choose Observation?

Common in product usability testing, communication and cultural studies, observation is useful when you want to understand thoroughly how research subjects act and interact with other persons or things. It's especially helpful for sensitive topics or when self-reporting does not produce accurate information. For example, people might not remember what steps they took before buying something. And some people might not be eager to discuss their exercise routine and eating habits, for obvious reasons. Observation is also relatively easy to do.

Open vs. Structured Observation – If you don't know much about your topic, open observations are useful. For example, multiplayer gamers adopted the streaming platform Twitch early on because they could monetize game play by growing fan bases. During the height of the COVID-19 global pandemic, musicians looking for new revenue sources began to use Twitch (Sisario, 2021). Researchers could use an open structure observation to see how musicians were using Twitch, with no predetermined behaviors to observe and no structure to the field notes. Open observations are just that – open. Their flexibility can lead to important unexpected information being discovered. Open observations also accommodate research questions that form or change as observers learn more about their study's participants.

Predetermined behaviors/interactions guide *structured observation*, often using an observation guide with specific tasks or other items to record. If multiple coders are involved, each coder needs to code the same way. Consistency helps when observing and counting certain recording procedures, such as speech events. Start with a research question, or at least an idea of what sort of behaviors/interactions you want to study, and identify what tasks or activities you want to observe.

Observation's Disadvantages – Observation is not a perfect method. Access can be a problem, especially if you want to observe professional and private settings, and gathering and analyzing data takes time. Observation often requires pre-interviews followed by multiple visits to locations, plus you can't determine someone's thoughts, values, attitudes, and opinions unless they are stated.

And someone aware of observation may act differently (the Hawthorne effect) (Figure 7.6), even saying what they think the researcher wants to hear. This *subject bias* happens when a research participant tries to anticipate and then deliver whatever it is that the researcher is after. *Demand characteristics* are the subtle cues researchers may give, consciously or not, that cause a participant to change behavior to respond to the

Figure 7.6 The Hawthorne effect is a type of observer effect (reactivity) in which people change their behavior when they know they're being observed.

imagined action. Another potential pitfall, social desirability bias, occurs when a participant decides to act differently to look good according to societal standards. Researcher bias can also hinder observation research, so researchers need to be open to everything they observe and not ignore something because it doesn't match their assumptions. Confirmation bias happens when a researcher focuses on things that confirm a belief and ignore alternative information.

How to Set Up an Observation Project

- Identify a research question or a behavior/interaction you want to observe
- Complete pre-observation activities: population and location selection
- Gather observations
- Analyze your data
- Report your findings (results)

Step 1: Identify a Research Question

Identify a research question or a behavior/interaction you want to observe. Chapter 2 will help you develop a research topic and Chapter 6 helps you develop your research question.

Step 2: Complete Pre-Observation Activities and Sampling Strategy

Most observations use small samples from a few people or small groups because observation is time consuming, often involving multiple observations.

Select participants who engage in the behaviors and other characteristics you want to study. Judgmental (or purposive) sampling allows a researcher to recruit and select participants based on specific characteristics. Another useful sampling technique, snowball sampling, tasks people with desired characteristics to identify others with those characteristics. For example, video gamers could identify others who play a certain game.

Recruiting – Posters, emails, and social media posts can promote your hunt for participants who fit your profile. If a particular group, such as a student club, fits the profile, talk to its leader(s) for help.

Access – If you are doing naturalistic or participatory observation, you will need participant's permission to watch/listen to their activities in non-public spaces, such as a person's home, office, or other private space. Activities that occur in public spaces like parks, beaches, and roads do not need permission.

Informed Consent – Before you collect any data for a college or university project, get permission from your ethics committee. In the United States, a college Institutional Review Board reviews and approves research proposals. Chapter 4 discusses informed consent's ethical issues and provides a weblink to informed consent templates.

You should address confidentiality in observation research because you are describing individuals' personal characteristics and activities in detail. Remove all identifying information – anything that could identify an individual, such as locations and participant names.

Other things to consider are the time involved and intrusions into private space. Observations can be "just once" or several times. Some people may not want multiple intrusions into their personal space.

Provide just enough information in a consent form to explain the research generally. Don't get too specific, since that could influence participant's responses.

Identifying the Tasks to Observe – Of the many options for focusing a task observation, here are a few:

- Characteristics of the person performing it
- Steps to complete
- Tools to complete
- Interactions with others while completing
- Environmental effects (interruptions, problems, etc.)

A good way to think about your observation more holistically is with the AEIOU organizing framework (Hanington & Martin, 2017) (Figure 7.7). AEIOU stands for activities, environments, interactions, objects, and users. Activities are the actual tasks observed. Environments (or context) are where those tasks are performed. *Interactions* are the back-and-forth actions between people, such as employee and customer. Objects are items used in interactions, or significant elements in the environment. Users, participants, are the people doing the tasks you're watching and listening to. In addition to the specific tasks, body language can provide helpful insights.

Step 3: Conduct the Observations

Field Notes – Field notes are hand-written descriptions and reflections of what you observe. They are your study's data. You write field notes while you are at the study's location, organizing them by describing the physical setting, the social environment (how people act in a particular environment), and the participant interactions (how people interact with others). Any tasks you plan to observe (see above) should be noted. The observer should also write down anything that strikes him/her as interesting, different, important, and confusing. Directly after an observation the researcher should flesh out the notes while the memory of the experience is still fresh.

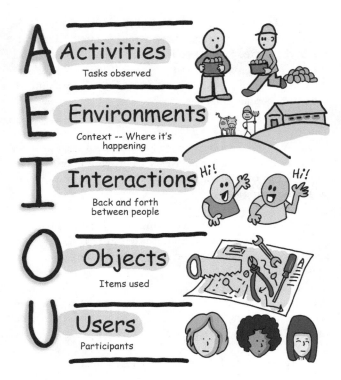

Figure 7.7 Organize your observations using Hanington and Martin's (2017) AEIOU framework: Activities, environments, interactions, objects, and users.

Recording Observations – Observations often are recorded as field notes, but video, audio, and/or photograph files are used, too. For online forum observations (see netnography below), conversations can be downloaded as cut-and-paste transcripts. Field notes are always encouraged because technology can fail. Organize the guide according to identified tasks you plan to observe.

How to be Unobtrusive – In nonparticipant observation, researchers need to be close enough to see and hear what a research participant is doing/saying but not close enough to make that person uncomfortable. Video and audio recording can help capture harder to hear/see actions, allowing you to keep your distance. Pre-interviewing participants offers a good way to ease the discomfort of dealing with a stranger and assure the participant that confidentiality will be a priority. Another way to encourage natural behaviors is to remain quiet; don't interrupt the participant's activities. Remain neutral in body language and expressions. Also, try to shield your note-taking from view, and write or keyboard quietly.

Step 4: Analyze Your Observations

Once you record observations you can analyze the data qualitatively (primarily using words) or quantitatively (mostly using numbers), or by mixing both methods. Most quantitative structured observations involve counting behaviors/interactions, similar to content analysis techniques. Qualitative observations seek patterns and meanings.

Thematic analysis techniques are common. Chapter 8 provides guidance on qualitative and quantitative analysis methods.

Step 5: Present Your Findings

Consult Chapters 9 and 11 for guidance on how to discuss and present your findings (results).

Academic Writing Examples

Example 1

Researchers (Ward et al., 2014) used nonparticipant observation to describe the proportion of park users engaging in moderate-to-vigorous physical activity (MVPA) in four cities over a three-year period.

Data were collected by using SOPARC {system for observing play and recreation in communities} in each of the 24 parks during spring, summer, and autumn seasons observing during four 1-hour intervals on 2 weekdays and 2 weekend days each season (Buehler, 2012). The hours were randomly chosen within segments of the day (morning, midday, afternoon, evening) covering daylight hours from 7 am to 8 pm. Each park was mapped and divided into discrete target areas (i.e., a predetermined observation area in which park visitors could potentially engage in physical activity) and then observed systematically by trained observers who rotated through each area using momentary time sampling (i.e., systematic and periodic scans were made of individuals and contextual factors). Target areas included outdoor facilities such as basketball courts, playing fields, picnic areas, and walkways, as well as indoor areas in recreation centers, such as gymnasiums, dance studios, and weight rooms.

Park neighborhoods were defined by a one-half-mile buffer around the park, about the distance of a typical walking trip (Yang & Diez-Roux, 2012). Because the population density of Chapel Hill is considerably lower than that of other cities, the block groups around the parks there were much larger. Only by including block groups with a centroid within four-fifths of a mile of the edge of each park was it possible to incorporate multiple block groups. Target areas in parks varied substantially in number and type, with a range of 23 to 33 areas in Chapel Hill, 17 to 30 in Albuquerque, 23 to 55 in Columbus, and 24 to 51 in Philadelphia. Target areas (N = 719) were visited a minimum of 16 times per season over 3 seasons, resulting in a total of 34,512 area visits (719 × 16 × 3) across all sites. During each visit, trained assessors first coded for the area characteristics (i.e., accessible, usable, equipped, supervised, organized) and then completed systematic scans separately for females and males according to an established protocol (Kaczynski et al., 2011). During a scan, the PA of each individual in a target area was coded as sedentary (i.e., lying down, sitting, or standing), walking, or vigorous.

Observers were trained first by studying the operational definitions, instrument notation, and coding conventions. They then practiced and received feedback on their scoring of video examples from the SOPARC training digital video disc (DVD), followed by practice during live observations in diverse park settings. Certification was conferred if an observer met an accuracy rate of greater than 90% for the number of people counted and 85% for all other categories except race/ethnicity and challenging situations (e.g., more than 5 people engaged in vigorous activity), where 80% reliability was accepted.

Example 2

The impact of mobile phones on family dining conversations was examined by researchers Kiefner-Burmeister et al. (2020). Typical of nonparticipant observation, the researchers did not actively participate with those being observed (Figure 7.8).

Using naturalistic, anonymous nonparticipant observation, 37 family meals were studied at a fast food restaurant in a large Italian city (N individuals observed = 129, see Table 1 for demographic information). The restaurant was chosen for its "family friendly" nature and its proximity to a metropolitan transit station, which afforded a large and diverse study population. Observations were performed on weekend days and weekdays in May and June. Observations were made on eight separate weekdays between 10 am and 2:30 pm, with most observations falling between the 12 pm to 1 pm lunch hour as this was the best opportunity to view families eating within the normative Italian meal schedule.

All observations were performed by a developmental psychologist specializing in child and adolescent health behaviors. Field notes were taken with pen and paper in a notebook. Most observations were made from a high-top counter in the middle of the restaurant, enabling clear observation of families within 20 feet of the examiner. During almost all observation days, the restaurant had either reached or was near seating capacity (roughly 300 patrons).

Families included any adult with a child (estimated age was pre-pubescent/0–11 years old) whose mealtime could be closely observed from beginning to end. Child and caregiver age was estimated based on height, body structure/proportion, and overall developmental status (Table 1). Following the methodology and field note structure used by (Radesky et al., 2014) family interaction during mealtimes were recorded via detailed notes regarding individuals' demographic information (including number of family members, ages, genders, and inferred relationship), eating/feeding behaviors, affect, communication behaviors, and mobile phone use.

Families to be observed were generally identified while in line to order food or while walking to a table. The crowded, large fast food restaurant was generally populated by adult groups without children. Roughly 10–20% of customer groups had a child in their family as determined from estimation performed on three random days of data collection. Families with children were therefore noticeable to the researcher and were identified immediately once the researcher had completed the last observation. The highest number of children and caregivers observed in one group was four. While no school groups were apparent, it is nevertheless possible that an unrelated group was determined to be a family. All observable groups with children were included with no exclusions made. Observations began once the family meal commenced and detailed notes were taken for at least ten minutes or until meal was completed. Start and stop times of the meal were recorded in the field notes. The average length of meals was 16 min, with two meals lasting under ten minutes (seven and nine minutes, respectively).

Figure 7.8 In example #2, a non-participant observation sought to determine the impact of mobile phones on family dining conversations (Kiefner-Burmeister, Domoff, and Radesky, 2020).

Activities

Conduct an Observation

Conduct an open observation of your college library for 30 minutes.

1. What behaviors/interactions did you see?
2. What were the contextual elements, relating to the situation, that you observed?
3. What conclusions can you draw from your experience?

Quantitative Observation

While most observation research is qualitative, it is possible to perform a more quantitative observation. Read Systematic Observation of Public Police: Applying Field Research Methods to Policy Issues, available at https://www.ojp.gov/pdffiles/172859.pdf.

1. How was systematic social observation (SSO) used in this study?
2. What did the researchers discover?

Netnography Project Ideas

Read Tenderich et al.'s (2019) study using netnography to better understand people with diabetes by observing online communities.

1. How might netnography be used for your topic? Suggest online communities you could observe.

2. What are the ethical issues involved in this method? For guidance, see Chapter 4.

Resources

- Communication Observation Methods Manual
  https://interruptions.net/literature/COM_Manual.pdf
- Data collection methods for program evaluation: Observation.
  https://www.cdc.gov/healthyyouth/evaluation/pdf/brief16.pdf
- Cottage Health Evaluation Toolkit: How to Plan and Conduct Direct Observation Center for Community Health and Evaluation
  https://www.cottagehealth.org/app/files/public/2253/Collect_Data_Plan_Conduct_Observations_Cottage_Health_Evaluation_Toolkit.pdf
- Observing Children
  https://hwb.gov.wales/api/storage/74f7c7cc-d337-4fd0-9604-27b3d1a5746d/observing-children.pdf
- Monitoring and Evaluating Life Skills for Youth Development: Volume 2: The Toolkit
  https://globaled.gse.harvard.edu/files/geii/files/jacobs_me_toolkit_e.pdf
- What are PWDs (People with Diabetes) Doing? A Netnographic Analysis
  https://www.ncbi.nlm.nih.gov/pmc/articles/PMC6399800/

References

Boehrer, J., and Linsky, M. (1990). Teaching with cases: Learning to question. *New Directions for Teaching and Learning*, 42, 41–57.

Buehler, J. W., & Centers for Disease Control and Prevention (2012). CDC's vision for public health surveillance in the 21st century. Introduction. *MMWR supplements*, 61(3), 1–2. PMID: 2283298

Hanington, B., & Martin, B. (2017). The pocket universal methods of design: 100 ways to research complex problems, develop innovative ideas, and design effective solutions. Rockport.

Harvey, S. A. (2018). Observe before you leap: Why observation provides critical insights for formative research and intervention design that you'll never get from focus groups, interviews, or KAP surveys. *Global Health, Science and Practice*, 6(2), 299–316. doi: https://doi.org/10.9745/GHSP-D-17-00328.

Kaczynski, A. T., Wilhelm Stanis, S. A., Hastmann, T., & Besenyi, G. M. (2011). Variations in observed park physical activity intensity level by gender, race, and age: Individual and joint effects. *Journal of Physical Activity and Health*, 8(2), 51–60. https://pubmed.ncbi.nlm.nih.gov/21918228/

Kiefner-Burmeister, A., Domoff, S., & Radesky, J. (2020). Feeding in the digital age: An observational analysis of mobile device use during family meals at fast food restaurants in Italy. *International Journal of Environmental Research and Public Health*, 17(17), 6077. doi: https://doi.org/10.3390/ijerph17176077r.

Radesky, J. S., Kistin, C. J., Zuckerman, B., Nitzberg, K., Gross, J., Kaplan-Sanoff, M., Augustyn, M., & Silverstein, M. (2014). Patterns of mobile device use by caregivers and children during meals in fast food restaurants. *Pediatrics*, 133(4), e843–e849. doi: https://doi.org/10.1542/peds.2013-3703.

Sisario, B. (2021, June 16). Can streaming pay? Musicians are pinning fresh hopes on Twitch. New York Times. https://www.nytimes.com/2021/06/16/arts/music/twitch-streaming-music.html

Ward, P., McKenzie, T. L., Cohen, D., Evenson, K. R., Golinelli, D., Hillier, A., Lapham, S. C., & Williamson, S. (2014). Physical activity surveillance in parks using direct observation. *Preventing Chronic Disease*, 11. https://doi.org/10.5888/pcd11.130147

Yang, Y., & Diez-Roux, A. V. (2012). Walking distance by trip purpose and population subgroups. *American Journal of Preventive Medicine*, 43(1), 11–19. doi: 10.1016/j.amepre.2012.03.015.

IN-DEPTH INTERVIEW

Figure 7.9 In-depth interviews are a great way to go deep on a topic.

What Is In-Depth Interview Research?

A simple yet powerful and popular qualitative method to gather data through conversations, in-depth interview research enables researchers to ask specific or topical questions in one-on-one interviews (Figure 7.9). Interview research can take other forms. Focus group research brings together 6–12 people who share similar characteristics for a group interview. Another type of interview research, *survey*, includes open-ended and forced response questions, among others. These methods will be discussed later in this book.

Three basic types of one-on-one research interviews – unstructured, semi-structured, and structured – should produce in-depth knowledge about a topic or questions. Generally, in-depth interviews last 60–90 minutes (Granot et al., 2012) (Figure 7.10).

Unstructured Interviews – Sensitive and little-known topics sometimes call for unstructured interviewing, in which a researcher talks to a person without preparing questions in advance. For example, in researching student cheating, social media addiction, and eating disorders, the technique enables participants to share deeply personal stories exactly how

they want to tell them. If necessary, a researcher can refocus an interviewee on the topic or get additional information in follow-up interviews. Grounded theory researchers often use unstructured interviews to build understanding from interview to interview (Corbin & Strauss, 2015).

One type of unstructured interview, ethnographic interviewing, takes place in a naturalistic setting with questions coming up based on what's happening around the researcher and subject. Examples: interviewing healthcare workers in a hospital setting during the COVID-19 pandemic, talking to fans watching a game, etc.

Semi-structured Interviews – In the most popular type of individual interview, the semi-structured (or guided) interview, researchers use a framework called an interview protocol, to guide the conversation. Through predetermined themes and open-ended questions this technique's flexibility generates new questions and uses *question probes* to get additional details. Researchers usually record these interviews and take field notes to fully capture body language, tone, and other context.

Structured Interviews – Structured interviews stick to questions contained in the interview protocol and are often comprehensive, posing many questions about a topic. Careful

Figure 7.10 An unstructured interview goes deep on a topic, a semi-structured one uses a list to start – with unexpected follow-up questions as needed, and a structure interviewed sticks to the approved questions no matter what.

advance preparation – and lots of questions – can reduce the need for follow-up interviews. And in a structure interview, it's common to record the interview *and* take notes so that everything is captured.

Why Choose In-Depth Interviews?

While observation research describes behaviors, interview research tells us what's behind them. Interviews can put behaviors in context, capturing lived experience to explain why and how participants did what they did. And since the more you ask, the more you find out, in-depth interviews help identify underlying causes of behaviors so researchers can better understand processes. For example, why do some kinds of advertising help people quit (or not start) smoking? How do Instagram celebrities build huge fan bases? How do minority students navigate discrimination in higher education?

Other reasons for choosing in-depth interviewing include:

- Understanding participants' personal perspectives, attitudes, and opinions
- Understanding sensitive topics, especially when participants would be uncomfortable in a group discussion
- Getting more detailed information (what researchers call *thick description*) about a topic
- Developing and refining better questions for surveys
- Providing flexibility to pursue unexpected findings (results) in open and semi-structured interviews

In-Depth Interview Method's Disadvantages – New researchers should be aware of the in-depth interview's disadvantages:

Time Intensive – Most interviews last 1–2 hours, and transcribing a one-hour recorded interview takes about four hours. Five in-depth interviews would take at least 20 hours just to transcribe. And that's just writing down all the words! You still have to schedule and do the interview, and then analyze all those hours of conversation.

Analysis – For new researchers, learning how to analyze qualitative data for patterns can be a challenge.

Representativeness – Because of small sample sizes, interview data can't be generalized to a larger population. One firefighter might have interesting stories to tell about work that may nor may not be true for all firefighters. You'll get indications and understanding, but not cause and effect.

Interviewing Skills/Aptitudes – Interviewing requires knowing how to conduct an effective interview and understanding how to make people feel valued and secure enough to share private information.

Confirmation Bias – Researchers might consciously or unconsciously ignore contradictory information that doesn't agree with their hypotheses. Other research biases are explained in Chapter 4.

Subject Bias – Interview participants might not answer a question truthfully. They may anticipate what they think the researcher wants to hear or what's considered socially acceptable.

Online Interviews

Online interviewing is growing. There are three basic types: synchronous, post-and-response synchronous, and asynchronous. Benefits include eliminating geographic barriers, reducing travel time, and maximizing convenience and comfort with a self-selected interview setting (Figure 7.11).

Email interviews have the added advantage of giving respondents more time to think about their answers and provide more detail and help those more inclined to express themselves in writing. Written email responses also reduce the time-consuming transcription process (Ratislavová & Ratislav, 2014). Researcher Dahlin (2021) provides guidance for conducting these types of interviews.

Online Synchronous – Synchronous interviews happen in real time with both the researcher and the interviewee

Figure 7.11 Online interviews eliminate geographic limitations.

together in conversation. While it's possible to do synchronous conversations via text/chat programs, a video conference allows the researcher to assess the participant's understanding and non-verbal communication.

Post and Response – Post-and-response synchronous interviews may or may not happen in real time, or parts can happen in real time or close to it. The interview starts with a posted question to be answered by the respondent. The researcher and respondent may engage in conversation in real time.

Asynchronous Email Interviews – Asynchronous interviews don't involve any real-time conversation. Questions are emailed, and the respondent answers each separately.

The two basic ways to document an interview – handwritten notes and recording – are frequently used together.

How to Set Up an In-Depth Interview Project

1. Start with a topic/theme you want to understand thoroughly
2. Select participants who best represent the topic/theme you are investigating
3. Train interviewers in interviewing techniques
4. Develop and pilot an interview guide for semi-structured and structured interviews
5. Conduct the interviews
6. Analyze your results
7. Present your data results

Step 1: Develop a Topic or Research Question

Observation research's flexibility allows a researcher to explore a topic without predetermined constraints. It also accommodates research question(s). Chapter 2 guides you in finding a research topic. Depending on the type of interview you use, questions will occur organically (unstructured) or be predetermined (semi-structured and structured) and come from the interview guide (a script containing the questions and other information). Try to use why and how questions.

Step 2: Create a Sampling Strategy

Participants should have first-hand experience of the topic/theme being investigated and a willingness to respond. This usually requires a purposive sample: participants are deliberately recruited based on specified characteristics that the researcher determines, such as current experience as a competitive esports video gamer, or an undergraduate student majoring in cybersecurity. For hard-to-find participants in new, niche, or sensitive topic areas, a snowball sampling technique asks individuals who fit the profile to identify others with similar characteristics or experiences. College students can recruit participants using social media, posters, or other means.

Sample Size – New researchers, especially at the undergraduate level, generally do five to seven in-depth interviews. Sample sizes have been justified for 5–50 interviews (Dworkin, 2012). Consider the so-called saturation technique, which says that once interviews don't produce new findings interviewing can stop (Kerr et al., 2010). Your instructor will help you determine the minimum sample size for your project (Figure 7.12).

Step 3: Develop Interviewer Skills

As the main instrument for data collection, an interviewer must be good at getting people to talk openly (Guion et al., 2011; Mack et al., 2005). In an interview, try to be:

Open minded – Stay, neutral, interested, and caring during an interview. Don't judge. If you agree or disagree with anything the participant says, don't let that show – it could change the interview's results.
Respectful – Remember, the participant is the expert. It's their story to tell.

Figure 7.12 What's an in-depth research project sample require? Start with 5–7 interviewees. When you get to the point where interviewing more people gives you no new information – saturation – stop.

Flexible – Researchers using open and semi-structured interviews don't have to follow an interview guide. They can ask unexpected questions as long as they are on topic.

Responsive – Good interviewers are quick and think fast. They can quickly reorganize interview questions and procedures as the need arises. They know when and how to probe for more information. Remember: Follow the respondent, not the interview guide (Strategies for Qualitative Interviews, n.d.).

An Active Listener – Careful listening is hard work. It requires your undivided attention (Mute your cellphone – and put it out of sight!) and neutral, supportive feedback. Nod, make eye contact, say "ok," or "I see," ask follow-up questions if necessary. You can also briefly summarize what was said to make sure you heard it right.

Patient – Some people get to the point quickly while others need more time. If a subject takes time to respond – even strays a bit and repeats things – don't interrupt. Use silence as a strategic tactic (West Virginia Public Broadcasting, 2015). Once you ask a question, don't rush to fill the silence. Give people the time they need. If you think they might have more to say, stay quiet a bit longer – just in case.

Observant – Interviews are valued for their rich insights. Some of that richness comes from context, which can be the participant's natural environment or historical, political, or cultural intersections. Be alert for environmental and other contexts.

Don't Inject Your Thoughts – Similar to leading questions that lead people to respond in a specific way, don't stick your thoughts into the participant's narrative. Arsel (2017, p. 946) provides a great example of how to probe for more information:

> *Interviewee: When I entered the coffee shop, it felt good.*
>   *You: So, you felt at home?*
>   *Bad…your response forces into your data the concept of "home," which should have emerged naturally through your participant's own volition. A better way to probe and open up the conversation would be, "So, tell me more about what was good. What do you mean by 'good'?"*

How to Build Rapport – Rapport is a trusted bond or connection made between two or more people. As an interviewer you can develop rapport with a participant by explaining the research study and why you think it's interesting. Also, say a little about yourself; in other words, "make yourself human" (Arsel, 2017, p. 945). But don't share your own opinions about the research topic.

How You Sound – How your voice sounds to the participant can speak volumes and can bias the interview. Tone is the volume and sound quality of your voice. Depending on the cultural context, a participant may interpret your voice quality in various ways – approval, disapproval, shock, even anger. Try to maintain a neutral-yet-interested tone of voice.

How Body Language Speaks – The body can communicate with gestures, posture, or movement. These can change meaning depending on the cultural context. An eye roll, a smirk, or a hand gesture can signal important information. Record these in your notes for further analysis.

Step 4: Design the Interview Guide

An interview guide provides the framework for semi-structured and structured interviews, including interview procedures, questions, possible follow-up questions, and a narrative script for what you say at the interview's beginning and end (Maier, 2016a). For example, an interview guide would detail the process for requesting and getting informed consent. It can also provide prompts ("Let's get back to the original question") for regaining focus of a conversation that has strayed off track (Arsel, 2017; Jacob & Furgerson, 2012).

Here is a suggested outline for your interview guide. A sample interview guide is available in the Resources section at the end of the chapter.

- Introductions, general study overview
- Informed consent review and acquisition
- Ground rules and roles for researcher and participant
- Participant's background ("Can you tell me about yourself?") and follow-up questions
- Study questions, ordered by themes, with potential follow-up and probe questions
- Conclude interview; thank participant, communicate if follow-up is needed

Creating Quality Questions – Your project's research question relates directly to the interview questions (Figure 7.13). Usually, a research question includes concepts that can be

Figure 7.13 In-depth interviews require open-ended questions. One-word responses often can be expanded through follow-up questions or question prompts.

Figure 7.14 Mirroring is an interview technique where the interviewer restates what the interviewee said to prompt more clarification or expand the answer.

broken down into multiple questions (Seidman, 2013). For example, "How do Instagram celebrities build a fanbase?" could lead to many additional questions about the ways of building a fanbase. Here's some tips to keep in mind:

- Interview questions should relate back to your topic or research questions.
- Write broad questions. Broad questions can be answered in several ways. "How" and "why" questions will do this. Example: How do you approach writing a novel?
- Write clear questions. Don't use technical language, acronyms, or jargon that your participants are unlikely to know.
- Write open-ended questions which encourage reflection and longer answers. Questions that start with phrases such as "Tell me about. . . What do you think about…" or "Describe what it was like to. . . " will produce rich, detailed description. Avoid closed-ended questions that lead to "yes" and "no" answers.
- Avoid leading questions. These are based on assumptions that push respondents toward a certain way of thinking. Example: "How happy are you with our product?"
- Anticipate possible answers for each question. Based on your literature review, what might be some additional follow-up questions should you ask?

Probe Questions – Probe questions are as vital as the key interview questions. Probes ask the participant to expand or clarify answers, and they often give you the rich detail you want (Maier, 2016b). Listen carefully and be ready to probe! Here are some probing questions:

- Can you give me an example?
- Can you expand on that idea?

- Can you explain that further?
- I'm not sure I understand what you're saying.
- Can you repeat what you just said?
- Is there anything else?

Mirroring Technique – Mirroring is a technique that helps clarify or expand what someone says. The researcher summarizes what a person says as a question (Rubin & Rubin, 2012). Example: "So you thought the product wasn't as good as the last model?" (Figure 7.14)

Step 5: Prepare for the Interview

Location Selection – Be sure that you have selected a private and quiet location to conduct your interviews. This might not be an option if you are conducting an interview in a participant's office or home. Always ask for a convenient time and, if possible, a quiet location that will prevent distractions.

Test Your Interview Guide – Test the interview guide (for semi-structured and structured interviews) with a friend unfamiliar with your research. This will also give you practice with interviewing. Check if the script's wording and vocabulary are appropriate for your research goals. Practice with classmates to get familiar with potential issues that participants might raise, like questions about informed consent or asking follow-up questions to clarify information or dig deeper.

Practice Using the Equipment – You should be familiar with how your recording equipment works. It's a good idea to have extra batteries, cords, or even a backup recording device.

If you're using your phone to record the interview, make sure it's charged or plugged in.

Note-taking Considerations – While it's hard to write down exactly what people say, notes are important because they can capture key phrases, speech emphasis, body language, and other things that in the moment may reveal important insights. Think of them as a yellow highlighter that can guide your recording transcript review. Use whatever kind of short-hand makes sense to you – acronyms, abbreviations, etc.

After an interview, while the conversation is still fresh, expand your notes with additional details and any thoughts. For example, you might start to see patterns from other interviews or new elements showing up. Be sure to note which things are your observations and thoughts, and what the participant said.

Notes are necessary because recording equipment doesn't always work. Hopefully your recording will turn out ok, but expanded notes can serve as a backup. They aren't part of your research paper, but they might form the basis for reflexive *memos* (see Chapter 8) which you can share with your research adviser. Notes also preserve nonverbal communication, environmental objects, and other context.

Digital Recording Considerations – Both note-taking and recording are standard for in-depth interviews. But recording (audio or video) requires consent that may not be spelled out in your informed consent document. Even if it is, the researcher should still ask if it's ok to record *before* starting an interview. Why? No matter what form someone fills out, when the time comes they might not want to be recorded – and if they're reluctant, being recorded might change the way they answer questions. Explain why a recording is needed (to make sure you get everything they say right) and describe safeguards in place to ensure confidentiality. Offer to answer any questions. But after all that, if you feel like a participant really doesn't want to be recorded – don't. In those cases, you'll need to take really good notes. To help that process along, say things like: "I'm sorry. Can you repeat what you just said?" or "Hang on. I need to write this down."

During a recorded interview, if you notice the participant is getting nervous about talking, especially about sensitive topics, you should ask if they would be more comfortable with the recorder turned off. Otherwise, you may not get the full story.

Send a Reminder – It's a good idea to remind your interviewee the day before the interview with an email or phone call.

Step 6: Gain Informed Consent

Before any interviewing happens, a college-based research project with human participants needs approval from the appropriate ethics committee, unless a classroom waiver has been approved.

Participants still must sign an informed consent form. It should clearly explain the research project's basic aim, emphasize that participation is voluntary, and disclose any potential risks and discomforts. Other necessary content: the project's potential benefits, researcher contacts, and confidentiality safeguards. Chapter 4 covers basic ethical considerations for a research project.

Researchers using the in-depth interview method should also consider:

- Potential power dynamics of interviews and how knowledge construction and subjectification could be a form of dominance and control.
- How questions are worded, to avoid the potential for symbolic violence. Sociologists have determined that a researcher from one group can unintentionally communicate harmfully to a subject from another group.
- Ways to carefully safeguard participants' identities to avoid putting them in a vulnerable situation when answers to your questions are published.
- Where you can conduct interviews in a private location with no outsiders present so that people feel that their confidentiality is completely protected.
- Counseling support during or after an interview for participants, especially if the interview topic could trigger unwanted emotional responses.

Step 7 Conduct the Interview

Show up on time to the interview. If the interviewee is coming to you, be available early. Show respect for the participant be dressing appropriately. Use the interview guide for your interaction with the participant but also use common sense. It's okay to start with some small talk but also be respectful of the person's time. Always end your interview with a thank you and ask if the person has any additional questions or concerns.

Steps 8 Analyze the Data

After the interview, carefully store your interview notes and recordings in a safe and secure location. Chapter 8 provides different ways to analyze your qualitative data.

Step 9 Present Your Findings

A discussing section (Chapter 9 "Writing the Discussion Section") in your research report allows you to explain your study results, including their significance and implications to the real world.

Chapter 11 "Presenting Your Research" shows you how to present your study results publicly.

Academic Writing Examples

Example 1

In-depth interviews were conducted with social media practitioners for health-related organizations to understand their strategy for promoting vaccinations and counterbalancing misinformation (Steffens et al., 2019):

Data collection

Both our research questions and risk communication principles informed semi-structured, in-depth interview questions (Additional file 1). Risk communication principles offer evidence-based best practices for engagement with the public about risks such as vaccination (Lowbridge & Leask, 2011), and are applicable to social media communication (Veil et al., 2011). Risk communication principles include communicating clearly, openly, and with compassion; collaborating with credible sources; listening to and involving stakeholders as partners; and planning thoroughly and carefully (Covello, 2003). Previous literature provided context for the interview schedule; due to the limited availability of similar research, it did not inform specific questions. Interview topics included purpose of social media activity; perceived role promoting vaccination; and strategies for engaging. We audio-recorded interviews between November 2017 and July 2018, and transcribed them using a confidential service. We collected additional data on participants' professional experience and training. We initially recruited 12 participants, identified emerging themes through analysis, then continued to sample, following identified leads until we reached thematic saturation.

Example 2

Fifty-nine adult smokers were asked to gauge the effectiveness of e-cigarette advertising for certain advertising elements related to the participant's peer crowd and non-peer crowd (Kim et al., 2020) (Figure 7.15).

Methods

Fifty-nine young adult tobacco users (18 to 29 years old) residing in California participated in an in-depth interview between January and August 2017. They were recruited through social media advertising. Eligible participants had used more than one tobacco product (cigarettes, e-cigarettes, and/or smokeless tobacco) within the past 30 days. Prior to the interview, participants completed a baseline survey that included the number of days they used each tobacco product during the past 30 days, socio-demographic characteristics, and peer crowd identification.

The semi-structured interviews lasted about 1 h and included both participants' experience using multiple tobacco products and responses upon

Figure 7.15 An electronic tablet was used to gather smoker reactions to particular features of smoking advertisements in semi-structured interviews (Kim et al., 2020).

viewing a set of four to five e-cigarette print advertisements. Most interviews were conducted face-to-face, with a minority completed over the phone. Participants received a $100 gift card. This manuscript is based on the part of the interviews wherein the participants were presented with e-cigarette advertisements featuring various characters representing different peer crowd groups and discussed their responses to the advertisements. The procedures are described more in detail below.

{Sections titled "Baseline Questionnaire," "Stimuli," and "Changes in Stimuli" were omitted.}

Interviews

Participants viewed the advertisements on an electronic tablet. After seeing an advertisement, participants were asked "what are the first few things you notice from the advertisement?" The interviewer did not direct the participant's attention to any specific aspect of the advertisement until they have finished discussing their first impression. This question was used to explore what features were the most salient to participants. Then, the interviewer asked more specifically about the characters shown in the advertisement. When necessary, additional probes were used to elicit responses to the characters and the advertisements, such as "do you think you would like (or be friends with) this person if you met them in real life?" or to learn more about perceptions of the type of people in the advertisements, "what kind of job/car do you think these people have?" Lastly, the interviewer asked "do you think this advertisement was made with people like you in mind? Why/Why not?" Additional probes included asking what the participants would change to make the advertisement more relevant to them, what kind of people they think the advertisement was made for, or which advertisement was their "favorite" and why. See the Additional file 1: for the interview guide.

During the conversation, the advertisement stayed on the screen, and participants could view or zoom in and out at will. When the discussion of an advertisement was finished, the participant moved on to the next advertisement by swiping the screen.

Activities

In-depth Interview with Your Professor

Read the interview tips in "Teaching Beginning Undergraduates How to Do an In-depth Interview: A Teaching Note with 12 Handy Tips" (Healey-Etten & Sharp, 2010) https://www.jstor.org/stable/25677744.

1. Come to class prepared to conduct an in-depth with the professor.
2. Your efforts can be evaluated by classmates who should offer helpful suggestions for improving your interview technique.

Quality Questions

Design ten questions for interviewing students about their preferences for student media (newspaper, radio, or television station).

1. Your questions should be:

   - Focused on the research topic
   - Open ended
   - Broad, asking how or why questions

2. Develop some prompt questions and mirroring phases for these questions.

Resources

- Data collection methods for program evaluation: Interviews
  https://www.cdc.gov/healthyyouth/evaluation/pdf/brief17.pdf
- Guide to Patient and Family Engagement – Draft Key Informant Interview Protocol.
  https://www.ahrq.gov/research/findings/final-reports/ptfamilyscan/ptfamilyapa.html
- Qualitative Research Methods: A Data Collector's Field Guide
  https://www.fhi360.org/resource/qualitative-research-methods-data-collectors-field-guide
- Sample In-depth Interview Guide
  https://www.nsf.gov/pubs/1997/nsf97153/c3app_b.htm
- Strategies for qualitative interviews
  https://sociology.fas.harvard.edu/files/sociology/files/interview_strategies.pdf
- Templates and examples – Recruiting Participants
  https://www.energy.gov/eere/communicationstandards/downloads/templates-and-examples-recruiting-participants
- Templates and examples – Preparing Test Materials
  https://www.energy.gov/eere/communicationstandards/downloads/templates-and-examples-preparing-test-materials
- User Experience Research Templates and Examples
  https://www.energy.gov/eere/communicationstandards/user-experience-research-templates-and-examples
- Workbook E: Conducting in-depth interview.
  https://www.wallacefoundation.org/knowledge-center/Documents/Workbook-E-Indepth-Interviews.pdf

References

Arsel, Z. (2017). Asking questions with reflexive focus: A tutorial on designing and conducting interviews. *Journal of Consumer Research, 44*(4), 939–948. https://doi.org/10.1093/jcr/ucx096

Corbin, J., & Strauss, A. (2015). *Basics of qualitative research*. SAGE Publishing.

Covello, V. T. (2003). Best practices in public health risk and crisis communication. *Journal of health communication, 8*(S1), 5–8. http://dx.doi.org/10.1080/713851971

Dahlin, E. (2021). Email interviews: A guide to research design and implementation. *International Journal of Qualitative Methods, 20,* https://doi.org/10.1177/16094069211025453.

Dworkin, S. L. (2012). Sample size policy for qualitative studies using in-depth interviews. *Archives of Sexual Behavior, 41,* 1319–1320. https://doi.org/10.1007/s10508-012-0016-6

Granot, E., Brashear, T. G., & Motta, P. C. (2012). A structural guide to in-depth interviewing in business and industrial marketing research. *Journal of Business & Industrial Marketing, 27*(7), 547–553. doi: 10.1108/08858621211257310.

Guion, L., Diehl, D., & McDonald, D. (2011). Conducting an in-depth interview. University of Florida. http://edis.ifas.ufl.edu/fy393

Healey-Etten, V., & Sharp, S. (2010). Teaching beginning undergraduates how to do an in-depth interview: A teaching note with 12 handy tips. *Teaching Sociology, 38*(2), 157–165. https://www.jstor.org/stable/25677744

Jacob, S. A., & Furgerson, S. P. (2012). Writing interview protocols and conducting interviews: Tips for students new to the field of qualitative research. *The Qualitative Report, 17*(T&L Art, 6), 1–10. http://www.nova.edu/ssss/QR/QR17/jacob.pdf

Kerr, C., Nixon, A., & Wild, D. (2010). Assessing and demonstrating data saturation in qualitative inquiry supporting patient-reported outcomes research. *Expert Review of Pharmacoeconomics & Outcomes Research*, *10*(3), 269–281.

Kim, M., Olson, S., Jordan, J. W., & Ling, P. M. (2020). Peer crowd-based targeting in e-cigarette advertisements: A qualitative study to inform counter-marketing. *BMC Public Health*, *20*(1), 32. doi: https://doi.org/10.1186/s12889-019-8126-x.

Lowbridge, C. P., & Leask, J. (2011). Risk communication in public health. *NSW Public Health Bulletin*, *22*(1–2), 34. https://doi.org/10.1071/NB10055

Maier, A. (2016a, June 20). Build empathy with stakeholder interviews. Part 1: Preparation. 18F. https://18f.gsa.gov/2016/06/20/build-empathy-with-stakeholder-interviews-part-1-preparation/

Maier, A. (2016b, July 22). Build empathy with stakeholder interviews. Part 2: Conversations [blog]. 18F. https://18f.gsa.gov/2016/07/22/building-empathy-with-stakeholder-interviews-part-2-conversation/

Ratislavová, K., & Ratislav, J. (2014). Asynchronous email interview as a qualitative research method in the humanities. *Human Affairs*, *24*(4), 452–460. doi: 10.2478/s13374-014-0240-y.

Rubin, H. J., & Rubin, I. S. (2012). *Qualitative interviewing: The art of hearing data* (3rd ed.). SAGE Publishing.

Seidman, I. (2013). *Interviewing as qualitative research: A guide researchers in education and the social sciences* (4th ed.). Teachers College Press.

Steffens, M. S., Dunn, A. G., Wiley, K. E., & Leask, J. (2019). How organisations promoting vaccination respond to misinformation on social media: A qualitative investigation. *BMC Public Health*, *19*(1), 1348. doi: https://doi.org/10.1186/s12889-019-7659-3.

Strategies for qualitative interviews (n.d.). Harvard University. https://sociology.fas.harvard.edu/files/sociology/files/interview_strategies.pdf

Veil, S. R., Buehner, T., & Palenchar, M. J. (2011). A work-in-process literature review: Incorporating social media in risk and crisis communication. *Journal of Contingencies and Crisis Management*, *19*(2), 110–122. https://doi.org/10.1111/j.1468-5973.2011.00639.x

West Virginia Public Broadcasting (2015, June 24). Death, sex, and money with Anna Sale – Live [Video, start 45:30]. YouTube. https://www.youtube.com/watch?v=oi5ufy3RguM&t=2728s

FOCUS GROUP

Figure 7.16 Focus groups are group discussions on focused topics.

What Is Focus Group Research?

Researchers use *focus groups* of 8–12 people with similar topic-connected characteristics to get information from their structured conversation about the topic. This qualitative exploratory research method uses in-depth interviewing techniques (see In-Depth Interviews, in this chapter) to understand thoroughly what motivates human behavior.

Focus groups could help researchers determine, for example, why Gen Zers favor electric cars or how they go about buying them. Focus groups, rather than surveys or experiments, provide rich understanding of actions, attitudes, and opinions. And like in-depth interviews, focus groups are flexible – able to capture unexpected insights due to semi-structured interviewing real-time feedback. Focus groups are popular in marketing, healthcare, and mass communication (Figure 7.16).

Why Choose a Focus Group?

Focus groups explore group norms, experiences, and decision-making processes especially those involving complicated social processes, including motivations for actions and decisions (Chang & Hsu, 2006) (Figure 7.17). Similar to in-depth interview research, focus groups are good for "why" questions, to better understand a particular group behavior, and "how" questions.

Focus groups explore values, attitudes, and opinions that lead to actions. Group discussions produce valuable insights when a group's dynamics:

- prompt forgotten memories
- encourage people to speak their truth
- explore and challenge values or beliefs.

Figure 7.17 Focus groups are valued for their ability to delve deeply into a topic.

In short, they can reveal new, unimagined ways for doing things that can be gamechangers. But focus groups have some disadvantages:

- Costly and time-consuming to arrange, conduct, and analyze
- Small sample sizes not representative of total population; results not generalizable
- Lack of anonymity can influence participant willingness to speak freely
- Artificial environment
- Poor group dynamics, such as aggressive, opinionated participants, can negatively influence discussion
- Moderator's unintentional actions can influence participant answers negatively
- Wrong or incorrectly worded questions can influence participant answers negatively

Online Focus Groups

Online focus groups are growing in popularity, thanks to the COVID-19 pandemic. The advantages include not having to travel to a research location and the ability to reach more diverse participants from a larger geographic region. Speed is another advantage because online focus groups can be organized quickly since travel is not a consideration. For online focus groups, be sure to consider the following:

Technology Access – Before you commit to an online focus group, consider your target populations' ability to access technology. Not everyone has a computer (or mobile device), reliable internet service, or the right software. If your study population, for example, is economically disadvantaged, a face-to-face focus group at a convenient location might be best.

Software Access – Make sure participants have access to the video conferencing software they'll need, so they can download it ahead of time.

Clear Meeting Access Instructions – Not everyone is technology savvy. Automatic emailed invitations for video conferencing may be confusing. They are generally information heavy. Send out a separate email before your session and provide simple access instructions.

Start Early – It's a good idea to start your video conference 10–15 minutes ahead of the scheduled session in case people unfamiliar with video conferencing log in early. If the conference hasn't started it may discourage people from participating.

Be Read to Troubleshoot – You should be familiar with the online software you are using to run your focus group because you will have to help trouble shoot participants' issues. For example, you might need to explain the location of the mic and video controls. Do a dry run with members of your research team to see what common issues are experienced by end users. Be able to clearly communicate the solution.

Unstable Internet Connection – An unstable internet connection can be a huge headache for online focus groups. Be sure to resolve your Wi-Fi before your focus group. Participants with unreliable internet or no computer access can use a cellphone and its data plan; they'll just need to download the video conferencing software app. Let participants know about this option well in advance so they can decide what will work best for them.

Recording the Discussion – Don't forget to remind participants that you plan to record the discussion and then – hit the record button! The recording consent should be part of the informed consent that is completed before the focus group starts.

Background Noise – Participants who have a lot of background noise (barking dogs, crying kids, construction hammers banging, etc.) should mute their mics unless they are talking.

Talking in Turn – Ask participants to make sure others are finished speaking before they talk. Also, read the "Optimizing the Chat Function" information below.

Optimize and regulate the chat function – Have the moderator emphasize that participating in the video and audio conversation is preferred, but the chat function can be used to weigh in and pose questions or comments, too. Mention that the chat needs to stay on topic!

Knowing the Software's Capabilities – Knowing the capabilities of video conferencing software expands your data collection options. Screen sharing, discussion groups, and emoticons can be useful in stimulating more discussion. Develop a plan to take full advantage of these features.

How to Set Up a Focus Group Project

Basic steps for designing a focus group are:

1. Develop a topic or research question (see Chapter 2)
2. Recruit participants based on demographic or other characteristics
3. Pick private and comfortable location, plan an incentive
4. Train moderator and notetaker
5. Develop and pilot moderator guide
6. Obtain informed consent
7. Conduct one or more focus groups, record discussions
8. Analyze discussion(s) (see Chapter 8)
9. Report findings/results (see Chapter 11)

Step 1: Develop a Topic or Research Question

Develop a topic or research question that you wish to explore.

Step 2: Develop a Recruiting Strategy

Think carefully about picking invited participants. They must reflect the key characteristics related to your topic or research question. If more than one focus group will be conducted, divide up groups based on characteristics such as gender, race, or class status (freshmen and seniors, for example).

Homogeneous Characteristics – Grouping strangers together and expecting them to quickly trust each other enough to share their inner thoughts and feelings is a tall order. Homogeneity (sharing common characteristics or experiences) helps participants start with some common ground, and they are more likely to feel comfortable and willing to talk freely about a topic. For example, female students might feel more comfortable talking with other female students about eating habits, communicating with intimate partners, or dealing with sexism on campus.

Participant Recruitment – Take recruitment seriously. Finding and then getting the right participants in a focus group can be hard. College focus groups can fail or fall short because participants sometimes don't show up. Assign recruitment to a research team member to make it a priority.

Sampling Techniques – A judgmental (or purposive) sample predetermines the participant characteristics you're looking for, such as demographics, hobbies, purchase history, etc. If your population is harder to find, use snowball sampling, which asks members of a particular population to identify others.

Publicizing Techniques – Use posters, news articles, social media posts, website notices, and even announcements on TV and radio (using college media) to recruit participants (Figure 7.18).

Figure 7.18 Focus group recruitment can include social media promotion.

Figure 7.19 Location, location, location. It's important to make a focus group location comfortable and convenient for participants.

Tracking Recruits – Make a list of recruit names and contact information – phone numbers and email addresses. Create three messages for each recruit: one thanking them for agreeing to participate, a reminder message the day before the focus group, and a last-minute reminder the day of the session. The second and third messages can be texts or phone calls.

Over Recruit – No-shows are a major problem, and you need at least six participants for a good discussion. Recruit 12 or 13 so even if several don't show up, you'll still have enough participants for robust discussion.

Incentivizing Attendance – Motivate attendance by explaining to recruits, in all communications and recruitment efforts:

- You will be part of something that matters
- Refreshments!
- You'll get a small gift and have a chance to win a gift card.

Incentives provided should not be large and/or expensive. You don't want grateful students offering only positive remarks in a focus group discussion because of unconscious gratitude.

Step 3: Pick a Location

The location for a focus group should be convenient and comfortable. A seminar room or small conference room are good options. Look for a room that offers privacy, to encourage open discussion, and avoid rooms with large windows that can lead to distractions. A conference table, rather than individual desks, provides a way for people to gather face-to-face to talk. Rooms near a restroom keep breaks short. Make sure the room has internet access and audio-visual support if you need them (Figure 7.19).

Step 4: Select and Train the Moderator and Notetaker

In addition to asking questions, the moderator creates a safe, comfortable, and private environment that encourages open and honest conversation. The moderator's performance often determines whether or not a focus group discussion produces rich data. To generate robust conversations, a moderator should have these qualities and abilities (Figure 7.20):

Reflects the Participants – To establish trust quickly, a moderator needs to reflect participant demographics and/or particular experiences. For example, if you want to learn about female experiences in college, it's best to have a female moderator.

Interpersonal Skills – The moderator keeps the group engaged and focused on the topic – discreetly and tactfully. That requires redirecting things when someone goes off topic, managing conversation "hijackers," and encouraging those not talking to contribute. The moderator also is the timekeeper and knows when to move on so there's time for all questions.

Builds Rapport – Moderators establish rapport (a positive relationship) with others by offering a brief personal introduction and by demonstrating interest in and understanding of the topic.

Respects Different Viewpoints – A moderator enforces respect for all opinions. When disagreements occur,

Moderator Characteristics

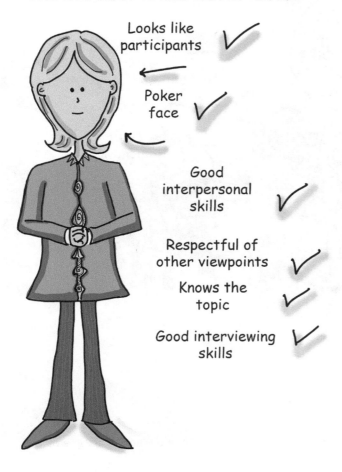

Looks like participants ✓

Poker face ✓

Good interpersonal skills ✓

Respectful of other viewpoints ✓

Knows the topic ✓

Good interviewing skills ✓

Figure 7.20 Effective focus group moderators have good interpersonal abilities and are skilled interviewers.

the moderator creates space so all participants feel safe and heard.

Maintains Neutrality – Moderators must maintain a neutral stance – no eyerolls, facial reactions, exclamations – because overreacting can shut down open, honest discussion.

Topic Knowledge – A moderator knows the topic thoroughly. In-depth knowledge shows effort and understanding that participants trust and respect. And since moderators can't know everything about the topic, they should encourage participants to dig deeper and explore unfamiliar concepts participants bring up.

Notetaker's Role

A focus group notetaker provides real-time analysis, recording first impressions and any notable items such as emerging themes. Notetaker and moderator roles are collaborative. The moderator manages the discussion and group dynamics while the notetaker carefully listens and observes the conversation's nuances. Similar to the notes taken during observation and depth interview research, in first-stage analysis focus group notetakers capture social and individual dynamics of the conversation.

Notes can be handwritten or entered into a computer or other device. A notetaker's work captures things recording devices can't. The notetaker actively listens and observes tone, non-verbal cues, body language, group dynamics, emerging themes or patterns, and other key insights. Did some group members not participate? Did some participants seem agitated or upset? Did the questions generate good discussion? Future focus groups may refine or add new questions or aim at different participant characteristics. Notetakers also identify direct, word-for-word participant quotes to illustrate key findings/results.

After the focus group is complete, the notetaker, moderator, and other members of the research team should meet to discuss the notetaker's first impressions. This meeting happens soon after the focus group concludes, so the focus group discussion is fresh in everyone's mind.

Team members will discuss

- How consensus did or didn't form around a topic or issue.
- Level of engagement with questions that seemed meaningful and/or important to participants. (The notetaker's observations will help guide this discussion.)
- Things about participant discussions that puzzled one or more research team members. (These can be followed up in future focus groups or with other data collection methods.)

Audio and/or video recordings are transcribed and carefully mined for more insights, especially those flagged by the notetaker. Together, the notetaker's notes and the transcription form the data analysis documentation (see Chapter 8 for techniques to analyze qualitative data).

Step 5: Design and Pilot the Moderator's Guide

A moderator's guide provides a framework for the overall discussion. This printed document can be a detailed, scripted narrative, or an outline format may help a moderator speak more smoothly and naturally. A moderator's guide template is available at in the Resources section of this chapter. Here's the basic framework:

Welcome – As people arrive, provide a warm welcome and introduce yourself. A consent form should be signed by each participant. Mention that demographic and/or psychographic surveys need to be filled out now. Encourage people to enjoy refreshments, and give a five-minute warning before starting the focus group discussion (Figure 7.21).

Figure 7.21 Participants tasted five different chocolate bars, one at a time, that presented a range of commercial chocolates to discuss.

Introductions – Again, welcome everyone, and briefly introduce yourself. State the general purpose of a focus group, since it's likely that many group participants have never before participated in one. Briefly explain the responsibilities of the moderator and notetaker. Explain how long the session will last, and don't forget to mention the restroom location.

After explaining the above items, ask if participants have any questions or concerns.

Group Guidelines – Suggested guidelines: explain measures for safeguarding confidentiality (see above); everyone participates; disagreement is allowed; no need to reach consensus; no right or wrong opinions; one person speaks at a time; be respectful, open and honest.

Participant Introductions – Ask for first names and one additional identifying item such as academic major or hometown, or a fun icebreaker as their current favorite show, song, video game, podcast, etc.

Warm-up Question Related to Topic – "When I say X, what's the first thing that comes to your mind?" For example, if you are exploring student experiences with a new tutoring service, ask: "When I say academic tutoring, what's the first thing that comes to your mind?" Think back questions recall positive and negative experiences related to a topic. Example: "Describe a typical day shopping with friends."

Guiding Questions – Questions that relate to your research question(s) should be carefully formulated and sequenced. Generally, six to eight questions will fill a 60–90 minutes discussion, but have some extra questions ready in case you need them.

Wrap-up Question – Once the key questions are discussed, offer participants the opportunity to mention something not covered in the discussion or to offer final thoughts: "What's the one suggestion you have…" or "Is there anything else you care to mention that hasn't been touched on yet?" or "In your opinion, what was the most important thing we discussed about X?"

Concluding Remarks – Thank participants for their time, and give them a name and contact information for follow-up questions or concerns. Remind participants to refrain from talking about the discussion or participant identities to outsiders.

Debriefing – If the focus group discussion deals with a sensitive topic, such as domestic abuse, racism, or

Figure 7.22 Focus group participation generally poses minimal risk to participants but you never know what may trigger unpleasant or unwanted feelings. Be prepared to offer appropriate counseling services when needed.

suicide, a counselor should be at the group discussion. The moderator should also provide contact information for counseling services should a participant have issues later.

Step 6: Gain Informed Consent

Informed consent should be gained before the focus group begins and includes: a general statement about the research's purpose, participation is voluntary, focus group length, a description of any possible risks or discomforts to the subject, how confidentiality will be protected, and any benefits of the research (Figure 7.22).

The moderator reviews the informed consent document, notes that everyone needs to sign one to take part, and ask if there are any questions. To encourage open and honest discussion, address exactly how you will protect confidentiality. Consider using the following measures:

- No participant names in the final report
- Participant direct quotes (or paraphrases) anonymous
- Session recordings stored securely, with access limited to research team members, and destroyed after the report is completed
- Participants encouraged not to discuss participant identities or information shared outside the session.

If a focus group deals with emotionally upsetting topics that may trigger distress or other discomfort in respondents, it's always a good idea to have a counselor available for a participant to access. Usually, this is provided in a separate private

room nearby. Another option is to provide a phone number for counseling assistance should a participant want it after the discussion has concluded.

Step 7: Conduct the Focus Group

Group Dynamics – Let's look at how the moderator keeps the group functioning and look more at the questions asked. Step 4 discusses the moderator's role in running a successful focus group. Moderator's sometimes must manage the group dynamic if people are being disrespectful, talking over others, dominating the conversation, or going off topic (Figure 7.23) This should be done diplomatically by politely intervening when necessary. When someone dominates the group discussion, the moderator can ask specific people to provide their views. When someone veers off track, the moderator can respond that the topic is interesting but due to time limits the conversation needs to focus on the question asked. If someone is disrespecting or bullying others, the moderator may need to ask the person to speak civilly or remind the person that the ground rules do not allow certain types of behavior. If the issue escalates, the moderator may ask the participant to leave.

Question Considerations – Step 5 discusses the development of the moderator's guide. It's important to think carefully about your questions. All questions should refer to your research questions. The phrasing, sequencing, and type of a question can greatly enhance or inhibit discussion. For more details on effective interviewing, read In-Depth Interviews, in this chapter. Here's some additional considerations:

Figure 7.23 Group dynamics, the attitudes or behaviors of participants, can sometimes hamper the effectiveness of a focus group.

Structuring – Use clear, easy-to-understand language rather than vague or technical language. Test your questions on people not involved in your research project.

Sequencing – Question order is important. Start with easy-to-answer "warm-up" questions first. Easy starter questions help participants get comfortable with others about sharing experiences, feelings, and opinions.

Open-Ended Questions – These can't be answered with "yes" or "no." Examples: "Can you give me an example of what happened to you…?" or "What was your experience with…?" or "How did you deal with…?"

Closed-Ended Questions – Closed-ended questions are yes/no questions or questions with very short responses such as, "How old are you?" Avoid them for focus group discussions.

Probing Questions – Probing questions provide an important method of making clear and/or expanding on what was said. A moderator needs to be alert for these opportunities. Examples: "Can you give me an example?" "Why do you think that's the case?" or "How did you decide…?"

Probing with Sensitivity – A moderator's expressions of concern may help participants move beyond facts, to feelings or emotions. For example, "I'm really sorry to hear that…" or "I can tell that was really difficult for you…"

Exit Questions – Final questions can include: "If you had one minute to tell [the organization, the individual, etc.] what would you say?," "What would be the main thing you'd like to emphasize about [the topic]?," "Out of all the things we discussed, what was the most important?" and finally, the last question could be "Have we missed anything?"

Step 8 Analyze the Data

Your data analysis will be qualitative. Two popular qualitative analysis techniques for determining your study's results/findings are discussed in Chapter 8.

Step 9 Report the Findings

Once your data is analyzed you should explain your findings/results. Chapter 9 explains how to write your discussion and conclusion section and Chapter 10 provides guidance on the formatting of your paper.

Add a Survey

Participant Survey – A participant survey is an optional data collection opportunity often conducted before a focus group begins its discussion. It can quickly obtain information describing the group's overall characteristics. Keep the survey easy to complete.

Demographic Information – Demographic information includes any characteristic that describes a population, including: sex, sexual orientation, gender identity, age, race, ethnicity, marital status, occupation, work status, household income, educational attainment, religious affiliation, political affiliation, etc.

Psychographic Information – Psychographic data identify hobbies, interests, attitudes, and values. These characteristics focus more on a person's internal self rather than more obvious external demographic attributes such as age, race, and occupation.

Add Focus Group Activities

In addition to questions, focus groups can accommodate all sorts of activities to gain insights into people's thinking. The activities in this section were adapted from researcher Colucci's (2007) research article "'Focus Groups can be Fun': The Use of Activity-Oriented Questions in Focus Group Discussions." Read her full text for more focus group activities.

Product/Usability Testing – Offer products that group members can experience and assess. Have enough product samples and necessary space for each participant. Products can include foods, drinks, or small items, such as technology gadgets, toys, or tools.

Message Testing – Campaign materials such as slogans, logos, commercials, websites, packaging, and other visual materials can be pretested by focus groups. Alternate messages can be assessed. A variation of picture sorting is choosing among alternatives (Figures 7.24 and 7.25).

Card Sorting – The "card-sort task" asks participants to sort cards with items (words, pictures, etc.) representing the discussion topic into similar and different piles.

Label Generation – This activity generates words, short phrases, or visuals based on a specific question, task such as "What words come to your mind when you think about…?"

Picture Sorting – This activity, which uses photographs or illustrations from magazines or other sources, works for groups or individuals. Participants select which visual best describes a statement or answers a question.

Figure 7.24 Message testing measures the overall effectiveness of marketing language.

Figure 7.25 Choosing among alternatives activity asks individuals to discuss various options based on certain criteria.

Technology Considerations

Technology plays a major role in focus group research because the discussion needs to be recorded. An audio or audio/video recording will yield a transcript of the discussion for the data analysis. Always assume the recording device or its user will fail, and plan accordingly to minimize recording problems.

Get Familiar with the Equipment – Reserve or purchase equipment well before the focus group session date, and practice using it in the room where the focus group session will happen.

Bring Extras – Dead batteries, broken microphones, too few or damaged memory cards, forgotten cables – disasters just waiting to happen. Check and double-check! Bring extras of everything including extension cords and surge protectors, and a secondary table mic to record soft-spoken people.

Academic Writing Examples

Example 1

Who says research can't be fun? For Brown et al.'s (2020) study, which focused on luxury chocolate consumer preferences, the research design explained its reasoning for male and female focus groups and the selection process for the study's chocolate brands. See original article for complete description of the research design (Figure 7.26).

Focus group design

A total of four focus groups lasting approximately 120 minutes each were conducted with 5–8 participants in January and February 2017. Each focus group was led by the first author and observed by the second and last authors. Discussions took place in The Pennsylvania State University Department of Food Science Focus Group Room, a

Figure 7.26 Brown et al.'s (2020) study, focus group participants tasted a range of commercial chocolates.

custom-built qualitative research facility located in the Erickson Food Science Building (University Park, PA, USA). All discussions were audio recorded with voice recorders (Sony ICDPX370, New York, NY, USA). The audio recordings were transcribed verbatim by a commercial transcription service (Landmark Associates, Phoenix, AZ, USA) and checked against the audio recordings to verify completeness. Immediately following each focus group, the moderator and two observers mapped each focus group for themes.

Because chocolate has been considered an aphrodisiac and American women have reported craving chocolate during perimenstruation, focus groups were divided by gender into two groups of all men and two groups of all women, to follow best practices and allow participants to feel comfortable discussing chocolate (Krueger & Casey, 2009a; Michener & Rozin, 1994; Rozin et al., 1991; Stewart & Shamdasani, 2015 and Zellner et al., 2004). Aside from basic demographic data collected from the participants based upon information they provided to the database, no information on profession, education, income, or otherwise, was collected from the participants.

The focus group questioning route was divided into three parts and sought to encourage a comfortable discussion of the research questions by beginning with general questions that eventually narrowed in focus (See S1 Appendix for Focus Group Moderator Guide) (Krueger & Casey, 2009b; Krueger, 2002). In part one, participants introduced themselves, recalled their most significant chocolate moment that they had articulated in the screener, explained their projective maps to the group, and described how they interpret chocolate quality.

In part two, participants tasted five different chocolate bars, one at a time, that presented a range of commercial chocolates…{excerpted}

Participants sampled one piece of each chocolate bar at a time and were given time to write down notes. Afterwards, in a group discussion, they described the product in terms of flavor, packaging, certification labels and other elements and attributes they found appealing and unappealing. For part three, participants discussed what encourages them to purchase a new food product and shared words they would use to describe the chocolates tasted. With four focus groups in total it was possible to identify key themes for the project within financial constraints (Charmaz, 2006; Guest et al., 2017; Krueger & Casey, 2009b) (Figure 7.27).

Example 2

A study that examined mobile health apps content and features that were most helpful to users (Peng et al., 2016) the researchers used a research quality checklist called the *consolidated criteria* for reporting qualitative studies (COREQ) to ensure that its study design elements were present. A section on "trigger materials" included screen captures of various app features.

Procedure

The institutional review board at Michigan State University approved the study. After acquiring their consent, each participant

Figure 7.27 Focus group participants were asked to recall "their most significant chocolate moment" (Brown et al., 2020). Participants were asked to discuss their most memorable chocolate memory.

first completed a questionnaire about demographics, smartphone and mobile app usage, and health status. The second author (female) served as the moderator and the third author (female) recorded the sessions and took notes. The fourth author (male) conducted the interviews. Both the moderator and the interviewer were doctoral students with a Master's Degree and were trained with qualitative research methods. The moderator and the interviewer did not have prior relationship with the participants. Nobody else besides the authors and participants were present during data collection. All the authors had a positive attitude towards health apps, but the authors strived to remain neutral in the conversations with participants. Each focus group session took place in a conference room and ran for about 40–90 minutes. Non-student participants were provided with a free meal and a $20 gift card for their time and student participants were provided with a free meal and extra course credit. The interviews were conducted by the last author, at participants' workplace, home or a nearby café. Each interview lasted for 30–45 minutes. The interviewees were provided a $40 gift card as incentive. All focus groups and interviews were audio-recorded and then transcribed verbatim. The anonymized transcriptions supporting the conclusions of this article are available at goo.gl/T9oZvk.

The moderator and the interviewer followed a discussion guide developed jointly by the authors (see Additional file 2) to direct the conversation. Participants were first provided an overarching introduction about the purpose of the study. They were then asked questions about their overall app usage, knowledge about health apps and their usage, and reasons for liking or disliking apps, including health apps. Participants freely discussed their own experiences without prompts.

Trigger materials

Next, in order to educate participants with no health apps and enlighten others about the wide variety of health apps, participants were exposed to a set of trigger materials (see Additional file 3). These materials included screen captures of various features of health apps based on Klasnja and Pratt's (2012) framework of the five behavioral intervention strategies enabled by smartphones: 1) tracking health information (a: goal setting, b: behavior monitoring and tracking, c: reminders, d: progress visualization), 2) involving health care team (e: sensing and information sharing with health care providers), 3) leveraging social influence (f: social networking), 4) increasing the

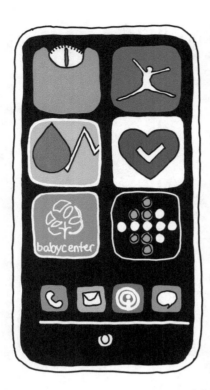

Figure 7.28 Mobile health app consumer preferences were examined in Peng's et al., 2016, study.

accessibility of health information (g: information such as tips, coaching, etc), and 5) utilizing entertainment (h: use of entertainment, i: use of gamification). The participants were exposed to the above categories and sub-categories of health apps, one at a time, and asked to discuss their thoughts about them. Since our study focused on the general usage of health apps in users' day-to-day lives, we did not include any medical apps in the trigger materials, which would be disease specific or apps connected to medical devices or for provider communication (Kamel Boulos et al., 2014; Spruijt-Metz & Nilsen, 2014). They were asked to go into as much detail as possible, explain what they liked or disliked, whether or not they had used that particular or a similar app before and what led them to continue or discontinue using it. The participants who did not have such an app were asked to provide reasons for non-use.

Activities

Create a Moderator's Guide

Develop a moderator's guide for a focus group on the campus dining experience. Include:

1. Introductions and discussion purpose.
2. Informed consent statement.
3. Ten or more questions that are open ended and sequenced from general to specific or east to difficult.
4. Participant activity, such as message testing.

Run a Mock Focus Group

Do a practice focus group using class members. Pick a topic that relates to some aspect of the student experience.

1. Develop a moderator's guide, including informed consent.
2. Develop 10 open-ended questions.
3. Select a moderator and notetaker; these roles can rotate to others during the discussion.
4. As you conduct the focus group, stop and discuss what works and what doesn't. How can you improve the conversation and data collection?

Resources

- Moderator Guide Example: Pew Research's Appendix A: Moderator guide for focus group discussions
https://www.pewresearch.org/internet/wp-content/uploads/sites/9/2016/07/PS_2016.07.26_Human-Enhancement-Focus_AppendixA.pdf
- Focus Group Checklist: Susan Bruce, University of Virginia's Center for Alcohol and Substance Education
https://ira.virginia.edu/sites/ias.virginia.edu/files/focus-groups_checklist.pdf

References

Brown, A. L., Bakke, A. J., & Hopfer, H. (2020). Understanding American premium chocolate consumer perception of craft chocolate and desirable product attributes using focus groups and projective mapping. *PLoS One*, *15*(11), e0240177. https://doi.org/10.1371/journal. pone.0240177

Chang, M. Y., & Hsu, L. L. (2006). Qualitative research: An introduction to focus group methodology and its application. *Hu Li Za Zhi*, *53*(2), 67–72. PMID: 16602049. https://pubmed.ncbi.nlm.nih.gov/16602049/

Charmaz, K. (2006). *Constructing grounded theory: A practical guide through qualitative analysis*. pp. 42–71. SAGE Publishing.

Colucci, E. (2007). "Focus groups can be fun": The use of activity-oriented questions in focus group discussions. *Qualitative Health Research*, *17*(10), 1422–1433. doi: 10.1177/1049732307308129.

Guest, G., Namey, E., & McKenna, K. (2017). How many focus groups are enough? Building an evidence base for nonprobability sample sizes. *Field Methods*, *29*, 3–22. https://doi.org/10.1177/1525822X16639015

Kamel Boulos, M. N., Brewer, A. C., Karimkhani, C., Buller, D. B., & Dellavalle, R. P. (2014). Mobile medical and health apps: State of the art, concerns, regulatory control and certification. *Online Journal Public Health Informatics*, *5*(3), 229. doi:10.5210/ojphi.v5i3.4814

Klasnja, P., & Pratt, W. (2012). Healthcare in the pocket: Mapping the space of mobile-phone health interventions. *Journal of Biomedical Informatics*, *45*(1), 184–198. doi: 10.1016/j.jbi.2011.08.017.

Krueger, R. A., (2002). Designing and conducting focus group interviews [PDF]. https://www.eiu.edu/ihec/Krueger-FocusGroupInterviews.pdf,

Krueger, R. A., & Casey, M. A. (2009a). Chapter 2: Planning the focus group study. In: Krueger, R. A & Casey, M. A. (Eds.). *Focus groups: A practical guide for applied research* (4th ed.) (pp. 17–33). SAGE Publishing.

Krueger, R. A., & Casey, M. A. (2009b). Chapter 3: Developing a questioning route. In: Krueger R. A, Casey M. A., (Eds.). *Focus groups: A practical guide for applied research* (4th ed.) SAGE Publishing.

Michener, W., & Rozin, P. (1994). Pharmacological versus sensory factors in the satiation of chocolate craving. *Physiological Behavior*, 56, 419–422. https://doi.org/10.1016/0031-9384(94)90283-6 PMID: 7972390

Peng, W., Kanthawala, S., Yuan, S., & Hussain, S. A. (2016). A qualitative study of user perceptions of mobile health apps. *BMC Public Health*, 16, 1158. https://doi.org/10.1186/s12889-016-3808-0

Rozin, P., Levine, E., & Stoess, C. (1991). Chocolate craving and liking. *Appetite*, 17, 199–212. https://doi. org/10.1016/0195-6663(91)90022-k PMID: 1799282

Spruijt-Metz, D., & Nilsen, W. (2014). Dynamic models of behavior for just-in-time adaptive interventions. *IEEE Pervasive Computer*, 13(3),13–17. doi: 10.1109/MPRV.2014.46

Stewart, D. W., & Shamdasani, P. N. (2015). Group dynamics and focus group research. In: Stewart, D. W. & Shamdasani, P. N. (Eds.). Focus groups: Theory and practice (3rd ed.) SAGE Publishing.

Zellner, D. A., Garriga Trillo, A., Centeno, S., & Wadsworth, E. (2004). Chocolate craving and the menstrual cycle. Appetite, 42, 119–121. https://doi.org/10.1016/j.appet.2003.11.004 PMID: 15036792.

CASE STUDY

Figure 7.29 The case study method uses multiple sources of data to answer a research question.

What Is Case Study Research?

Case studies are everywhere. Medical and psychology professionals have long used case reports to describe single patient incidents, and businesses use them to spotlight services or products. But those two kinds of focused reporting differ from case study research.

Case study research is both a qualitative method of inquiry (a data collection technique) and a methodology that fully justifies what and how data is obtained and analyzed (Yin, 1994). As a methodology it has research questions, a data collection protocol, and analysis plan.

Using multiple sources of evidence, case study research investigates complex, human activity in its natural environment. An incident investigated is time bound, with a beginning and end, and has happened recently. Cases can focus on individuals, small groups, or organizations.

A key feature is the use of multiple sources of evidence such as interviews, observation, documents, and artifacts (human-made objects). This method relies on the researcher to determine what data is collected and through which lens to interpret the data. In other words, the researcher is the primary research instrument (Figure 7.30).

Researcher as Primary Research Instrument

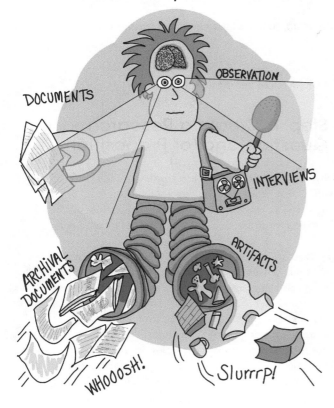

DOCUMENTS

OBSERVATION

INTERVIEWS

ARCHIVAL DOCUMENTS

ARTIFACTS

WHOOOSH!

Slurrrp!

Figure 7.30 Case study research's primary instrument is the researcher, who determines what data to gather – and how to interpret its meaning.

This method accommodates single and multi-case studies.

Why Choose a Case Study?

The case study method combines the power of observation and interview techniques with other sources of naturalistic data collection to create deeply rich understandings of complicated situations (Yin, 1994). Researchers can explore, describe, and explain the *how, what,* or *why* of a situation/case in a certain context (Baxter & Jack, 2008; Hancock & Algozzine, 2016).

A case study could help researchers figure out why a program succeeded or why an organizational crisis happened. When something goes wrong at a company, its history, employees, and work practices all could have played a part. A researcher using the case study method applies the time, freedom, and flexibility to explore the situation in-depth using data from multiple sources (Figure 7.31). Experiencing people in their natural setting gives a researcher a holistic and realistic look at social behaviors, and researchers may take weeks or months to conduct their investigations. The method's built-in flexibility allows capture of unexpected events and information throughout.

Finally, the method can be conducted at one or multiple sites. Multiple-site case studies typically compare and contrast program or other organizational practices at two or more similar sites.

Types of Case Studies – Researchers adopting the case study method can choose one of three types: explanatory, exploratory, or descriptive. Explanatory case studies focus on explaining possible causal links between events through research questions and propositions. When little is known about an event or situation, exploratory case studies produce deep understanding about it. Descriptive case studies provide rich description of the situation in its natural context.

Of the many approaches to case studies, three popular approaches are intrinsic, instrumental, and collective. Intrinsic case studies focus on a unique instance, instrumental case studies apply a typical example, and collective case studies compare multiple cases (Stake, 1995). Case studies may also be classified as: best, worst, comparative, typical, or unique.

Disadvantages – Case study research takes time and money because of its:

- Emphasis on gathering multiple data sources
- Substantial time purposely spent at a site
- Required access to the people and/or organization
- Potential for researcher and subject bias problems

The last of these points can affect reliability. The researcher's prejudices and/or biases can interfere with the study's design,

Case Study Research

Figure 7.31 Case study relies on multiple sources of data, such as interviews and observation.

implementation, and interpretation, and participants may adjust their behaviors if they know they are being studied. External validity (how to extend the findings/results to similar situations) can also be difficult. Reliability and validity issues are discussed below in Criteria for Trusted Findings.

How to Set Up a Case Study Project

Once you have determined an epistemological stance (see Chapter 3) and a question, you are ready to set up your case study. Develop your research questions, propositions (if applicable), identify the unit of analysis, and determine data sources and the protocol for data collection and analysis. A case should have a defined beginning and end (Yin, 1994). Conduct a case study after the situation, such as a project, program, or a crisis, has concluded or a specified time period has passed, such as a program's first year of operation. The case situation should be recent enough that people can recall details clearly.

- Develop a research question/proposition
- Determine the case(s) and gain access
- Collect the data

- Analyze the data
- Report the findings/results

Step 1: Create a Research Question and/or Proposition

Research questions for case studies usually seek to answer *how*, *why*, or *what* questions about a topic. Chapter 6 will help you develop a focused research question. A theoretical perspective to frame a study is helpful but optional.

A case study can include a proposition statement, which (like a hypothesis) suggests a link between two concepts that relate to the research topic/questions. A proposition (what the researcher expects to find) can be used for explanatory studies; it's optional for both exploratory and descriptive studies. A proposition example: "Innovative companies encourage employee's artistic development." A case study's findings/results could prove or disprove (accept or reject) that proposition. A case study can also be descriptive and exploratory.

In one case study, for example, researchers investigated public participation in one community where hazardous waste from

Figure 7.32 A case study using multiple sources of data provided an in-depth analysis of public participation in a local hazardous waste dispute involving a closed oil refinery.

a chemical plant was seeping into a neighborhood (Culley & Hughey, 2008). This three-year case study used depth interviews and multiple documents to analyze the social power dynamic (Figure 7.32).

Step 2: Select the Case(s) and Gain Access

Your research question will help you determine the unit of analysis (the thing that is analyzed), which can be an individual, a social group, or a whole organization. Examples: an organization's human resources department, a family with small children, or an event such as an organizational crisis.

The type of case study you choose (see Types of Case Studies above) determines the sample size at one or multiple sites. Look for situations that match the study's characteristics in the research question. Sample sizes for multiple-site case studies usually range from 2 to 10.

For case selection, use judgmental (purposive) samples that allow you to specify the study's necessary characteristics. Convenience sampling is acceptable too as long as the necessary sample characteristics are present. For example, if you want to explore cybersecurity breaches the organization must have experienced one. Convenience sampling selects a case that meets research criteria and is nearby or otherwise convenient to access.

Gain Access – Organizations may be uncomfortable opening their operations and documents to outsiders, but a researcher with some connection to the group can help get access. In other situations, the organization itself wants the in-depth study. Whatever the challenges, researchers need permission before conducting a case study. Specifically, a site must be

accessible to researchers for data collection. Key informants or other knowledgeable people should be willing and able to participate. Access to relevant documents and artifacts is also a must.

Reluctant organizations may be swayed by the in-depth investigation's benefits, such as improving some aspect of their work. A well-constructed research proposal with clearly communicated informed consent procedures, especially voluntary participation and confidentiality protections, (see Chapter 4) can ease management's discomfort.

College Research Projects – For case studies in a college class, consider researching a person or organization on campus, or a local business with a family connection. You need both access to the person or thing being studied – in the natural setting – and the ability to use multiple data sources. Here's an example: How do campus media (newspaper, radio, magazine, etc.) operate under college administrative oversight?

Step 3: Gain Informed Consent

Depending on the data collection methods used for a case study, any method that uses human subjects (such as in-depth interviewing, focus groups, surveys, etc.) should include acquiring informed consent before any data is collected. This is a general statement about the research's purpose, participation is voluntary, length, a description of any possible risks or discomforts to the subject, how confidentiality will be protected, and any benefits of the research. Informed consent is detailed in Chapter 4 "Thinking Ethically" or you can look at individual data collection methods in this chapter.

Step 4: Collect the Data

Accessing Multiple Data Sources – Unlike other methods, case study research uses multiple methods for data collection (Rashid et al., 2019). These multiple data sources and types provide different perspectives that deepen the researcher's understanding of the topic. This process is referred to as triangulation and may verify patterns or rule out alternative explanations. Data sources may include:

- Documents – brochures, policies, manuals, legal and financial records, advertisements, videos, photographs, diaries, emails, websites, social media posts, etc.
- Archival records – meeting minutes, historical records, newspaper clippings etc.
- Interviews – in-depth interviews
- Observation – direct and participant observation
- Artifacts (objects) – any human-made or used object significant to the research topic, such as work uniforms, office decorations, etc.

Building Trustworthy Results

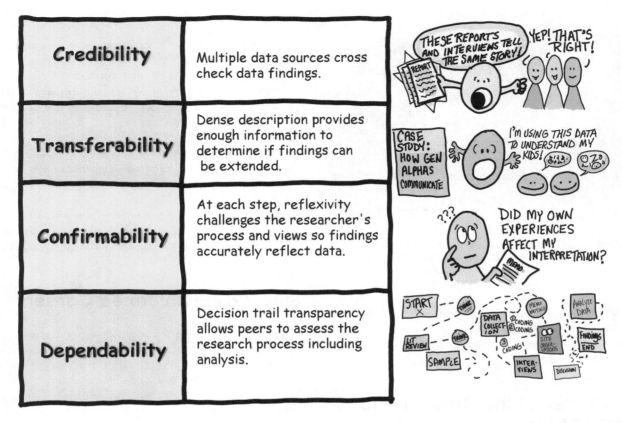

Credibility	Multiple data sources cross check data findings.
Transferability	Dense description provides enough information to determine if findings can be extended.
Confirmability	At each step, reflexivity challenges the researcher's process and views so findings accurately reflect data.
Dependability	Decision trail transparency allows peers to assess the research process including analysis.

Figure 7.33 Case study, as a type of qualitative research, relies on the researcher's ability to adopt rigorous techniques to ensure data findings are trustworthy.

Criteria for Trusted Findings – A qualitative researcher's role as the primary research instrument increases the need for showcasing project's accuracy and trustworthy features (Figure 7.33). How do we convince others that our case study findings can be trusted? Lincoln and Guba (1985) suggested embedding four design features: credibility (use data triangulation – with different data sources – to deepen understanding about the topic and crosscheck a researcher's interpretations); transferability, (enhance the description of research context and findings so readers can extend the results to similar situations); confirmability (demonstrate researcher neutrality through research process transparency); and dependability (confirm the study's replicability with peer consultant research review).

Confirmability can be demonstrated with an audit trail, a sequentially organized and detailed record that connects each link of the research process with corresponding documents or other evidence. Audit trails provide transparency by openly exposing the data collection, analysis, and interpretive processes to outsiders. Do this by offering documentation, such as interview notes, and a daily field journal that discusses how you maintained self-awareness of your role as the main research instrument to guard against personal biases.

Beyond Lincoln and Guba's trust model, Merriam (1985) provides additional measures to increase a case study's rigor and trustworthiness:

- Prolong the data gathering at the site to increase the chances that no stone was left unturned. Case studies require evidence in the form of multiple data sources. Ensuring that all available evidence was collected increases the confidence that the researcher's interpretations were based on adequate information.
- Supplement site data collection with referential materials. Seek previous research studies and other evidence.
- Share your research interpretations with those who actively provided the data to the researcher. These member checks can help corroborate the data interpretation.

Step 5: Analyze the Data

In case study research, analysis begins during data collection. It is not unusual for new variables to crop up as more data is analyzed.

There are two general ways to interpret the case study data: Holistically or with coding.

Holistic analysis starts with determining the big picture first, identifying and understanding the key concepts involved, and how individual data points connect and build the interpretation (Smith & Fletcher, 2004).

Coding methods include thematic coding and qualitative content analysis, which looks for patterns within the text. These approaches are described in Chapter 8. Other analytic methods are explanation-building, time-series analysis, and logic models.

Step 6: Present the Findings

Case studies are written using a story structure with basic chronology – a beginning, middle, and end. Narrative techniques such as rich description of the place and events, character development and dialogue, and exposition help tell the story effectively (Boehrer and Linsky, 1990). A case study's findings – the results described at the end of the story – focus on answering the research questions, exploring any patterns or themes that researchers found. How to discuss and present your data findings are explained in Chapter 9.

Academic Writing Examples

Example 1

Researcher Buschow (2020) wanted to know why "digital-born news media" ventures failed within the German market. Buschow selected 15 media companies to study in depth. Here's how the 15 companies were selected and the type of data collected for the case study.

3.1 Sample

Because of the volatility and opacity of the field under investigation, three complementary pre-studies (a standardized survey of 29 German media experts, a systematic analysis of trade media coverage as well as an investigation of investors, media industry congresses, and awards/prizes) were triangulated to identify a population of around 200 German news ventures. From this population, 15 cases were selected for in-depth research.

Case selection was based on a most-different design reflecting the following consideration: If the same entrepreneurial activities and challenges occur in a broad variety of disparate organizations, this should increase the generalizability of the empirical findings. The diversity of the cases was determined by the following three criteria, that were determined prior to the in-depth investigation:

1. company status (for profit vs. not-for-profit; identified by corporate form);
2. type of media product(s) produced (digital pure player vs. hybrid media products, e.g., both online and print publications);

3. audience scope (broad general coverage vs. specialized niche journalism).

All start-ups investigated were a maximum of four years old and in one of the following three early stages differentiated by van Gelderen et al. (2005): concept development, resource allocation, or first market operations.

To reduce "survival bias" – a bias toward organizations that have succeeded (Parker, 2009, p. 8) – ventures that (at the time of investigation) either struggled with their business or had already been shut down were included as well. Even though this study focuses on failure, it was not only failed cases that were examined: This was to provide a retrospective view of the entire process of venture creation and to identify critical turning points in the history of companies. Due to the number of cases investigated, no longitudinal research framework could be applied. Despite their diversity, what these companies share is that, overall, they have a small workforce size (typically only founders and a network of supporters), achieve low audience reach and – even if they work for profit – do not generate a major surplus for their founders. Table 1 gives a more detailed overview of the cases examined in this study.

3.2 Data Collection

The 15 selected cases were examined in-depth, based on the triangulation of 22 qualitative, semi-structured interviews with founders (approximately 32 hours of audio material), 164 external and internal documents and, where possible, short site visits.

To address the research question, interviews were primarily aimed at a detailed reconstruction of the organization's early start-up phase with its every-day activities and events, decisions, as well as the barriers it faced. Documents used included internal (e.g., strategy papers, business plans) and external (e.g., interviews with founders in trade media, manifestos) texts by and about the organization, which had been produced without researcher's influence; they were included to gather further information from the company's past as well as indications of the intentions, goals, and objectives of the start-ups. Site visits focused on working procedures and organizational structures (by means of observable artefacts) and were recorded in the form of field notes. Data collection took place in 2015 within a broader research project (Buschow, 2018). The case studies had to be anonymized to prevent any harm to the organizations involved, even if this reduces the research's reliability.

Example 2

Researchers Kim and Woo (2021) used the case study method to examine how global fashion retailers (Zara, H&M, and Uniqlo) responded to their internal and external stakeholders during the COVID-19 pandemic. Here's how they described their method of data collection (Figure 7.34):

In order to address the proposed research questions, this study implemented a case study approach. The case study method is a prominent tool in social science studies (Zainal, 2007), and refers to select and compare certain

Figure 7.34 Three global fashion brands' Covid-19 pandemic related messaging was examined by Kim and Woo (2021).

small numbers of cases (Bennett, 2004). It is also an effective method by which to understand complex issues in contemporary real-life phenomena through relevant cases (Zainal, 2007). For this reason, this study chose a case study approach in order to explore global fashion retailers' (i.e., Zara, H&M, and Uniqlo) responses during the pandemic.

In order to address the research questions, information about the three retailers' responses during the pandemic was collected from various secondary sources, such as news articles, the companies' official websites, and corporate magazines. The data collection period was from February to June, 2020, during the "peak" of the COVID-19 pandemic crisis, when the official death toll was drastically increasing worldwide between March and May (World Health Organization, 2020), and companies were actively releasing their responses toward the crisis. Researchers used Google search engine, and utilized diverse combinations of keywords, including the brand names (i.e., Zara, H&M, and Uniqlo), subject (i.e., COVID-19), and verbs related to the brands' issues and responses (i.e., donate, supply, layoff, etc.). After discovering information

related to the research purpose, all data links were saved and classified as relevant to each of these brands (see Appendix).

Activities

Identify Campus Case Studies

What kind of communication-oriented case studies could you do on your campus? Here are some starter ideas:

1. Campus media (newspaper, radio, magazine, etc.)
2. Campus marketing-communication office
3. Communication-related majors
4. Campus communication recruitment program

Turn Your Research Topic into a Case Study

1. Using your research topic or questions, how could you develop a case study?
2. What case or cases would you select and why?
3. What data sources would you include in your case study?

Resources

Here are some video lectures about the case study research method by Graham Gibbs.

- Types of Case Study. Part 1 of 3 on Case Studies
  https://www.youtube.com/watch?v=gQfoq7c4UE4&t=31s
- Types of Case Study. Part 2 of 3 on Case Studies
  https://www.youtube.com/watch?v=o1JEtXkFAr4
- Types of Case Study. Part 3 of 3 on Case Studies
  https://www.youtube.com/watch?v=b5CYZRyOlys

References

Baxter, P., & Jack, S. (2008). Qualitative case study methodology: Study design and implementation for novice researchers. *Qualitative Report, 13*(4), 544–559.

Bennett, A. (2004). Case study methods: Design, use, and comparative advantages. In D. F. Sprinz & Y. Nahmias-Wolinsky (Eds.), *Models, numbers, and cases: Methods for studying international relations.* (pp. 19–55). New York: University of Michigan Press.

Boehrer, J., & Linsky, M. (1990). Teaching with cases: Learning to question. *New Directions for Teaching and Learning, 42,* 41–57.

Buschow, C. (2020). Why do digital native news media fail? An investigation of failure in the early start-up phase. *Media and Communication, 8*(2), 51–61. https://doi.org/10.17645/mac.v8i2.2677

Buschow, C. (2018). *Re-organizing journalism: A study on the formation of new media organizations.* Wiesbaden: Springer VS.

Culley, M. R., & Hughey, J. (2008). Power and public participation in A hazardous waste dispute: A community case study. *American Journal of Community Psychology, 41*(1–2), 99–114. https://doi.org/10.1007/s10464-007-9157-5

Hancock, D. R., & Algozzine, B. (2016). *Doing case study research: A practical guide for beginning researchers*. Teachers College Press.

Kim, S., & Woo, H. (2021). Global fashion retailers' responses to external and internal crises during the COVID-19 pandemic. *Fashion and Textiles*, 8(1), 1–26. https://doi.org/10.1186/s40691-021-00260-x

Merriam, S. B. (1985). The case study in educational research: A review of selected literature. *Journal of Educational Thought*, 19(3), 204–217.

Parker, S. (2009). *The economics of entrepreneurship*. Cambridge University Press.

Rashid, Y., Rashid, A., Warraich, M. A., Sabir, S. S., & Waseem, A. (2019). Case study method: A step-by-step guide for business researchers. *International Journal of Qualitative Methods*, 18, 160940691986242–160940691986242. https://doi.org/10.1177/1609406919862424

Smith, D. V. L., & Fletcher, J. H. (2004). *The art & science of interpreting market research evidence*. Wiley.

Stake, R. E. (1995). *The art of case study research*. SAGE Publishing.

van Gelderen, M., Thurik, R., & Bosma, N. (2005). Success and risk factors in the pre-startup phase. *Small Business Economics*, 24(4), 365–380.

World Health Organization. (2020). *WHO COVID-19 dashboard*. https://covid19.who.int/.

Yin, R. K. (1994). *Case study research: Design and methods* (2nd ed.). SAGE Publishing.

Zainal, Z. (2007). Case study as a research Method. *Jurnal Kemanusiaan*, 5(1). https://jurnalkemanusiaan.utm.my/index.php/kemanusiaan/issue/view/44

CONTENT ANALYSIS

Figure 7.35 Any content that has been recorded (print, video, sound, etc.) can be researched using a content analysis method.

What Is Content Analysis Research?

Any publicly and privately available communication that is in recorded form can be analyzed (Figure 7.35). Broadly, content analysis is "any technique for making inferences by objectively and systematically identifying specified characteristics of messages" (Holsti, 1969, p. 14). An expanded definition calls it "a research technique for making replicable and valid inferences from texts (or other meaningful matter) to the contexts of their use" (Krippendorff, 2013, p.24).

The content comes from existing media sources, not from people newly interviewed or observed. Content includes documents, such as newspaper articles, social media posts, website content, and diaries, along with other media that can convey something important about a culture – music, movies, artwork, and fashion. An inference, an educated guess, enables a researcher to use evidence and reasoning to build a kind of conclusion about the analyzed content.

The technique accommodates either qualitative or quantitative analysis (Kleinheksel et al., 2020). It could be as simple as counting the number of times a certain word or image appears in newspapers or movies or finding deeper, less obvious, even hidden meanings in messages.

Communication researchers use content analysis to examine words/phrases, themes, or concepts (power, gender, etc.) to identify trends and patterns. What's the "big message" being communicated over time? Are there trends? (Figure 7.36) Examples:

- A researcher might look at Hollywood-produced films over the years to analyze the race and ethnicity of movie directors. These frequencies may communicate a cultural message about how the film industry values diversity.
- Content analysis has been used to show the growth of film and TV product placement advertising.
- A content analysis can compare how movies and television do or don't mirror the real world.

While a content analysis cannot determine the beliefs or motivations of the person creating the message (unless he or she explicitly states it), it provides evidence that can be applied to other research efforts. For example, the frequency of video game violence can be used to explore end-user effects (media effects) with in-depth interviews.

Types of Content Analysis – Content analysis can be performed as a qualitative, quantitative, or mixed method using both qualitative and quantitative content analysis approaches.

Trends in Reality Food TV

Figure 7.36 Content analysis can detect trends over time.

Content analysis generally is classified as either conceptual or relational:

- Conceptual (thematic) analysis looks for the appearance of certain words, phrases or concepts. A concept can't be touched – it's not a solid, physical thing – it's abstract, like the idea of "masculinity." The presence of patterns provides indications about the text's conceptual/thematic meaning.
- Relational content analysis extends conceptual analysis by looking for relationships between two or more concepts. Smoking terms (smoked, vaped, exhaled, etc.) found alongside words indicating stress (worried, overworked, etc.) may imply a relationship.

Why Choose a Content Analysis?

All kinds of texts and cultural artifacts are readily available in our media-rich world, and enormous amounts of content are uploaded and printed every day. Some of these texts are hugely influential on societies and individual thinking and behavior. A celebrity's social media can inspire millions of followers, and a science fiction film franchise can make fantasy cool.

Unlike face-to-face data collection that requires informed consent, content analysis is unobtrusive – it doesn't rely directly on humans for data collection.

Examples of Content to Analyze

Figure 7.37 Song lyrics, social media texts, television violence, textbook information, and television crime reporting are just a few examples of content analysis research.

Content Analysis Disadvantages – Content analysis, when done manually, takes a lot of time. And since you only know what the text *says*, you don't know the *why* – what motivated the author to create what he/she did. (You can infer meaning – make an educated guess – but you can't be sure) (Krippendorff, 2013). Similarly, message effects on consumers remains a mystery. To get those insights, a researcher would have to ask people what they're thinking. While content analysis does not rely on human participants, the data collected is created by individuals so care is required to protect privacy. Research examining social media posts, for example, should consider how to protect the poster's identity. Even though many internet sites are public, people may not want their content included in a research project. See Chapter 4 for online ethics suggestions (Figure 7.37).

How to Set Up a Content Analysis Project

Content analysis is versatile because it accommodates qualitative and quantitative approaches. The approach you take will depend on your epistemological stance (see Chapter 3). The basic elements for a content analysis project are found in both qualitative and quantitative approaches.

Here's how a content analysis works:

1. Choose a research topic or question, or hypothesis
2. Determine a sampling strategy and recording unit
3. Determine the analysis plan
4. Collect and code the recording units
5. Analyze the data
6. Present the findings/results

Other Considerations – Content analysis, as mentioned can be quantitative or qualitative, or both. Each will be described in detail below. Some common issues for both approaches include:

Manifest vs. Latent Content – Generally, researchers choose to do either a manifest (surface-level) or a *latent* (below-surface) analysis. Manifest content examines what you can see and is common with quantitative approaches using frequency – how many times you can see something. Qualitative researchers often include latent (hidden) content that might have coded references or multiple, contextual meanings. However, researchers sometimes do both – this is the mixed methods approach (Gray & Densten, 1998). Using variations of both methods is common and may supply cross support for both sets of findings/results.

Ethical Considerations – Researchers using content data analysis should consider ethical issues. A researcher's preconceived ideas or expectations can lead to researcher bias, when data is ignored or miscoded. Collecting publicly available internet content, such as discussion group dialog and social media posts, can infringe on users' privacy – since many don't understand what they're giving up when they click "I Agree" to a software platform's user policy. Embarrassment or other negative consequences can result when people's sensitive information can be recognized in research studies taken from "public" information on the internet. Even removing people's names associated with internet content does not ensure privacy because they sometimes can be traced back to the original post. Chapter 4 discusses the ethical issues of internet research in more detail.

Sampling Strategy – Different sampling options are discussed at the start of this chapter. What you choose depends on accessibility to materials, your time constraints, comfort level with sampling, and project requirements.

Qualitative Content Analysis

A qualitative researcher functions as a central data instrument, using knowledge and skills to look beyond the words and consider their deeper meanings (Bengtsson, 2016). The researcher keeps an open mind about the text and considers possible below-the-surface latent meanings. This technique offers flexibility to consider any concept that emerges. Texts are coded, often thematically, and the researcher interprets the meaning using words rather than numbers.

Basic Steps for Qualitative Content Analysis

Here are the basic steps for planning a qualitative content analysis:

1. Create research aim/questions
2. Select the materials to analyze
3. Define the recording units
4. Develop an analysis plan
5. Code and analyze the data
6. Report the findings/results

Step 1: Create a Research Aim/Question

Qualitative researchers should have a broad idea, an *aim*, of what they intend to accomplish in a topic area. Research questions are used too, but can change as more data is analyzed. Chapter 6 helps you with creating a research question.

Step 2: Select Materials to Analyze

This is your data sample. It can be any type of media (newspapers, radio, television, internet websites, social media posts, brochures, speeches, music lyrics, books, movies, diaries, etc.) and cultural artifacts, such as art. The sampling strategy can include probability or nonprobability samples. Refer to the sampling section discussed at the start of this chapter.

Step 3: Define the Recording Units

A recording unit is the specific feature examined for coding. If your sample is Instagram posts, you must decide what to look at: the whole post, or just part of it: text, photo, video, etc. Samples and recording units can be the same or different. If you researched how *The New York Times* covers climate change your *sample* is *New York Times* publication over a given period of time. Your *recording unit* could be the entire newspaper sample content. Or, it could be just climate news articles in the newspaper sample (not advertising or opinion columns) or a recording unit could be limited to the headlines of climate editorials. Assign a code to each recording unit (Figure 7.38).

Step 4: Develop Your Analysis Plan

Qualitative content analysis happens at the same time (*concurrent*) as data collection. Researchers take notes about any significant ideas while gathering data and then read the whole text for an overall understanding. Once familiar with a text, the researcher begins coding. Qualitative analysis avoids predetermined categories. Instead, categories emerge from careful reading and interpretation of latent material.

Step 5: Code and Analyze the Data

Coding and data analytic techniques are discussed in Chapter 8. While coding is *reductive* (simplified) it often uncovers deep data patterns that can be obscured by large data sets. Codes condense recording units while maintaining their essence. Codes are short one-to-three-word labels. Related codes form categories, and two-to-three related categories form themes. Themes represent behaviors, experiences, or emotions that come from related categories. One or more themes can identify central tenets of a phenomenon – what it's all about in principle. Together, they should produce a framework to understand what's happening.

Step 6: Report the Findings

Qualitative research reports with words, not numbers. Summarize data findings/results based on your analysis. Thick, detailed description is a common feature of qualitative analysis, particularly to support the interpretive nature of *latent* (below-surface) meaning of texts. Illustrative quotes can be used to support findings. Chapters 8 and 9 discusses how to analyze and report your findings/results.

Producing Trustworthy Results – Maintaining research standards and credibility throughout the research process

Sampling Unit: Any climate-related article in newspaper X for the past 6 months.

Recording Unit: First 3 paragraphs of each climate article.

Figure 7.38 A recording (coding) unit is the specific thing a research looks at to code. In this case, the researcher is coding the first three paragraphs of a climate story. The sample is News Hound newspapers. A sampling unit is a single newspaper that contains the recording unit.

ensures trustworthy results. Every aspect of the research design should embed strategies to maintain rigor (accuracy) and credibility (believability) with convincing procedures and findings. Krefting (1991) suggested many ways to improve trustworthy results for qualitative research based on Lincoln and Guba's (1985) trust model.

- Use dense description of research methods
- Select samples that are an appropriate fit for the research question.
- Create accurate codes that genuinely describe the source material.
- Use code-recode procedure. The researcher codes twice separated by a period of time and the results are compared.
- Maintain a field journal to record your thinking and experiences about the research process. As a tool reflexivity considers the researcher's positionality and personal values that can affect the research process.

Before data is collected, ask research peers to examine the research design.

Quantitative Content Analysis

Quantitative content analysis starts with research questions and, sometimes, hypotheses. Sometimes relying on previous research and theoretical frameworks, researchers predetermine the study's categories and variables before data collection with protocols and coding definitions. This structure ensures that multiple coders code consistently and reliably. Words, phrases, and concepts are coded as frequencies using descriptive statistics (Figure 7.39).

How to Set Up a Quantitative Content Analysis Project

The eight steps to conduct a quantitative content analysis are:

1. Create a research question/hypothesis
2. Identify the variables

Message Features

Ethos: Person delivering message (our dead guy) is credible since he's a former smoker.

Pathos: Emotional (fear...it kills! A visual of a dead guy.)

Logos: Uses facts: it's expensive: $1.9 million

Visual Cues: Dramatic visual. Picture of a dead guy with lighted cigarettes.

Language Cue: The word "kill" is intense and quickly and clearly communicates. "Get the Patch" is easy to remember.

Message Sidedness: This message offers only one side of the issue -- it's really bad for you.

Evidence: This ad offers evidence such as CDC data: smoking kills you and it's really expensive.

Self Efficacy: The 1-800 number is an easy way for a person to change his/her behavior.

Figure 7.39 Messages can be analyzed in a variety of ways. This anti-smoking advertisement has several message features that can be classified.

3. Select the materials to analyze
4. Define the recording units
5. Develop an analysis plan (codebook and coding form)
6. Code the data
7. Analyze the data
8. Report the findings/results

Step 1: Create a Research Question/Hypothesis

Quantitative content analysis should have questions that focus the research, and your study should answer those questions. Questions contain variables, things that are measured and have varying states, or values. Variables give your study its data. A *hypothesis* is a specific statement that tests the relationship between two variables, independent and dependent variables. These are constructed as if-then statements that can be tested. For example, IF effective navigation features (independent) are present THEN it will be a highly rated website (dependent).

Step 2: Identify the Variables

Variables can be easily identifiable variation of things — such as different types of dogs or cats. To measure concepts, you have to turn them into variables. That's the main difference between a concept and a variable: you can't measure or see a concept, but you can observe and measure its variable. For example, if you want to investigate website usability, a concept, then variables might include certain navigation and content features. Another concept is economic class that can be defined by lower, middle, and upper classes (Figure 7.40).

Step 3: Select the Materials to Analyze

Content analysis materials can be any type of recorded communication (newspapers, radio, television, internet websites, social media posts, brochures, speeches, music lyrics, books, movies, diaries, etc.) and cultural artifacts, such as art.

Character Classification

| [1] OCCUPATION | [2] FINANCIAL SECURITY | [3] MATERIAL POSSESSIONS |

Working Class   **Middle Class**   **Upper Class**

PAYCHECK TO PAYCHECK

#?!@!

JERK!   401K

SEE YA AFTER WORK!

Figure 7.40 In one study, coding determined a character's social class in primetime TV by considering the character's occupation, financial security, and material possessions (Behm-Morawitz et al., 2018).

After determining what *type* of items you're going to study, the next step is choosing specific items to look at. If the material belongs to a much bigger group of items, such as *The New York Times* archive, it makes sense to select a portion of the total.

Probability and nonprobability sampling options are described above.

Step 4: Define the Recording Units

A *recording unit* is the specific feature examined for coding. While a sample might include each *New York Times,* issue published in a month, the recording unit might be the same or different. If it's the same, the recording unit is the entire content of each newspaper issue (articles, photos, and advertising); if it's different, it could be just the editorials.

Step 5: Develop an Analysis Plan

An analysis plan outlines what data will be analyzed and how you'll do it. Two key documents are used in a quantitative content analysis plan: a coding book and coding form. Do you need one coder or several? Using multiple coders can increase reliability (see Reliability below). Finally, pretest the coding form to ensure definitions are clear and workable.

Step 6: Create a Codebook

To help maintain consistency when multiple coders are used in quantitative content analysis, codebooks often contain the code name/label/numerical codes, brief and full definitions, inclusion and exclusion criteria, and examples.

The coding book offers definitions and classification rules to assign coding units to particular categories, and those rules should guide what's included and excluded. How to handle *manifest* (surface-level) and latent (below-the-surface) analyses is explained. Manifest data, such as the presence of the word "tax" (and its variations) in a speech is easy to do.

Beyond manifest content – what is easily observable, researchers Potter and Levine-Donnerstein (1999) note two types of latent content: pattern and projective content. Pattern content asks coders to examine more concrete content cues that together add up to something recognizable. For example, to determine a person's fashion (formal/causal) coders look at all pieces (a pattern) of clothing people wear. Projective content relies more heavily on a coder's personal experiences to judge the content's symbolic nature. Judging a person's attractiveness will involve more individual interpretation regardless of coding rules. To improve consistency, all coders should be assigned to the same overlap content to test how consistent coders are coding and also compare coding results to expert standards.

McQueen et al. (1998) suggest that the structure of codebooks should consist of six components, including the code name/label, brief definition, full definition, inclusion criteria, exclusion criteria, and examples.

A study that examines the type of social media platforms used on hospital websites could include a category called "social media" with the possible variations including Facebook, Twitter, Instagram, YouTube, Snapchat, TikTok, and blogs.

Blogs would be included because of their ability for dialog between the author and readers. Another category could take a closer look at the blogs, specifically their type as possible variables. Medical blog variables could be, for example, authored by patient, physician, or staff. Another variable could be type of physician blogger, and variations could include various medical specialties such as oncology, surgery, neurology, etc. What variables you choose to include will depend on your research questions. Codebooks ensure that coding directions are crystal clear.

Creating a Coding Form – This is the companion to your codebook. A *coding form*, which could be a sheet of paper or a digital spreadsheet, is your data document – the actual tool used to code the content observed. Like the codebook, the coding form is described but not included in the written method section of your research report. For first-time coders, this textbook recommends separate, physical coding sheets for each sampling unit. For example, if you were researching hospital website homepage features, you would need a separate coding sheet to record each hospital's homepage features in your sample. Be careful, though – this approach could mean hundreds of individual sheets of paper, if your sample included hundreds of hospital homepages. (And save a tree – use both sides of the sheet!)

A simple example of coding a variable would be a study looking at newspaper editorials written about climate change. A variable called "climate change cause" could have just two values: 0 = not human caused, 1 = human caused. Another variable could look at newspaper stories written about climate change called "type of climate change story" with several options: 0 = no specific focus, 1 = rising oceans/flooding, 2 = rising temperatures, 3 = forest fires, 4 = extreme weather, 5 = climate policy/regulations, 6 = alternative energy, 7 = health effects.

Digital coding forms created using spreadsheet software are popular. Microsoft Excel, Google Sheets, and other spreadsheet programs allow you to share collaboratively and edit online. But problems can happen when inputting computer data – crashing hard drives, stolen laptops, lost thumb drives, corrupted files, etc. If you decide to record your data directly to a software program, back it up. You can always email the file to yourself and/or create a shared Google folder.

Creating Coding Forms that Work – Your coding scheme contains the coding categories for your variables; coders should be able to assign each piece of a content a value that is mutually exclusive, exhaustive, and independent from other pieces of content. Good category systems are:

- **Mutually Exclusive** – Coding units can fit in only one scoring dimension, not two or more. In a study that codes different types of message appeals, the options might be either emotional or rational. In a sample of newspaper editorials on abortion legislation the options could be coded for its position/stance as either pro-life or pro-choice. The coder must select just one option for each coding unit.

- **Exhaustive** – All possible variations or attributes of variables should be included in your categories. To ensure that you have captured all possible variations, include "other" or "none" in your coding choices for each variable.
- **Independent of Each Other** – This refers to the coding process in which the assignment of data to one category does not affect the assignment of other data to a category.

Step 7: Code the Data

Content analysis coding can be accomplished manually or with a computer

Manual coding requires the researcher to go through the text line by line to code and categorize the information. While it takes time, manual coding's close and careful reading of texts may be needed to find conceptual patterns undetected by computers.

Computerized coding uses digitized transcripts for organizing and categorizing data. It can search for specific word frequencies or keywords in context, meaning that words surrounding a specific word are also captured. For example, a keyword could be "duty" and two words before and after that word are also captured to better understand the contextual meaning of "duty." Visual software can also distinguish faces and other common items. While they can't analyze data the same way as manual coding, computers can speed up the process.

Reliability and validity are stressed for producing trustworthy results.

Validity – This refers to how well the measuring system and results reflect reality. One type of research validity, construct validity, determines how well the study was designed to collect quality data. In content analysis, construct validity evaluates how closely the indicators measuring the abstract concepts mirrored the real world. Using proven research protocols, such as codebooks, and established data collections tools, such as coding forms developed by other researchers, can help achieve construct validity.

Reliability – In content analysis coding consistency is important to obtaining reliable (stable) *data*. Reliability can be supported by effective coder training, using clear coding rules that eliminate broad-based judgment calls, two or more coders who code independently of each other, and pretesting the appropriateness of coding categories, coding instructions, and – before data collection starts – the reliability of coders to code consistently prior to data collection.

Pretesting Interrater Reliability – *Interrater reliability* focuses on the coders: Do they get the same results when coding the same content independently of each other? If there are unclear definition of categories, confusing instructions, incompetent coders, or inadequate coder training, the data

Figure 7.41 Multiple independent coders should classify content according to research protocols. Reliable coding requires coder training and checking coder consistency using the same overlap materials.

Figure 7.42 One content analysis study looked at the prevalence of alcohol in UK television.

results will be flawed. Training the coders is essential to eliminate subjective content interpretation, and a pretest will show how closely multiple coders classify data the same way. The acceptable 80–100% range of coder agreement means that two coders independently code the same content exactly the same way at least 80% of the time (Figure 7.41). Pretest results can guide revision of definitions and/or make additions or deletions to coding categories and coding units. A pretest called an interrater reliability test can use Cronbach's kappa or Scott's pi, either of which is useful for nominal level variables, although there are many agreement indices to choose from.

Step 8: Analyze the Data

A quantitative analysis summarizes data in numeric form using percentages. Other statistical functions can be used. Data analysis is covered in Chapter 8.

Step 9: Report the Findings

Data findings (results) for quantitative studies are numeric. The numbers are embedded in a narrative summary, often with tables and charts. Ways to report your findings/results are covered in Chapter 9.

Academic Writing Examples

Example 1

Not surprisingly, alcohol imagery was frequently portrayed on UK television, according to a content analysis done by Barker et al. (2019). Researchers recorded the presence or absence of audio-visual alcohol content every 1-minute for four categories (Figure 7.42).

Methods

All programmes and advertisements/trailers broadcast on the five national UK free-to-air channels in the UK (BBC1, BBC2, ITV1, Channels 4 and 5) were recorded during the peak viewing hours of 6–10 p.m. capturing data on the 3 h before and 1 h after the Office of Communications (OfCom) 9 pm watershed. All programmes, and all advertisements and/or trailers for other programmes broadcast in these time intervals were recorded in three separate weeks (Monday–Sunday) in 2015, with a 4-week gap between each (21–27 September, 18–25 October, 16–22 November). At the time of the study these five channels were the most watched channels in the UK (British Audience Research Board, 2017) and remain so today (OfCom, 2017). Two of the channels, BBC1 and BBC2, are public service channels with no commercial advertising, while ITV1, Channels 4 and 5 all feature commercial advertising. All recorded footage was viewed and coded using the 1-minute interval period method previously described by Lyons et al. (2014). The method includes recording the presence or absence of audio-visual alcohol content every 1-minute and in the following categories:

Actual use: Use of alcohol on screen by any character
Implied use: Any inferred alcohol use without any actual use on screen.
Other alcohol reference: The presence on screen of alcohol or other related materials
Brand appearance: The presence of clear and unambiguous branding

Alcohol appearances were recorded if they appeared on screen in any 1-minute coding period. Multiple instances of the same category in the same 1-minute period were considered a single event, however, if two instances of different categories occurred this was recorded as two different events (e.g. actual alcohol use and inferred use). When the same appearance transitioned into a new 1-minute period it was coded as two separate events as the appearance occurred in two, 1-minute intervals. We categorized the genre of each programme based on information from Box of Broadcasts (The British Universities and Colleges Film and Video Council, 2017) and the researcher's discretion when genre not available. The periods between programmes containing trailers for forthcoming broadcasts on BBC1 and BBC2, and those including trailers and/or commercial advertising between or within programmes on ITV1, Channel 4 or Channel 5 were coded separately from programmes as a single category of advert/trailer content. One-third of the recorded footage was coded separately by two authors (A.B. and K.W.) to ensure accuracy and reliability in the coding method. Data were analysed descriptively with separate analyses conducted to compare content broadcast before or after the 9 pm watershed, between the five channels, and between the programme genres observed.

Results

A total of 611 programmes and 1140 advert/trailer periods comprising 27 083 1-minute intervals (22 960 from programmes and 4123 from adverts/trailers) were recorded during the peak viewing hours of 6–10 pm from Monday to Sunday in 3 separate weeks. The most frequent programme genres were News and Current Affairs, Documentaries, and Soap Operas (totalling 137, 126 and 76 programmes respectively). The genres accounting for the greatest broadcast time were Documentaries, News and Current Affairs, and Entertainment, with 5482, 3573 and 2408 min, respectively.

Any Alcohol Content

Any alcohol content appeared in a total of 3734 intervals (14% of the total) (Fig. 1). Of the 611 programmes broadcast, 412 (67%) contained any alcohol content, occurring in 3002 (14% of all intervals from programmes) 1-minute intervals. Of advert/trailer periods, 524 (47%) contained any alcohol content, occurring in 732 (18% of all intervals from advert/trailer periods) 1-minute intervals.

The channel broadcasting the greatest number of alcohol appearances was ITV, which accounted for 1081 intervals (29% of all alcohol intervals) and with alcohol appearances occurring in 226 programmes (62% of all broadcasts on ITV). ITV also had the most alcohol appearances in both programmes (20% of all intervals from programmes, 83% of all programmes) and advert/trailer periods (55% of all advert/trailer periods, 18% of all intervals from advert/trailer periods containing alcohol). The lowest number of alcohol appearances occurred on BBC2, with 508 intervals (14% of all alcohol intervals) across 91 broadcasts (40% of all broadcasts). BBC2 also had the lowest number of alcohol appearances in both programmes (63% of all broadcasts, 10% of all programme intervals containing alcohol) and advert/trailer periods (15% of all advert/trailer periods, 7% of all intervals from advert/trailer periods containing alcohol; see Table S1 in the online Supplementary file 1). "Other Alcohol References" were the most frequent form of alcohol appearance on each channel. When compared to an earlier analysis of UK TV footage using the same methods, the results appear to be virtually unchanged, see Fig. 2.

The proportion of programme genres containing the highest alcohol content, defined by any alcohol content in the show, were Cookery (all cookery programmes included alcohol content), Soap Opera (99% included alcohol content) and Drama (94% included alcohol content) (Fig. 3; note that the high proportion of Education programmes containing alcohol arises from a single programme).

Of the 1120 advert/trailer periods analysed, 524 (47%) contained any alcohol content, occurring in 732 (18%) of 4123 1-minute intervals. The 75% of programming in our sample broadcast before the 9 pm watershed contained 78% of the broadcast alcohol appearances in 1-minute intervals.

Example 2

A qualitative and quantitative content analysis examined 1,5040 Twitter posts of five stakeholder groups to gauge perceptions about people centered care (van Diepen & Wolf, 2021) (Figure 7.43).

2. METHODS

2.1. Data collection

The PCC-related Twitter search was conducted in the Twitter Application Programming Interface (API) called Mozdeh (Statistical Cybermetrics Research Group. Mozdeh, 2014) which is one of the many freely available programmes. The search terms consisted of "Person-Centred Care" translations from 16 European languages (Supplementary Table 1). These search terms were compiled from the Cost Action 15222 COST CARES network in which stakeholders from each country offered their local term for PCC.

The API collected PCC-related tweets posted between 1 October and 31 October 2019. Besides the PCC-related content of the tweets, the data derived from the API encompassed an ID-number, a timestamp, name, username and language.

The API generated 3,632 tweets consisting of 1,231 original tweets, 1,878 retweets and 523 replies. Only the original tweets and replies were used in this study and accumulated to a sample of 1,754 tweets for the content analysis. The flow chart (Fig. 1) presents the steps of this study

Figure 7.43 Stakeholder Twitter posts about patient-centered care were examined by researchers van Diepen and Wolf (2021).

For the content of the tweets, we applied the content analysis method as described by Graneheim & Lundman (2004). The tweet's content was read line by line and coded by the first author, whereby meaning units were created and categorized. All tweets could only fit one category to avoid over over-calculation of the number of tweets. When the tweets did not contain the search term in the order of the concept (e.g. "Communities of care centred around the patient/person"), not refer to the concept of Person-Centred Care (e.g. "I don't care for this self-centred person") or contained no more than the concept (e.g. "Person-centred care?"), they were coded as "other" and not included in the results.

For the quantitative analysis, we started by allocating the author posting the tweet to stakeholder groups with "individual" as standard. This allocation was based on the name, username or explicit content of the tweet. If there was no clear indication of the stakeholder group, the author remained an "individual." This group of "individuals" could contain a wide variety of Twitter users. We also grouped the tweets into the common topics, see Figure 2.

In the qualitative content analysis, the tweets were further coded to interpret the meaning within their topic. These topics can be understood as the latent content of the text (Graneheim and Lundman, 2004, p. 107). The purpose of this analysis was to explore the perceptions of PCC expressed in the tweets. Consequently, the different topics were scrutinized for content that encompassed a perception of PCC. Two topics (i.e. Opinions & Experiences) were eligible for the qualitative content analysis into the perceptions and experiences of PCC on Twitter. An example of the coding scheme is shown in Table 1.

Activities

Defining What You Mean

Abstract concepts like "framing" or "agenda setting" are hard to define. Definitions help identify them so we can recognize them when we see them.

1. What are abstract ideas in your research question or topic?
2. What strategies can you use to define these abstract concepts?
3. Write a definition for your concepts. If there are real-world indicators for these concepts, provide them.

Determine the Recording Unit

Once you have a sample, you need to determine what specifically will be observed for your data collection. The sample and the recording unit can be the same thing. For example, you may collect a sample of 500 tweets. The tweet post would be your sample as well as your unit of analysis. Another example involves newspapers. Your sample could include specific full newspaper issues. The unit of analysis, however, could be headlines of environmental stories. It also could be the headline and the complete story. Or it could be the first paragraph of a newspaper article. What makes the most sense to answer your research question(s)?

1. Determine the coding unit for the proposed study.
2. What might be some alternative coding units for the study?
3. Justify how the coding unit will adequately measure your concepts.

Coding Practice

Once you have identified a recording unit, try coding. Codes are one-to-three-word labels that condense the meaning of the recording unit.

1. Code some of your materials. For example, music lyrics, newspaper articles, etc.
2. Do any codes relate to each other? For example, social media fan engagement might have several different yet related strategies for engaging fans.
3. Ask a classmate to independently code the same material.
4. Compare your results with your classmate's efforts. Discuss the differences.

Resources

- Content analysis: A methodology for structuring and analyzing written material.
  https://www.gao.gov/assets/pemd-10.3.1.pdf
- Graham Gibbs has a number of videos on coding. "Grounded Theory – Line-by-Line Coding," for example, explains the open coding technique.
  https://www.youtube.com/watch?v=Dfd_U-24egg&t=1s
- Methods 101: What is machine learning, and how does it work?
  https://www.youtube.com/watch?v=A4KIW4O8bYM

References

Barker, A. B., Smith, J., Hunter, A., Britton, J., & Murray, R. L. (2019). Quantifying tobacco and alcohol imagery in Netflix and Amazon Prime instant video original programming accessed from the UK: a content analysis. *BMJ open*, *9*(2), e025807. http://dx.doi.org/10.1136/bmjopen-2018-025807

Behm-Morawitz, E., Miller, B. M., & Lewallen, J. (2018). A model for quantitatively analyzing representations of social class in screen media. *Communication Research Reports*, *35*(3), 210–221. https://doi.org/10.1080/08824096.2018.1428544

Bengtsson, M. (2016). How to plan and perform a qualitative study using content analysis. *Nursingplus Open*, *2*, 8–14. https://doi.org/10.1016/j.npls.2016.01.001

British Audience Research Board. *Share by Broadcaster* (2017). http://www.barb.co.uk/

Graneheim, U. H., & Lundman, B. (2004). Qualitative content analysis in nursing research: concepts, procedures and measures to achieve trustworthiness. *Nurse Education Today*, *24*(2), 105–112. https://doi.org/10.1016/j.nedt.2003.10.001

Gray, J. H., & Densten, I. L. (1998). Integrating quantitative and qualitative analysis using latent and manifest variables. *Quality and Quantity*, *32*(4), 419–431. https://doi.org/10.1023/A:1004357719066

Holsti, O. R. (1969). *Content analysis for the social sciences and humanities*. Addison-Wesley.

Hsieh, H. F., & Shannon, S. E. (2005). Three approaches to qualitative content analysis. *Qualitative Health Research*, *15*(9), 1277–1288. https://doi.org/10.1177/1049732305276687

Kleinheksel, A. J., Rockich-Winston, N., Tawfik, H., & Wyatt, T. R. (2020). Demystifying content analysis. *American Journal of Pharmaceutical Education*, *84*(1), 127–137. https://doi.org/10.5688/ajpe7113

Krefting, L. (1991). Rigor in qualitative research: The assessment of trustworthiness. *American Journal of Occupational Therapy*, *45*, 214–222. https://doi.org/10.5014/ajot.45.3.214

Krippendorff, K. (2013). *Content analysis: An introduction to its methodology* (3rd ed.). SAGE publications.

Lincoln, Y. S., & Guba, E. G. (1985). *Naturalistic inquiry*. SAGE Publishing.

Lyons, A., McNeill, A., & Britton, J. (2014). Alcohol imagery on popularly viewed television in the UK. *Journal of Public Health*, *36*(3), 426–434.

MacQueen, K. M., McLellan, E., Kay, K., & Milstein, B. (1998). Codebook development for team-based qualitative analysis. *CAM Journal*, *10*(2), 31–36. https://doi.org/10.1177/1525822X980100020301

OfCom. *PSB annual research report 2017*. (2017). https://www.ofcom.org.uk/__data/assets/pdf_file/0019/103924/psb-annual-report-2017.pdf

Potter, W. J., & Levine-Donnerstein, D. (1999). Rethinking validity and reliability in content analysis. Journal of Applied Communication, *27*(3), 258–284. https://doi.org/10.1080/00909889909365539

Statistical Cybermetrics Research Group. Mozdeh (2014). http://mozdeh.wlv.ac.uk/

The British Universities and Colleges Film and Video Council (Sept. 27, 2017). *Box of broadcasts*. https://www.learningonscreen.ac.uk/ondemand/

U.S. General Accounting Office (1996). Content analysis: A methodology for structuring and analyzing written material. GAO/PEMD-10.3.1. Washington, D.C. https://www.gao.gov/assets/pemd-10.3.1.pdf

van Diepen, C., & Wolf, A. (2021). "Care is not care if it isn't person-centred": A content analysis of how person-centred care is expressed on Twitter. *Health Expectations: An International Journal of Public Participation in Health Care and Health Policy*, *24*(2), 548–555. https://doi.org/10.1111/hex.13199

SURVEY

Figure 7.44 Survey development is easy and hard at the same time!

What Is Survey Research?

Surveys are often designed as quantitative, rather than qualitative data collecting instruments. Most questions or statements are designed to be reported out numerically rather than in a word format.

Survey research is "the collection of information from a sample of individuals through their responses to questions" (Check & Schutt, 2012, p. 160). Survey research does offer qualitative options such as focus groups, in-depth interviews, and open-ended questions in questionnaires, but this textbook focuses on quantitative survey research.

Surveys typically use samples instead of a census, which asks questions of everyone in a population. The survey research process and its tools include polling, a survey method that researchers used to measure public opinion; and questionnaire, a question form for data collection.

Survey Administration – Surveys can be administered two ways: through the personal approach with face-to-face or phone surveys; or self-administered with online/email or pencil-paper modes. The personal approach has someone who reads the question to the respondent. Self-administered surveys require the respondent to fill out the survey independently. Any of these survey types can be longitudinal, collecting data from the same people over time, or cross-sectional, collecting data once to provide a point-in-time snapshot of people's thinking.

Survey Types – Surveys generally are quantitative, meaning most of the data collected results in numeric data. Surveys often include a few open-ended questions, which provide qualitative data that results in worded data. A common open-ended qualitative question found at the survey's end is "Do you have anything else you want to say?"

Why Choose a Survey?

Studying a large population often makes a census impractical or impossible, so surveys provide efficient, accurate, and affordable alternatives.

Reliability – Quantitative surveys can be highly reliable in understanding people's behaviors, opinions, and attitudes. If a survey uses a representative subset of the population, the results can help show relationships between variables.

Fast – Online surveys can produce fast results. Third-party providers make this method easy, providing customizable templates, survey distribution, and results analysis.

Respondent Privacy – Keeping respondents' personal information private or anonymous increases participation. Surveys conducted online, that automatically strip away identifying

Figure 7.45 Anonymous data means that even the researcher doesn't know the identity of the person's data.

information, can be anonymous meaning no one knows you filled out the survey. Respondent identification can be protected by keeping consent forms and surveys separate. A researcher knows you filled out a survey, but he/she will not have your survey data associated with your name or other personal data (Figures 7.45 and 7.46).

Minimal Cost – Sampling surveys, especially online or via phone, are cost-effective.

Response Collection Options – Surveys can be self-administered or interviewer-administered. Depending on the delivery method, the results can be collected online, via mobile and email, face-to-face, etc.

Wide Distribution – Surveys can reach remote audiences via phone and online (email, text, and web posting) techniques.

Figure 7.46 Only the researchers can identify the participant's identity for confidential research data.

Survey Disadvantages – Just like any research method, surveys have disadvantages. Here are some of the common ones:

Asking the Wrong People – Choose the right population to produce accurate results. Using random sampling will improve accuracy.

Asking the Wrong Questions – The biggest drawback to survey research is that you're stuck with the questions you ask. If you don't ask the right questions (or they're worded badly) the responses will be unreliable.

Researcher Bias – Speaking of badly worded questions, a researcher's personal views can result in biased question construction (see below for how to write effective questions).

Response Rates – People who say "no" to taking part in a survey lower the overall response rate. Pew Research Center noted that telephone response rates were 6% (Kennedy & Hartig, 2019) but found overall accuracy did not suffer as a result. There is no agreement on how high the response rate should be to ensure quality outcomes (Response Rates – An Overview, n.d.) More important is that the sample population reflects the characteristics of the study population.

Self-Reporting Bias – A respondent may not answer truthfully. When people tell a researcher what they think other people would approve of (Do you eat vegetables every day?) rather than just telling the truth, that's called social desirability bias. And how well someone's memory works can result in recall bias. For example, asking someone how often they ate vegetables last month, or their recollection of some other past behavior, might not get you 100% accurate results.

Inability to Answer – Sometimes, the respondent does not understand the question or does not have the ability (lack of knowledge or experience, memory recall, etc.) to answer it.

Online Survey Considerations

The advantages of online surveys include access, time, and cost (Wright, 2006) plus customization (Rubin, 2019) and HTML linking options. The technique has some challenges, too.

Access to Unique Populations – Some populations exist only in online virtual communities, so they're geographically dispersed. Online communities can receive surveys by emailed or posted survey invitation links in online communities.

Time – Readily available software, such as Google Forms, Qualtrics, and SurveyMonkey, automate tasks such as questionnaire design, previewing, testing, distribution, and reporting results. Using one of these options speeds up the process so researchers can work on other tasks.

Cost – Some third-party survey businesses offer free options, such as 20 questions and a total of 100 responses. Amazon offers Mechanical Turk that provides people willing to fill out a survey or perform other research tasks (Amazon Mechanical Turk, n.d.).

Design Customization – Some third-party survey tools allow for great design customization (Rubin, 2019). Skip logic lets respondents go to another set of questions if they don't meet certain criteria, and branching filters respondents into different questions depending on their answers. Piping allows surveys to insert new questions depending on a respondent's answer.

Anonymity – Online surveys can ensure participant names and personal information stay private, removing any information that digitally connects to a person's identity. This protection may encourage respondents to participate and answer truthfully.

HTML Linking Capability – Online surveys can include links to visual content, such as a proposed video commercial, website, or photos, for specific content or other questions.

Problems with Online Surveys – In a time when it seems *everything* is online, surveying there still has some drawbacks:

- Not everyone is online, which makes reaching certain populations challenging.
- Since respondents are self-reporting answers, it's hard to know if demographic and other characteristics are accurate.
- Generalization of results is difficult because random sampling requires access to a sampling frame (a list of all members in a population). For online communities, or website survey popups, that's usually impossible.

How to Set Up a Survey Project

1. Develop the research question/hypothesis
2. Select the sample
3. Recruit the Sample
4. Develop and test the questionnaire
5. Gain informed consent
6. Administer the questionnaire
7. Follow-up with nonresponders
8. Analyze the data
9. Report the findings/results

Step 1: Develop the Research Question/Hypothesis

Every study needs a purpose, and the research questions and hypothesis provide one. For guidance, read Chapter 6.

Step 2: Sample Selection

Sampling techniques are explained at the beginning of this chapter. Quantitative survey samples should reflect the whole population's characteristics. Samples can be further divided as subsamples. If you're studying a student tutoring program and the entire sample consists of male and female students using the program, you would choose only females for a subsample examining female student satisfaction with the program.

Sample selection sizes are often 10% of an entire population but usually no more than 1,000 potential respondents. You can use a sample size calculator to help figure out the best number for a project. Online options include Creative Survey Systems (Sample Size Calculator, n.d.).

Sampling Options – Sampling strategies are discussed at the beginning of this chapter. When possible, it's best to select a probability sample.

Step 3: Recruit the Sample

Communication – When recruiting people to take your survey, explain the potential benefits, ease, and any incentives. This can be done in a variety of modes: posters, letters, emails, pop-up internet ads, and text messages.

Incentives – Since low response rates are a growing challenge for researchers (see Response Rates above), the best way to increase engagement is through monetary and nonmonetary incentives (AAPOR Guidance for IRBs and Survey Researchers, n.d.). Cash, gift cards, or items such as food or t-shirts are acceptable. The American Association for Public Opinion Research recommends limiting cash incentives of $25 or less unless the target population represents a higher economic group like engineers. For college campus research involving students, $10 gift cards or food such as soda and pizza are more common.

Amazon's Mechanical Turk – If you don't have participants for your survey, consider using the Mechanical Turk, an online, crowdsourced pool of people who sign up to do simple tasks, like answer survey questions for a small fee (Getting started with surveys on MTurk, 2019). You can add eligibility requirements, such as age or industry occupation, for an added customization.

Step 4: Develop and Test the Questionnaire

This is your data collection instrument. When coming up with the survey *questionnaire*, the document containing your questions, pay close attention to question types, survey wording, and other considerations. The questions you ask and how you ask them will determine the quality of the survey data.

Basic Tips

Here are some basic tips for successful questionnaire development:

Limit the Number of Questions – People are busy. Keep the number of questions to what could reasonably be answered in 10 minutes, usually 20–25 questions. Focus on the most important information you need related to your research questions.

Keep it Simple to Complete – Focusing on what you really need to know can help you come up with questions that are short, easy and fast to answer. Fixed response statements/questions such as multiple choice or simple rating scales are easy and fast.

Keep it Easy to Understand – Use language familiar to respondents. No theoretical terms, acronyms, or technical language, and if you have to use an unfamiliar term be sure to include a simple definition with the question.

Overcome Inability or Unwillingness to Answer – There are many reasons why people don't answer survey questions. A respondent, for example, might not know anything about your topic (use a screening question to ensure they qualify for the survey). Other issues include the respondent's fear that his/her privacy might be jeopardized (emphasize data safeguards); his/her inability to remember an experience (include visual aids or other descriptions to aid recall); or a question is too sensitive or too hard to answer easily (limit data collection to easy to answer questions and limit private data collection) (Figure 7.47).

Question Ordering – Sometimes you have to ask harder questions that involve more effort (recall questions, etc.) or sensitive questions (income, race, religion, etc.). Start the questionnaire with easy-to-answer questions, work your way up to harder ones, and put demographic questions at the end.

Screening, Filter and Skip Logic Options – Screening questions determine eligibility trequirements. Are you 18 years or older? Do you own a car? etc. If the requirement is not met, the survey ends. Filters can route a participant to follow-up questions depending how he or she answers the question. For example, if you own a car, you may get more questions about your car. or the respondent skips over certain questions Just as filters can route respondents to additional questions, skip functions can move a respondent more quickly through a survey if certain questions don't pertain to the individual. This kind of customized path is easier to do with online questionnaires (Figure 7.48).

Pretest – Once questions are constructed, ask a friend who doesn't know anything about your project to take the survey. Use the feedback to revise any questions that your friend found confusing or especially hard to answer. In addition to the questionnaire, make sure you pretest mobile and online distribution methods to make sure everything works right.

Figure 7.47 Careful screening of participants and careful wording of questions can eliminate people's inability to answer questions.

Third-Party Survey Tools – Online questionnaires tools (Survey Monkey, Google Forms, Qualtrics, SurveyGizmo, and others) provide survey templates, easy-to-use tools to construct and distribute questionnaires anonymously, and analytic help.

Different Question Types – Different types of questions will provide different types of data, categorical or numerical. The type of data generated by a question determines what level of statistical analysis you can perform.

Data is classified by four levels of measurement: nominal, ordinal, interval, and ratio. Nominal and ordinal are categorical, focusing on the characteristics of the data, and interval and ratio are numerical (either discrete or continuous) data. Chapter 8 covers levels of measurement in more depth.

Open and Closed Ended Questions

Questions can be classified as either *open* or closed. Open-ended questions can be useful at the end of a survey (Is there anything else you care to comment on?), and they can be good follow-up probes to closed-ended questions (multiple choice or rating scales). Open-ended questions are at the *nominal* level of measurement.

Closed-ended questions provide response options that a user chooses from, like multiple choice. The level of measurement that closed-ended questions generate can be either nominal, ordinal, interval, or ratio. Here are some closed-ended question types:

Yes-No Questions – Sometimes a *yes/no question* is necessary as an opening filter (e.g., Are you 18 years or older?) to make sure you get the respondents you want. For web-based surveys, if a respondent doesn't meet the requirements the survey automatically moves to the end. Avoid yes/no questions if you are trying to gain deeper understanding of behaviors, attitudes, and opinions. Yes/no questions are at the nominal level of measurement.

Multiple Choice – Guided by previous research, *multiple choice questions* usually provide about three options that cover most anticipated responses. Sometimes a fourth response like "other" should be provided. Multiple choice questions are at the nominal level of measurement.

Screening and Filter Questions

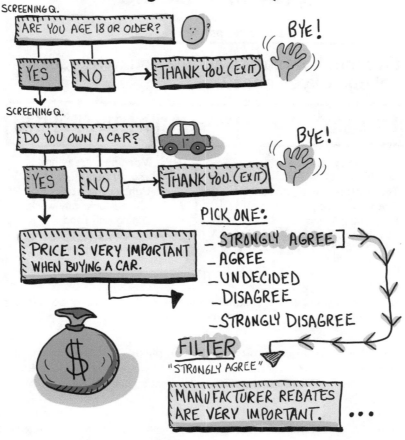

Figure 7.48 A screening question helps ensure that the appropriate person is taking the survey. Filter questions redirect respondents to questions that apply to them.

Rank Order Scales – Rank order scales, comparing different items to one another, can determine preference, importance, or other qualities about products and services. Variables are ordered but the distance between each is unknown. The Likert scale and other rank order scales are treated as categorical data, but they have some numeric value, too. They are at the ordinal level of measurement but are often analyzed at the interval level (Figure 7.49).

Rating Scales – Rating scales measure the direction and intensity of attitudes or opinions using a Likert or other common scale, and asking respondents to rate something from 1 to 10 or 1 to 100. Rating scales are at the ordinal level of measurement but are often analyzed at the interval level.

Constant Sum Scales – To understand what a person values, constant sum scales ask the respondent to assign points or cents to characteristics of a product, service, or other item that add up to 100 points or $1. Constant sum scales are at the ordinal level but are often analyzed at the interval level.

Semantic Differential Scales – These scales use word opposites on a five- or seven-point scale to gauge the strength of the respondent's attitudes or opinions about a product, service, or item. Semantic differential scales have been treated as both ordinal and interval data.

Wording Issues

Survey Wording – Question wording is full of possible traps for first-time researchers. Consider these common issues questions, and take the time to pretest your survey questions.

Leading Questions – Leading questions prompt the survey respondents to answer in a certain way. They cultivate bias because they include an element of tone, conjecture, or assumption that *leads* respondents to a certain kind of answer. Example: How amazing was your research class? (Figure 7.50).

Loaded/Assumptive Questions – Loaded questions contain an assumption about the survey respondent's habits or perceptions. The respondent might inadvertently agree or disagree with an implied statement (When did you stop cheating on exams?) that does not reflect their situation or opinion.

Likert Scale

Figure 7.49 Likert scales involve a series of statements that respondents can choose to rate attitudes, values, knowledge, etc.

Two Questions in One – Double-barreled questions try to force a survey respondent to answer two questions at once, like Example: Do you like pizza and beer? Only one question per question, please! (Figure 7.51).

Absolute Questions – Beware of *absolute* terms such as *always*, *never*, and *all*. Absolutes in questions are not useful because there are usually exceptions, especially when it comes to daily behavior. Survey respondents will struggle with what you really want to know. Example: Do you always eat breakfast?

Jargon – Acronyms and technical language – jargon – confuse survey respondents. Use language that is clear and concise. Example of jargon use: How satisfied are you with QIMCO's WYSIWYG user interface?

Complexity – Ask questions that respondents can easily answer. Memory and lack of exposure to the information can prevent accurate responses.

Biased Language – Use neutral language. Biased language can lead people to react negatively. Biased language includes words or phrases that demean or exclude people because of age, sex, race, ethnicity, social class, or physical or mental traits. Example: What's your opinion of policemen? (The neutral term "police officers" is preferred.) A full list of resources for avoiding biased language is provided in this text's web resources.

Exhaustive and Mutually Exclusive Responses – When response options are exhaustive that means they includes

Leading Question

Figure 7.50 A leading question pushes respondents to answer in a certain way.

Figure 7.51 A double-barrelled question asks for feedback on two different things. You can usually spot one if it contains an "and" or an "or" in the question.

Answers Should be Collectively Exhaustive

Figure 7.52 Make answer options collectively exhaustive. Every survey taker should be able to answer every question, which often means including an "I'm not sure" and an "Other (please describe):" response.

everything possible. Include the response option of "other." When a response is mutually exclusive that means responses don't have overlapping categories. For example, for age responses don't overlap ages like this: 18–24; 24–35; 35–45, 45–55; 55–. Instead: 18–24; 25–34; 35–44; 45–54; 55– (Figures 7.52 and 7.53).

Step 5: Gain Informed Consent

Informed Consent – College survey research projects are subject to ethics committee approval since they involve human subjects. Informed consent is necessary for every respondent before taking a survey. Informed consent generally includes: a general statement about the research's purpose, notification that participation is voluntary, an estimate of time to complete the survey, a description of any possible risks or discomforts to the subject, how confidentiality will be protected, and any benefits of the research.

For more guidelines on informed consent and privacy consideration see Chapter 4 "Thinking Ethically."

Step 6: Administer the Questionnaire

A questionnaire can be self-administered or interviewer-administered. In an interviewer-administered survey the interview can help when a respondent is having difficulties with a question.

Surveys can be distributed online (including email), or via mobile, mail, and face-to-face. A group whose members provide email addresses makes an email survey easy to administer. Internet surveys hosted on a website, such as a college campus website, are convenient but are subject to sampling error, since you can't control who responds. Mobile surveys require access to people's cell phones. Snail-mailed and face-to-face surveys can be expensive with larger samples. College campus projects should determine what mode (or multiple modes) will get the highest response from the chosen population.

Make Answer Options Mutually Exclusive

Generally, how many hours daily do you play video games?

Figure 7.53 Make sure all answer options are mutually exclusive; answers only fit in one option (e.g. 3-6 and 6-9 hours should be 3-5 and 6-9 hours) to avoid confusion – and respondent churn.

Step 7: Follow-Up with Nonresponders

Develop a strategy for contacting people who haven't responded to your questionnaire. Depending on how the survey was distributed, a reminder can be as simple as an email or text message.

Step 8: Analyze the Data

Statistical analysis can be used with quantitative data, and theme analysis is used on open-ended questions. Determining how to analyze quantitative data depends on the type of question asked and the level of measurement involved. Chapter 8 provides techniques and tools to analyze the data.

Step 9: Report the Findings

The final step is presenting the findings/results. Numeric data is presented in a narrative summary, often with tables and charts. Qualitative data is organized by themes. Ways to discuss and report your findings/results are covered in Chapters 9 and 11.

Academic Writing Examples

Example 1

Hung et al. (2017) conducted a national telephone survey of adolescents to measure an anti-tobacco campaign ("The Real Cost") ad and slogan recall and attitudes toward smoking products. Here's how they set up the research:

3. Measures

3.1. The Real Cost Ad and Slogan Recall

For the four The Real Cost ads that aired in the initial phase of campaign, we assessed aided recall of the ads by giving participants a brief verbal description of an ad and then asking whether they had seen or heard of the ad ("Yes" coded as 1, "No" coded as 0). Two of The Real Cost ads centered on the theme of physical appearance: the "Tooth" ad where a young man pulls his tooth out with pliers and the "Skin" ad where a young woman pulls some skin off her face. Two ads centered on the theme of loss of control: the "Bully" ad where a tiny man bullies a teenager and the "Alison" ad where a high school girl sits at a lunch table and talks about a bad relationship. The campaign was launched in February 2014 (10 months prior to the survey) across multiple media platforms. Campaign ad airtime varied between 6 and 10 months, with one ad, "Bully," on air during our data collection. We created an ad recall index (range 0–4) which indicated the number of

ads that a participant recalled, which was also dichotomized to indicate whether adolescents recalled any of the four ads. We assessed aided recall of The Real Cost campaign slogan with the following question: "Have you ever seen or heard any ads on television or radio with the slogan The Real Cost?"

3.2. Attitudes

For participants who recalled each ad, they were asked about how they felt about tobacco products after seeing or hearing that particular ad. For participants who recalled the slogan, they were asked about how they felt about tobacco products after seeing or hearing the slogan. Responses were dichotomized into "more negative" (coded as 1) versus "more positive" or "no difference" (coded as 0) for analysis.

3.3. Risk Perceptions

Perceived likelihood of harm about cigarette smoking (risk perceptions) was assessed by asking all participants "If you smoked cigarettes regularly for the next 10 years, how likely do you think it is that you would develop serious health problems?" Responses were dichotomized to reflect perceived likelihood, "not at all likely" (coded as 0) vs. "somewhat likely" or "very likely" (coded as 1).

3.4. Smoking Status

Participants were categorized into three groups by smoking status: non-smoking adolescents who were not susceptible to using cigarettes, non-smoking adolescents who were susceptible to using cigarettes, and current cigarette users (i.e., smoked in the past 30 days). Two susceptibility questions were asked of all youth who had not used cigarettes in the past 30 days (Pierce et al., 1996; Thrasher et al., 2009): "Do you think you will smoke a cigarette in the next year?" and "If one of your best friends were to offer you a cigarette, would you smoke it?" Participants who chose "definitely yes," "probably yes," or "probably not" to any of the two questions were classified as susceptible to cigarette smoking, while participants who chose "definitely not" to both questions were classified as not susceptible. Adolescents who reported using cigarettes in the past 30 days were categorized as current cigarette users.

3.5. Sociodemographics

Sociodemographic variables included sex (male, female), age (13–17 years), race (White, Black, all other races), ethnicity (Hispanic, non-Hispanic), and parental education (high school graduate or less, associate's degree or some college, bachelor's degree or above).

Example 2

A survey method was used to collect data from young females who subscribed and observed makeup tutorials on social media platforms. Researchers Hassan et al. (2021) examined the social media influencers' credibility traits, such as knowledge, attractiveness, and relatability to measure the influencers' ability to influence young millennials (Figure 7.54).

Figure 7.54 Hassan et al. (2021) examined the social media influencers' credibility traits to measure the influencers' ability to influence young millennials.

Methods

A survey instrument was developed to collect responses from female youths aged above 18 in Malaysia who had subscribed and watched video tutorials of makeup gurus on social media such as YouTube, Instagram, Twitter, and Facebook. Furthermore, a non-probability purposive sampling method was chosen to collect data through online platforms. The purposive sampling technique, also known as judgment sampling, involves identifying and selecting competent and well-informed participants with a subject of interest (Creswell & Clark, 2011). In addition to knowledge and experience, the availability and willingness to participate and communicate their experiences and opinions in an articulate, expressive, and reflective manner are also essential. Thus, for the purpose of this study, only respondents who followed and watched video tutorials of makeup gurus were selected.

The questionnaire was divided into several sections, in which the consent statement was first included in the survey form. The respondents were assured that no personal information would be made public, while the data would be kept strictly confidential and would exclusively be used for this report. Next, they were required to tick their consent agreement to answer the questionnaire, where they will be unable to continue answering the questionnaire if they choose the disagree option, and the survey process will be terminated. The second section of the questionnaire addressed independent variables: relatability, knowledge, helpfulness, confidence, articulation, and perceived authenticity. The independent variables were measured using a 5-point Likert scale, which is widely used in research and extensively tested in the social science literature. Meanwhile, the items of the influencer's cosmetic choice were measured using a 7-point Likert scale. The last section of the questionnaire showed the demographic profiles of the respondents.

This questionnaire included five social media influencers' characteristics: knowledge, relatability, helpfulness, confidence, and articulation. Firstly, the items for knowledge were taken from Chen et al. (2019),

followed by Kim and Park (2010), while the items for relatability were constructed from Fastenau (2018). Simultaneously, the items for helpfulness were adapted from Filieri et al. (2018), and the questions for confidence originated from Greenacre et al. (2014). However, certain items for articulation were adapted from previous studies, such as McMillan and Hwang (2002) and Ki (2018). Additionally, there were three dimensions of trust in this study: benevolence, integrity, and competence, all of which were adapted from Lu et al. (2016). Lastly, the items for the influencer and their recommendation to cosmetics purchase decisions were adapted from Flavián et al. (2006), Halim (2006), Xiao et al. (2016), and Gecti and Zengin (2013).

The sample size is viewed, considering the number of variables observed. According to Kline (2015), a minimum sample size of 200 or 5 times the number of parameters is required to test Structural Equation Modelling. For this study, the model had 53 parameters or items with the minimum sample needed for about 265 ($53 \times 5 = 265$). Overall, our sample satisfied these minimum requirements and a final total of 271 usable questionnaires were gathered and analyses.

The data was entered into Statistical Package for the Social Sciences (SPSS), and later, Structural equation modelling (SEM) was conducted using the Analysis of Moment Structures (AMOS 26) is a visual statistical program for structural equation modelling (SEM) (Byrne, 2001). The measurement model describes the relationships between the latent variables included in the analysis and their observed indicators to test the hypotheses stated (Fig 7.1). Overall model fit statistics and significance tests were generated for each path within the model. Several indices of model fit were used to examine the model, including the Tucker-Lewis Index (TLI), Comparative Fit Index (CFI), Root Mean Squared Error of Approximation (RMSEA), and Standardised Root Mean Squared Residual (SRMR) and Chi-square (McDonald & Ho, 2002).

Activities

Survey Considerations

Think about your research question or topic. How could you design a survey project for it? Briefly describe and justify the following design considerations:

1. Population's characteristics
2. Sampling method
3. Mode of administration
4. Questions

Develop a Short Questionnaire

Using your knowledge and/or experience of your campus dining facilities, design a short questionnaire that gauges student attitudes about:

1. Food quality
2. Variety
3. Facility

Resources

- Methods 101: Random Sampling
  https://www.youtube.com/watch?v=sonXfzE1hvo
- A Survey in 10 Steps
  https://www.youtube.com/watch?v=U1MYM35q
  Ur8&t=9s
- Best Practices for Survey Research
  https://www.aapor.org/Standards-Ethics/Best-Practices.
  aspx
- Question wording
  https://www.youtube.com/watch?v=eFzGdQrr2K8
- Evaluating Survey Quality in Today's Complex
  Environment
  https://www.aapor.org/Education-Resources/Reports/
  Evaluating-Survey-Quality.aspx
- 7 Tips for Good Survey Questions
  https://www.youtube.com/watch?v=Iq_fhTuY1hw
- What are Nonprobability Surveys?
  https://www.pewresearch.org/methods/2018/08/06/
  video-explainer-what-are-nonprobability-surveys/
- Mode effects
  https://www.pewresearch.org/fact-tank/2019/02/07/
  phone-vs-online-surveys-why-do-respondents-answers-
  sometimes-differ-by-mode/

References

AAPOR guidance for IRBs and survey researchers (n.d.) American Association for Public Opinion. https://www.aapor.org/Standards-Ethics/Institutional-Review-Boards/Full-AAPOR-IRB-Statement.aspx

Amazon Mechanical Turk (n.d.) https://www.mturk.com/

Byrne, B. M. (2001). Structural equation modeling with AMOS, EQS, and LISREL: Comparative approaches to testing for the factorial validity of a measuring instrument. *International Journal of Testing*, *1*(1), 55–86. https://doi.org/10.1207/S15327574IJT0101_4

Check, J., & Schutt, R. K. (2012). Survey research. In J. Check, & R. K. Schutt (Eds.), *Research methods in education* (pp. 159–185). SAGE Publishing.

Chen, J., Wang, H., & Gao, W. (2019). How do goal and product knowledge specificity influence online channel choice? A polynomial regression analysis. *Electronic Commerce Research and Applications*, *35*, 100846.

Creswell, J. W., & Clark, V. L. P. (2011). *Designing and conducting mixed methods research*. SAGE Publishing.

Fastenau, J. (2018). Under the influence: The power of social media influence, in Dostopno prek https://medium.com/crobox/under-the-influence-the-power-of-socialmedia-influencers-5192571083c3

Filieri, R., McLeay, F., Tsui, B., & Lin, Z. (2018). Consumer perceptions of information helpfulness and determinants of purchase intention in online consumer reviews of services. *Information & Management*, *55*(8), 956–970.

Flavián, C., Guinalíu, M., & Gurrea, R. (2006). The role played by perceived usability, satisfaction and consumer trust on website loyalty. *Information & management*, *43*(1), 1–14. https://doi.org/10.1016/j.im.2005.01.002

Gecti, F., & Zengin, H. (2013). The relationship between brand trust, brand affect, attitudinal loyalty and behavioral loyalty: A field study towards sports shoe consumers in Turkey. *International Journal of Marketing Studies*, *5*(2), 111.

Getting started with surveys on MTurk (2019, July 1). Amazon Mechanical Turk. https://blog.mturk.com/getting-started-with-surveys-on-mturk-e2eea524c73

Greenacre, L., Tung, N. M., & Chapman, T. (2014). Self confidence, and the ability to influence. *Academy of Marketing Studies Journal*, *18*(2), 169. https://www.researchgate.net/profile/Luke-Greenacre/publication/286318041_Self_confidence_and_the_ability_to_influence/links/577f3a2608ae5f367d33ed47/Self-confidence-and-the-ability-to-influence.pdf

Halim, R. E. (2006). The effect of the relationship of brand trust and brand affect on brand performance: An analysis from brand loyalty perspective (A case of instant coffee product in Indonesia). *Behavioral & Experimental Economics*. SSRN: https://ssrn.com/abstract=925169 or http://dx.doi.org/10.2139/ssrn.925169

Hassan, S. H., Teo, S. Z., Ramayah, T., & Al-Kumaim, N. H. (2021). The credibility of social media beauty gurus in young millennials' cosmetic product choice. *Plos one*, *16*(3), e0249286. https://doi.org/10.3390%2Fijerph14010042

Joint American Statistical Association/AAPOR statement on use of incentives in survey participation (2016, Oct. 24). American Association for Public Opinion. https://www.aapor.org/Publications-Media/Public-Statements/AAPOR-Statement-on-Use-of-Incentives-in-Survey-Par.aspx

Ki, C. W. (2018). The drivers and impacts of social media influencers: The role of mimicry [Unpublished doctoral dissertation]. University of Tennessee. https://trace.tennessee.edu/utk_graddiss/5070

Kim, K., & Park, J. S. (2010). Message framing and the effectiveness of DTC advertising: The moderating role of subjective product knowledge. *Journal of Medical Marketing*, *10*(2), 165–176.

Kennedy, C., & Hartig, H. (2019, Feb. 27). Response rates in telephone surveys have resumed their decline. Pew Research Center. https://www.pewresearch.org/fact-tank/2019/02/27/response-rates-in-telephone-surveys-have-resumed-their-decline/

Kline, R. B., (2015). Principles and practice of structural equation modeling. Guilford.

Lu, B., Fan, W., & Zhou, M. (2016). Social presence, trust, and social commerce purchase intention: An empirical research. *Computers in Human Behavior*, *56*, 225–237. https://doi.org/10.1016/j.chb.2015.11.057

McDonald, R. P., & Ho, M. H. R. (2002). Principles and practice in reporting structural equation analyses. *Psychological Methods*, *7*(1), 64. PMID:11928891

McMillan, S. J., & Hwang, J. S. (2002). Measures of perceived interactivity: An exploration of the role of direction of communication, user control, and time in shaping perceptions of interactivity. *Journal of Advertising*, *31*(3), 29–42.

Pierce, J. P., Choi, W. S., Gilpin, E. A., Farkas, A. J., & Merritt, R. K. (1996). Validation of susceptibility as a predictor of which adolescents take up smoking in the United States. *Health Psychology*, 15, 355–361. doi: 10.1037/0278-6133.15.5.355.

Response rates – An overview (n.d.) American Association for Public Opinion Research. https://www.aapor.org/Education-Resources/For-Researchers/Poll-Survey-FAQ/Response-Rates-An-Overview.aspx

Rubin, R. (2019, June 8). The best online survey tools. PC Magazine. https://www.pcmag.com/picks/the-best-online-survey-tools

Sample size calculator (n.d.) Creative Research Systems. https://www.surveysystem.com/sscalc.htm

Thrasher, J. F., Sargent, J. D., Huang, L., Arillo-Santillán, E., Dorantes-Alonso, A., & Pérez-Hernández, R. (2009). Does film smoking promote youth smoking in middle-income countries? A longitudinal study among Mexican adolescents. *Cancer Epidemiology Biomarkers & Prevention*, 18(12). doi: 10.1158/1055-9965. EPI-09-0883.

Wright, K. B. (2006). Researching internet-based populations: Advantages and disadvantages of online survey research, online questionnaire authoring software packages, and web survey services. *Journal of Computer-Mediated Communication*, 10(3). https://doi.org/10.1111/j.1083-6101.2005.tb00259.x

Xiao, L., Guo, Z., D'Ambra, J., & Fu, B. (2016). Building loyalty in e-commerce: Towards a multidimensional trust-based framework for the case of China. *Program*, 50(4), 431–461. https://doi.org/10.1108/PROG-04-2016-0040

EXPERIMENT

Pavlov's Dog's Experiment

Figure 7.55 Who says researchers can't learn new tricks?

What Is Experimental Research?

People use the word "experiment" all the time to describe something they're going to try, to see if it works. In research, the word has a specific meaning: an experiment explores possible relationships between two things that can or could change, the independent and dependent variables (Coleman, 2018; Figure 7.55).

To be valid in the research world, a true experiment must include random selection and group assignment, manipulation of the independent variable, and comparable treatment, and control groups (Figure 7.56).

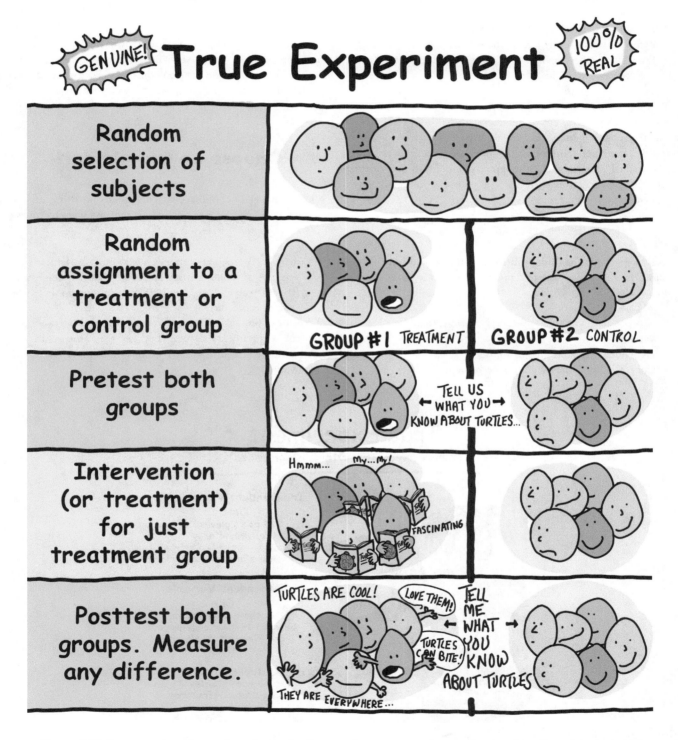

Figure 7.56 True experiments used random selection, random group assignments, use of treatment and control groups, an intervention/treatment (brochure for Group #1), and pretest and posttest. "Knowledge about turtles" is the variable measured.

Here's how it works. The researcher manipulates the independent variable (the "I do" variable) systematically to see if the dependent variable changes as a result. For example, you could experiment with an online financial planning module (the independent variable), by:

- offering it to one (treatment) group but not a second (control) group, group members would be randomly assigned;
- measuring both groups' financial planning knowledge; and
- comparing the results. Any change in financial planning knowledge (the dependent variable), would be the effect between two variables.

To get the most accurate results, researchers try to control extraneous variables, any other variable that could affect an experiment's outcome. In the example above, researchers could control for (eliminate) the presence of any workplace educational materials, such as posters, employee newsletter articles, and brochures with financial planning info – all controlled variables (Figure 7.57).

All other factors are controlled.

Every experiment has independent, dependent, and controlled variables, and a good way to remember their differences is: *It's not all about me, it's "all about I"*:

- Independent variable – *What **I** change* (it's the "I do" variable)
- Dependent variable – *What **I** observe*
- Controlled variables – *What **I** keep the same*

The independent variable can test more than one thing by including different conditions. In the example above, the researcher could set up an experiment to measure outcomes from three levels of online financial planning coursework (conditions) to three different groups, with a fourth (control) group getting no training at all. At the end of the experiment, the knowledge of the three groups would be compared to the group that received no training.

Common communication research experiments look at how a communicator puts together information (*message characteristics*) and the message delivery. Take any message you plan to send, and consider whether you construct it with rational or emotional content – and compare how well each approach was received, understood, and/or remembered.

Why Choose an Experiment?

When you need to know conclusively if one thing affects another, true experiments can answer that question (or questions) (Bechhofer & Paterson, 2000).

- **Control** – A true experiment's *control* of all variables is its biggest advantage; that control is what can determine conclusively a cause-and-effect relationship between two or more variables.
- **Replication** – Other researchers can duplicate original experiments. When they get the same results, it builds confidence in the relationship between the tested variables.

True Experiment
(Where Nearly Everything is Controlled)

Independent Variable:
Time
14 hours playing
Halo Infinite daily
or
hours daily playing

Dependent Variable:
GPA
Is there a difference
between 14-hour daily players
and 2-hour daily players?

Controlled Factors
Gender - males
Class Status - freshman
undergraduates
Credits taken: 15 credit hours

Figure 7.57 The independent variable is manipulated (changed) to reveal an effect on another variable (the dependent variable).

Generalizable Findings/Results – As more experiments produce similar results, researchers can generalize the results to populations larger than the research groups.

Natural or Lab Conditions – This method can be used in the "real world" or (especially for greater control) in an artificial, laboratory environment.

Quantitative Results – The quantitative (numeric) data produced by an experiment can be analyzed using statistical methods.

Disadvantages – Nothing is perfect, including experimental research. Some possible pitfalls:

Human Error – Experiments, like other methods, are prone to human errors. Mistakes can happen at every stage of design, data gathering, and analysis.

Too Artificial – If a researcher tries to control every variable, the experiment might be so controlled that it's doesn't mirror the real world.

Researcher Bias – Sometimes a researcher may consciously or unconsciously send signals to participants that will affect their behavior.

Demand Characteristics – Participants who know they're in an experiment will often try to figure out what's being tested. And depending on what they think, they might change their behavior one way or the other. Not good.

Time Consuming/Costly – Some experiments eat up a lot of time and cost a lot of money, especially if you try to test several conditions of the independent variable. Creating the experiment, recruiting participants, executing the experiment, analyzing the results – the time factor can be a problem.

Explanation – True experiments provide causal (cause-and-effect) evidence (Figure 7.58). Did X affect Y? Yes/No. Either way, true experiments don't explain the *why* – especially when dealing with human behavior!

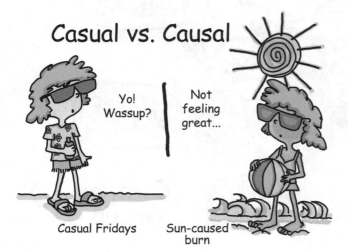

Casual vs. Causal

Yo! Wassup?

Not feeling great...

Casual Fridays

Sun-caused burn

Figure 7.58 Make your professor's day. When you write about cause and effect between the independent and dependent variables in an experiment, it's called a "causal" effect - not casual. That's a little too informal!

That's why adding other research methods (focus groups, depth interviews, surveys) to any investigation is a really good idea.

Experimental Design Options

What's described above, a true experimental design, is considered the most trustworthy causal data collection method because it can control all variables within comparable, randomized groups. Other research designs associated with true experiments produce significantly less valid results. Pre-experimental designs, for example, are exploratory, not causal research. Remember, the words "experiment" and "experimental" are often used in everyday conversation to describe something that's not a true experiment.

Pre-Experimental Designs – Pre-experimental designs share some features with true experiments, but again – they're not causal. Think of them in medical research, a kind of exploratory pilot study where a researcher tries a treatment (intervention, program, or event) to see if a disease responds. Pre-experimental designs could lead to the design of a true experiment, and they are acceptable when time, money, or comparable group participants aren't immediately available to conduct a true experiment.

- **One-Shot Case Study** – With no pretest or comparison group, a small test group receives treatment, and a posttest is conducted to see if anything changed. An example: Smokers view interviews with a lung cancer survivor. A week after the interviews, smokers are asked if they had quit smoking. Since it wasn't designed as a true experiment, the results wouldn't indicate if the smokers had already decided to quit smoking or if some other unknown variable influenced their decision.
- **One Group Pretest, Posttest Design** – This design offers a pretest before the experimental treatment and posttest afterwards to see if there was any change. Without a comparison group, it's impossible to know if other factors affected the group. An example: Smokers are pretested about their attitudes toward smoking. They watch interviews with lung cancer survivors. A week later, smokers are checked to see if they are still smoking. Without a comparison group, it is hard to know if the interviews or some other factor caused the participants to keep smoking or stop.
- **Group Design** – This design measures two groups, treatment and no-treatment (control group) at the same time. No random assignment, no pretest; and without a pretest it's unknown if the two groups are comparable.

Quasi-Experimental Designs – Quasi-experimental designs have a lot in common with true experiments because both seek a cause-and-effect relationship between two variables, include pre/post treatments, measure treatment outcome, and compare results to similar groups (Levy & Ellis, 2011; Reichardt, 2019) (Figure 7.59).

Quasi-Experiment

Figure 7.59 Non-experimental research doesn't randomly select participants or randomly assign participants to groups. Researchers can make after-treatment observations only, or both before and after treatment.

- **Pretest/Posttest Design** – Participants get a pretest to measure baseline information related to the treatment. After the treatment is administered, a posttest measures any changes compared to the pretest. A control group is optional.
- **Nonequivalent Group Design** – A common option in school/college settings, in which the researcher doesn't randomly assign participants to the treatment/control group but rather assigns the treatment to the groups. In college, this could include two class sections of an oral communication course. One class gets the treatment, the other doesn't.

- **Interrupted Time Series Design** – Similar to a pretest/posttest design, but with multiple pretest/posttest measures. The treatment happens at some determined point in a defined period. For example, the researcher pretests students every week to measure their knowledge about a historical event. After five weeks of pretests, the students are given a lecture on the specific historical event (treatment). Students are posttested for five more weeks.

True Experimental Design – True experiments test one or more independent variables, use randomized samples, control groups, and a controlled treatment and setting (Figure 7.60).

Figure 7.60 A true experiment has a treatment group and a control group with randomly assigned members. Above, both groups have the same demographic characteristics, but the treatment group members were given masks and " how to wear your mask" instructions. The control group received no intervention (no masks or instruction). True experiments text whether an intervention caused an effect – a "causal" effect.

The key differences between quasi-experiments and true experiments are as follows:

- True experiments randomly assignment participants to treatment/control groups. Quasi-experiments don't use randomization for group assignments.
- True experiments use a control group (participants who don't get the treatment). In quasi-experiments, control groups are optional.
- True experiments use treatments designed by a researcher; quasi-experiments study preexisting groups that received different treatments after the fact. Quasi-experiments are often natural (real world) experiments, occurring outside a laboratory setting.

Factorial Designs (True Experiment) – The simplest true experiment is one that tests one independent variable. If two or more independent variables need to be tested, a factorial design is needed. That requires four or more groups with at least two independent variables called factors. For example, a 2 × 2 factorial design would test two treatments (independent variables) with four groups: product packaging color (red or blue) and different typography (Helvetica or Arial fonts).

How to Set Up a True Experiment Project

1. Start with a theoretical framework
2. Develop a hypothesis and research question
3. Create the treatment and experimental conditions
4. Pretest and pilot the experiment; revise as necessary
5. Recruit participants
6. Gain informed consent
7. Conduct the experiment
8. Analyze the data
9. Report the findings/results

Step 1: Theoretical Framework

Pick a theory that best explains the phenomenon you're investigating. A theory, usually based on previous studies, predicts how something happens, and it has variables that can be tested.

Step 2: Hypothesis and Research Question

Based on a theory, a researcher comes up with a hypothesis, a kind of prediction in the form of a "if this, then that" statement that contains two types of variables. The independent variable is what the researcher changes (the cause) and the dependent variable is what the researcher observes (the effect). See Chapter 6 for more information.

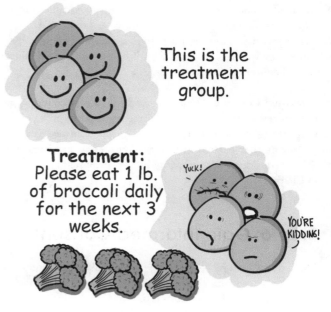

Figure 7.61 A treatment in an experiment is the independent variable (eating lots of broccoli) that may cause an effect (better health).

Step 3: Create a Treatment and Experimental Conditions

For social science experiments, the independent variables are often some type of information (treatment) provided to participants in a situation. If you're new to this method, consider limiting your experiment to one independent variable (Figure 7.61). You can include different conditions, variations of the independent variable. Develop protocols that include what roles researcher and their associates play. Experiments require clear instructions for what the participants will do.

Step 4: Pretest/Pilot the Experiment

Pretesting the treatment activities (such as instructions and tasks) with friends, fellow students, other people can help you spot changes that might need to be made. Pilot *tests* are a bit more involved than a simple pretest, since they try out aspects of the design, the instructions, tasks, equipment, environment, and use of associates (those supporting a researcher's experiment) to make sure they check out.

Step 5: Develop a Sampling Strategy

True experiments use random assignment to decide who goes in what group, treatment or control. Random assignment means that every person in the population has an equal chance of being selected for either group. The most common random-based techniques, probability samples, are simple, systematic, stratified random selection. Nonprobability samples, techniques that don't rely on random sampling. These nonrandom techniques (convenience, purposive, quota, and snowball, to name a few) are less accurate. Sampling options are explained at the beginning of this chapter.

Informed Consent – Human-based research at colleges and universities require ethics committee approval to protect participant rights, which are outlined in an informed consent document that participants must sign before participating. Ethical considerations including informed consent are covered in Chapter 4.

Step 6: Gain Informed Consent

Informed Consent – College experimental research projects are subject to ethics committee approval since they involve human subjects, unless your classroom has obtained an IRB waiver. Informed consent is necessary for every respondent before participating in an experiment. Informed consent generally includes: a general statement about the research's purpose, notification that participation is voluntary, an estimate of time to complete the survey, a description of any possible risks or discomforts to the subject, how confidentiality will be protected, and any benefits of the research.

In addition to informed consent, here are some additional considerations:

- **Cover Story** – A cover story disguises the experiment's real purpose so that participants are unaware of its true goal – and act more genuinely that they might if they knew what was really being studied (Lavrakas, 2008). Beyond just describing a cover story, you may need to include some non-study related alternative tasks that participants think are the actual experiment. An effective cover story with appropriate tasks increases internal validity (Figure 7.62). A cover story may be provided that disguises the true purpose (true hypothesis) of the experiment from the participants. Avoid disclosing to them the true hypothesis being investigated. This type of deception is generally fine especially when participants' behavior might change if they knew the true purpose of the study.
- **Volunteers** – Ethically, research participation must be voluntary. But research shows that volunteer participants tend to be more educated, more sociable, come from a higher social economic class, are more approval motivated, etc. (Rosenthal & Rosnow, 1975) So they may not truly reflect the larger population being studied, and that can threaten external validity.

For more guidelines on informed consent and privacy consideration see Chapter 4 "Thinking Ethically."

Figure 7.62 A cover story disguises the true intent of the experiment so that participants don't guess the real goal. If participants knew the experiment's goal, they might alter their behaviors. This deception should be balanced with participants' right to know and should not greatly increase their risks. A debrief with participants should happen as soon as possible.

Step 7: Conduct the Experiment

True experiments offer tight control of variables, allowing researchers to confidently investigate cause and effect between two variables (Field & Hole, 2003). Before and during an experiment, it's important to make sure it's conducted with precision. (Careless work or "I guess that's good enough" lowers confidence in the results.) Internal validity deals with how well a study was performed (see Internal Validity, below). Take the time to administer the experiment carefully so no mistakes are made.

Internal and External Validity – Internal validity relates to how well the study was conducted; how confident we are in the cause-and-effect relationship. External validity is about a study's ability to extend to other situations and populations. Some common validity issues for experimental research include:

Control Group – A comparable control group, which does not receive the experimental treatment, helps improve internal validity because both groups share similar key characteristics and experiences.

Randomization – Random selection and randomized group assignments ensure study participants are representative of the target population. This increases internal validity.

Establish, Test, and Follow Protocols – Following strong study protocols increases internal validity. Pretests, pilot tests, training of researchers in the administration of the experiment – together, all these strengthen overall quality (Mitchell & Jolley, 2004).

Step 8: Analyze the Data

Experiments create quantitative data to analyze. Some of the key analyses are hypothesis testing, such as the standard error of the mean, and statistical testing such as ANOVAs or t-tests to establish the significance of observed differences. Quantitative data analysis is discussed in Chapter 8.

Step 9: Report the Findings

The final step is presenting the findings/results, telling the story. A narrative summary usually includes tables, charts, and other ways of showing the numbers – the numeric data. Qualitative data is usually explained with a longer, more thorough narrative, often organized by themes. Ways to discuss and report your findings/results are covered in Chapters 9 and 11.

Academic Writing Examples

Example 1

Researchers Lewandowsky and Yesilada (2021) used an experiment to test whether or not viewing an informational video could counter the spread of Islamophobic and radical-Islamist disinformation (Figure 7.63). Read the full article to see how the experiment was carried out.

The study used a 2 × 2 between-subjects design, with variables training (no intervention vs. inoculation) and misinformation (Islamophobic Misinformation vs. radical-Islamist misinformation). Participants were randomly allocated to one of the 4 groups (see Table 1 for the number of participants per group). Dependent variables were perceived accuracy of the target video, feelings of anger, likelihood to share the target video, extent of agreement and extent of support for the target video, and next-video preference (expressed by choosing another video from a "recommender system").

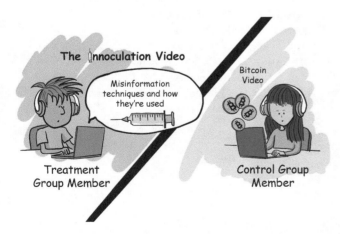

Figure 7.63 Lewandowsky and Yesilada (2021) used an experiment to test whether or not viewing an informational video could counter the spread of Islamophobic and radical-Islamist disinformation.

Design Procedure

Figure 1 *provides an overview of the procedure. Participants first answered demographic questions, including about their religious orientation. Participants then either watched the training material (inoculation condition; see below for details) or content about an unrelated issue (control condition). The control condition video taught participants about the use of bitcoin and the origin of money and was the same length as the inoculation video. Participants then watched the target video, which depending on random assignment either displayed content comprising a conduit to radical-Islamist content or Islamophobic content. All participants were then presented with a mock YouTube sidebar with a recommender tab of 5 videos (see Fig. 2) that, depending on condition, displayed Islamophobic or radical-Islamist video titles. The titles and thumbnails were arranged on an ordinal scale of extremism, from benign content to extreme content. Participants were asked to select from the recommender tab what video they would like to watch next.*

Following their next-video selection, participants responded to questions about the target video. All questions used a 5-point Likert scale, with the exception of agreement, which used a 6-point scale. The first question investigated participants' likelihood of sharing the video via social media platforms (response options ranging from highly unlikely to highly likely). The second question inquired about the extent to which participants believed the video to be reliable (response options ranging from highly unreliable to highly reliable). The third question aimed to determine participants' level of anger after watching the video (response options ranging from none at all to a great deal). The fourth question queried the extent to which participants agreed with the video (response options ranging from "I accepted all of the points made in the message" to "I argued against all of the points made in the message"). The fifth and final question aimed to determine participants' level of support for the ideas presented in the video. Instead of a 5-point scale, this question used a slider from 0-100. The slider was positioned at 0 at the outset.

Participants were then asked to watch a debrief video and read a debrief sheet. The debrief video consisted of the inoculation video and a video explaining the push and pull factors involved in radicalization. Participants who did not watch the debrief video were sent an invitation to complete the study by watching the debrief video. Fifteen participants were sent an invitation to watch the debriefing video. Thirteen of these participants completed the debrief upon receiving the invitation. Data from participants who did not watch the debrief video during the experiment were included, irrespective of whether or not they subsequently followed the invitation.

Example 2

Researchers Bellman et al. (2018) used an experiment to test the effects of program quality and content – particularly violent, sexual or extremist content – on pre-roll ads (the ads placed before the video). Read the full article to see how the authors developed the sample, stimuli, training video for the inoculation condition, and the target videos for the experiment.

Design

A laboratory experiment tested the effects of different types of short video content (less than 5 minutes in duration, like most YouTube videos) on pre-roll advertising. The experiment's participants watched eight short videos, two each (a high- and a low-budget version) of four content types (neutral, violent, sexual, extremist). Before each short video, participants watched a pre-roll ad. The pre-roll ads in this experiment could not be skipped, but to reproduce the typical viewing time for a YouTube pre-roll ad, we used short seven-second ads. A seven-second ad is just longer than the six-second duration of most YouTube pre-roll ads, which are skipped as soon as ad-skipping becomes possible, after five seconds (Campbell et al., 2017). Before each pre-roll ad, participants watched 30-seconds of relaxation video to relax their emotional response after the previous content. After watching all eight short videos, participants completed a questionnaire measuring responses to each video context and then to each pre-roll ad.

This study used a powerful repeated measures design that compares participant content differences rather than group differences (Potter and Bolls, 2012). This design controls for individual difference effects such as age and gender (which varied widely in the non-student sample). As within-participant designs are vulnerable to order effects, randomizing the video presentation-order and the pre-roll ad assignments to the eight videos controlled for order effects. Two sets of eight short videos (both sets had a high and low budget version of four content types, G, V, S, and E) provided replication and generalization, as otherwise significant effects might have been due to the specific experimental stimuli (Potter and Bolls, 2012). Randomly allocated to one of these two video-content groups, one participant group saw one set of eight videos; the other group saw the other set. Both groups saw the same eight pre-roll ads.

Activities

Create a Research Question and Hypothesis

Using your research topic, develop the following design elements:

1. Create a research question related to your research topic.
2. Create a hypothesis with independent and dependent variables related to your research question. This can be written in an if/then statement format. The independent variable is what you change and the dependent variable is what you observe. Included control variables – those that you keep the same.
3. Based on the hypothesis, what prediction can you make?

Create Quasi-Experimental and True Experimental Designs

Based on your research topic, questions or hypothesis:

1. Select a quasi-experimental design and explain the treatment/ intervention.
2. Create a true experimental design and explain the treatment/ intervention.
3. Explain the advantages and disadvantages of each approach.

Simple Controlled Experiment: A/B Testing

A popular way to assess websites and other marketing materials is a simple controlled experiment called A/B testing. All variables are controlled except one – the independent variable. A website, for example, can create two versions of a landing page and ask viewers which one they prefer. Watch: A/B Testing Tutorial: A Short How-to-Guide at https://www.youtube.com/watch?v=jauOqdNtkhQ.

1. Create an A/B testing experiment for a company such as a new logo or a new slogan.
2. What is your independent variable?
3. How would you evaluate the experiment?

Resources

Duke University's social science research center offers *Causal Inference Bootcamp: Experiment Basics*, with helpful videos that look at the experimental process.

- Causal Inference Bootcamp: Experiment Basics (15 videos) https://www.youtube.com/playlist?list=PL1M5TsfDV6VtNeC13g4hb5PEYSq24KXfd
- Research Methods: Experimental Design https://www.youtube.com/watch?v=qtLnBz6lbRQ
- A/B Testing Tutorial: A Short How-to-Guide https://www.youtube.com/watch?v=jauOqdNtkhQ
- A/B Testing Tips Proven to Increase Advertising ROI https://www.youtube.com/watch?v=oyoGU6wRsn4&t=17s

References

Bechhofer, F., & Paterson, L. (2000). *Principles of research design in the social sciences* (Series: social research today). Routledge.

Bellman, S., Abdelmoety, Z., Murphy, J., Arismendez, S., & Varan, D. (2018). Brand safety: The effects of controversial video content on pre-roll advertising. *Heliyon, 4*(12), e01041. https://doi.org/10.1016/j.heliyon.2018.e01041

Coleman, R. (2018). *Designing experiments for the social sciences: How to plan, create, and execute research using experiments.* SAGE Publishing.

Campbell, C., Mattison Thompson, F., Grimm, P. E., & Robson, K. (2017). Understanding why consumers don't skip pre-roll video ads. *Journal of Advertising, 46*(3), 411–423.

Field, A., & Hole, G. (2003). *How to design and report experiments.* SAGE Publishing.

Jeong, M., Zhang, D., Morgan, J. C., Ross, J. C., Osman, A., Boynton, M. H., Mendel, J. R., & Brewer, N. T. (2019). Similarities and differences in tobacco control research findings from convenience and probability samples. *Annals of Behavioral Medicine: Society of Behavioral Medicine, 53*(5), 476–485. https://doi.org/10.1093/abm/kay059

Lavrakas, P. J. (2008). *Encyclopedia of survey research methods.* SAGE Publishing, Inc.

Levy, Y., & Ellis, T. J. (2011). A guide for novice researchers on experimental and quasi-experimental studies in information systems research. *Interdisciplinary Journal of Information, Knowledge, and Management, 6,* 151–161. https://doi.org/10.28945/1373

Lewandowsky, S., & Yesilada, M. (2021). Inoculating against the spread of Islamophobic and radical-Islamist disinformation. *Cognitive Research: Principles and Implications, 6*(1), 57. doi: https://doi.org/10.1186/s41235-021-00323-z.

Mitchell, M., & Jolley, J. (2004). *Research design explained* (5th ed.). Wadsworth.

Potter, R. F., & Bolls, P. D. (2012). *Psychophysiological measurement and meaning: Cognitive and emotional processing of media.* Routledge.

Reichardt, C. S. (2019). *Quasi-experimentation: A guide to design and analysis* (Methodology in the social sciences). The Guilford Press.

Rosenthal, R., & Rosnow, R. (1975). *The volunteer subject.* John Wiley & Sons.

8

Writing the Results

Numbers Rule!

The Pen is Mightier than the Sword!

Figure 8.0 Quant and qual fighters at it again…

DOI: 10.4324/9781003214489-8

QUALITATIVE DATA ANALYSIS

Figure 8.1 Qualitative analysis promises rich data findings...and a few skeletons!

ANALYSIS TIME

"I was just looking for an easy research project and thought, Gee--the more interviews, the better! What do I do with the data?"

Figure 8.2 It's easy to get overwhelmed with lots of textual qualitative data.

Making Sense of Qualitative Data

The results section (sometimes called the findings) forms a written description of data findings told narratively. Succinct and clear writing are important. The results should explain your understanding of the pattern-based themes and organized concepts about a topic or research question. Vivid illustrative quotes are frequently used to provide additional evidence for themes and concepts (Figure 8.2).

This information can be visualized in textual (and sometimes numeric) tables, matrices, and models. Other illustrative material may be used to support the narrative. Visual models often show how themes connect and form an organizing concept.

The goal is to find the underlying story of your data. Always seek to move beyond mere data summarization and attempt to link patterns together that explain or illuminate a phenomenon.

Qualitative Approaches

Now that you have collected your qualitative data, what do you do with it? Sometimes, the sheer amount of data — many, many pages of recorded interviews, for example – can be daunting. This book reviews two popular qualitative analytic approaches for qualitative data analysis: reflexive thematic analysis (RTA) and directed qualitative content analysis. There are many qualitative analytic approaches and variations so if these two approaches featured are not right for your research project pursue other approaches. Some of those include grounded theory, discourse analysis, narrative analysis, and interpretative phenomenological analysis, among others.

Reflexive Thematic Analysis

Thematic analysis is a catch-all term for several qualitative analytic approaches that look for patterns across datasets in human-produced data:

- Interviews, focus groups, diaries, and open-ended surveys
- Secondary sources such as websites, online forums, blogs, newspaper articles, etc.
- Communication that exists in visual or audio form such as film, photography, art, etc.

As long as the communication can be observed in text, audio or visual form, it can be analyzed.

Thematic analysis looks for similarities, "patterns of shared meaning" (Braun & Clarke, 2019, p. 593) and groups them, through coding, into themes. Themes can combine into a central organizing concept.

Coded data chunks can be as small as a single word, entire paragraphs, or longer. Thematic analysis answers how or what questions best: How do people/groups experience life? What shapes processes? How do people's viewpoints differ on particular topics? Thematic analysis can answer all these and more (Figure 8.3).

Figure 8.3 Reflexivity is used by researchers to check their assumptions and reflect on both their past experiences, and anything else that might bear on a research effort that relies on their interpretive skills.

Reflexive Thematic Analysis – RTA puts the researcher center stage to generate a systematic, rigorous, yet highly interpretive analysis from the data – one not predetermined by existing theory or coding schemes (Braun and Clarke, 2013). Data is assigned codes that are grouped into themes to describe a central, unifying concept or a theory. This analytic technique considers a researcher's assumptions, experiences, and disciplinary knowledge part of the data analysis. Researchers using this method recognize and embrace their role in the research process. Beyond just reflecting on the work's soundness, this method asks researchers to go deeper and be reflexive, questioning their assumptions and actions, in how the data is gathered and interpreted.

How Reflexive Thematic Analysis Works

The following is adapted from Braun and Clarke's (2012) six-step analytic technique (Figure 8.4).

Pre-steps – Because RTA is an analytic technique only, these pre-steps should occur before you analyze the data:

- Establish your philosophical framework that explains your research approach (see Chapter 3). Your epistemological view explains the underlying assumptions that guide your research.
- Develop a research question or topic and a research design with a sampling strategy and data collection method (depth interviews, focus groups, etc.)
- Collect the data and create transcriptions of the data.

Step 1: Data Familiarization

Read and re-read the data (transcripts) so that you are completely familiar with the content. Take enough the time to absorb what the data says and how it might be interpreted. Don't be content with just surface meaning. Make marginal notes as you read – tracking your questions, connections, and hunches. Throughout this process, consider how your own experiences, knowledge, and assumptions affect your work.

Step 2: Generate Codes

Once you're familiar with the data, it's time to code. Think of coding as an analytic strategy (Bazeley, 2021, p. 2) to interrogate and challenge the data (by "loosening" and "breaking apart" the data). Coding reduces data by labeling information relevant to the research question. Don't worry if you don't know exactly how it connects. Coding assigns short, multi-word descriptors that mark or summarize data – word-by-word, line-by-line, paragraph-by-paragraph, or some other

data-chunking system. Surface-level (manifest) and below-the-surface (latent) meanings are coded. Latent data's value may be less obvious because it can contain more complex and hidden meanings. Go through the data at least twice to make sure you've captured anything that looks relevant to the research question. Group similar coded meanings together. Your coding orientation can be inductive (a close bottom-up examination of the data) or deductive (top-down), using theory or concepts to guide the examination. Similarly, coded items grouped together will start to reveal patterns in the data (Auerbach & Silverstein, 2003) (Figure 8.5).

Step 3: Generate Initial Themes

Grouped codes with things in common that connect to your research question become your initial themes. While the frequency of certain codes can signal something important, it's not the only way to determine a theme. Some frequently mentioned items may have nothing to do with the research question, and at the opposite end of the spectrum a single coded item can be a theme if it helps explain the phenomenon (Adu, 2019).

Themes should represent higher-level conceptual thinking rather than just descriptive labels. Themes are "patterns of shared meaning" supported or united by a "central organizing concept" (Braun and Clarke, 2019, p. 593). Together, these "building blocks" start to tell a story about the phenomenon – how something works, how people cope, what people think, etc. (Braun, Clarke, Hayfield and Terry, 2019, p. 855). Linked themes should start to explain what or how something happens better than simple information summaries. It's okay to dig deep and use your interpretative skills to develop a cohesive narrative (Figure 8.6).

Step 4: Review Themes

It's possible – but unlikely – that your initial themes will produce the final unified concept that answers your research question. Most qualitative analysis involves a lot of back-and-forth consideration and reflection to determine meaning from the data. Themes can be refined or dropped, and new ones can pop up. Researcher's assumptions, motivations, and experiences should be assessed, because this self-check may reveal missed or overvalued data. And talk to others about your analysis to see what they think.

Step 5: Define and Name Themes

Complete a visual map connecting themes and subthemes to a unifying concept, and continue this individual theme analysis and refinement until the "essence" is clear (Braun & Clarke, 2006, p. 92). Consider "concise, punchy" names for each theme (Braun and Clarke, 2006, p. 93). Strong themes are

REFLEXIVE THEMATIC ANALYSIS

PRE-STEPS:
- ESTABLISH A RESEARCH APPROACH.
- DEVELOP A RESEARCH QUESTION OR TOPIC.
- COLLECT YOUR DATA/TRANSCRIBE DATA.

STEP 1 — GET FAMILIAR WITH YOUR DATA

TRANSCRIPTS — READ THEM! HIGHLIGHT INTERESTING STUFF.

WHAT DOES IT MEAN?

REFLECT — THINK ABOUT IT. WHAT DOES IT MEAN?

STEP 2 — LABEL DATA

CODING
HA HA — Humor Reduces Stress
HA HA — Fun Memories
HA HA — Funny Teacher

ASSIGN LABELS TO DATA CHUNKS. LOOK FOR PATTERNS, KEY IDEAS. EX: HUMOR AND SOCIAL SUCCESS.

STEP 3 — CREATE INITIAL THEMES

CODE (HUMOR) "Reduces Stress"
CODE (HUMOR) "SO MUCH FUN!"
THEME: HUMOR
CODE (HUMOR) IN COMIC BOOKS
CODE (HUMOR) "KEEPS ME HEALTHY"

GROUP SIMILAR CODES TOGETHER TO FORM THEMES. EXAMPLE: CODES ABOUT HUMOR.

STEP 4 — EVALUATE AND REVISE

CODE (HUMOR) "Reduces Stress"
CODE (HUMOR) "Increases my happiness"
THEME: HUMOR
CODE (HUMOR) "EASES PHYSICAL PAIN"
CODE (HUMOR) "KEEPS ME HEALTHY"

REMOVED "COMIC BOOKS" AND "SO MUCH FUN!" AND ADDED "EASES PHYSICAL PAIN" AND "INCREASES MY HAPPINESS."

STEP 5 — DEFINE AND NAME THEMES

STEP 6 — TELL THE DATA STORY

THEME: HUMOR + THEME: SOCIAL SUCCESS

HUMOR HELPS DEVELOP SOCIAL SUCCESS (ANOTHER THEME).

Figure 8.4 Reflexive thematic analysis is an interpretive approach to finding patterns (themes) in qualitative data. Because the researcher plays an active role in knowledge production, researchers use reflexive (thoughtful and reflective) actions to remain faithful to the data.

conceptual and always connect back to data patterns or other significant data points, and they also come together to tell an overall story. Often, two or three themes can form the unifying concept for an undergraduate research project.

Step 6: Write the Results

Once the final themes are ordered and linked to a central unifying concept, it's time to develop a written narrative that

WHAT IS A CODE?

Easy! I'm a label. For a subset, y'know, a chunk of data.

Don't look at me like that! How about: "A single or multiword descriptor that marks or summarizes data." ??

Ok, try this: "The person TOTALLY didn't get qualitative coding." I would code that as "coding confusion."

Figure 8.5 A code is a label assigned to content (a word, words, phrases, etc.) that allows the researcher to condense text into categories so that patterns emerge.

WHAT IS A THEME?

REPEATING PATTERN

In thematic analysis, "themes are actively constructed patterns (or meanings) derived from a data set that answer a research question, as opposed to mere summaries or categorizations of codes. Themes can be generated inductively or deductively."*

It just means that when data repeats, that's a pattern. Put some patterns together, and you've got a theme that answers a research question.

If your research question asks: Why are students uninterested in research, you might find a pattern of people telling you that video gaming is way more fun than research. So, a potential theme might be "lure of leisure pursuits" to explain the lack of research interest.

That's all I got. Go play video games.

*Michelle E. Kiger and Lara Varpio (2020) defined themes in thematic analysis as "actively constructed patterns" by the researcher.

Figure 8.6 A theme can be based on a single code or similar codes grouped together that create a concept that represents an important element in the data.

Directed Qualitative Content Analysis

Content analysis started as a quantitative method (Krippendorff, 2018). Over time, qualitative approaches to content analysis emerged. Instead of focusing on counts and frequencies, qualitative content analysis looks at the explicit (obvious) and implicit (less obvious) characteristics of textual content. Implicit communication requires a researcher's interpretative skills to determine the implied meaning of text so it can be classified correctly.

Qualitative content analysis is used to examine mostly text-based data. It differs from quantitative content analysis because counting frequencies is secondary to understanding

explains and justifies the themes – and how they consolidate into a unifying concept that answers your research question. This resulting effort should be situated within the research topic's current literature. Strengthen the narrative by selecting relevant, revealing quotes and/or informational abstracts that reinforce your assertions. Even at this final stage of analysis you can revise, add, or delete themes if new considerations arise and make good sense.

the "characteristics of language" (Hsieh & Shannon, 2005, p.1278). There are different approaches in qualitative content analysis ranging from fully inductive to fully deductive, and hybrid methods.

A directed qualitative content analysis is focused on the explicit and implicit characteristics of textual content in addition to counts and frequencies (Hsieh & Shannon, 2005). It's a deductive approach that starts with a theory or framework and codebook with definitions to guide its efforts. If new codes emerge, they are included in the analysis. Data patterns that emerge from the codes and frequencies are analyzed and compared to the theoretical framework. New data is evaluated to see if it can expand or modify the framework.

How Directed Qualitative Content Analysis Works

Step 1: Create a Research Question

A specific research question, not just a topic, is created (Figure 8.7).

Step 2: Link Research Question to a Theory

Research questions are linked to a theory to guide the research process.

Step 3: Determine a Coding Framework

A theory, theoretical framework, or other research findings/results will help you develop a codebook with initial categories and subcategories, coding definitions, coding rules, and anchor examples.

Step 4: Determine Sampling Strategy and Sampling Unit

Samples are subsets from your population you want to study. Sampling techniques include randomized sampling to samples that don't use randomization such as judgmental or snowball sampling. Convenience sampling should be avoided because research subjects need to possess common experiences or characteristics the researcher is interested in exploring. Samples sizes for qualitative research are generally smaller than quantitative studies. In interview research, for example, once you reach the point that interviews don't generate anything new, it's considered the saturation point and interviewing can stop.

A sampling unit refers to sample subset selected, such as elderly male and female Americans who smoke. A recording unit (or unit of analysis) is an object that is observed or measured and data collected, such as interview transcripts of elderly smokers.

Step 5: Collect the Data

Data collection for a qualitative content analysis often includes interviewing (in-depth or focus groups) and generating transcripts. Artifacts, such as diaries, books, music lyrics, or social media feeds, can be collected via a sampling strategy for analysis.

Step 6: Data Familiarization

Familiarize yourself with the content by reading and highlighting data chunks that align with your predetermined coding scheme.

Step 7: Code the Content

Apply your predetermined coding scheme to the content. Assign codes to content (words, phrases, sentences, paragraphs, etc.) to analyze. Any content that relates to the theory but does not fit the coding scheme should be highlighted and developed into new codes. Manifest (explicit meaning or actual words) and latent content (underlying meaning of words/phrases) should be coded. Latent content requires a researcher's interpretative skills. Similar codes are grouped into subcategories and/or categories. If you are new to textual coding, *The Coding Manual for Qualitative Researchers* is a helpful and accessible resource about the coding process (Saldaña, 2015).

Step 8: Connect, and Make Conclusions

Once content coding is completed, the researcher uses the coding results to make connections and conclusions. Often, researchers classify similar codes into related categories. A single category or categories can be combined into themes that describe phenomenon. Another option is to use software to analyze frequencies, sentiment, and other characteristics of the data. A free software option is Mozdeh (Mozdeh, n.d.; Thelwall, 2020) which can perform time series graphs, sentiment analysis, and keyword and word association searches.

Step 9: Report the Findings

Report your findings/results based on the themes generated from the study. Your results should be compared to the theory or theoretical framework that developed your project's coding

DIRECTED CONTENT ANALYSIS

1. CREATE A RESEARCH QUESTION

2. LINK YOUR QUESTION TO A THEORY

THEORY?

3. DETERMINE A CODING FRAMEWORK

CODE BOOK

4. DETERMINE A SAMPLING STRATEGY

5. COLLECT THE DATA

6. GET FAMILIAR WITH THE DATA

HELLO!

7. CODE THE CONTENT

CODES

8. CONNECT & MAKE CONCLUSIONS

Figure 8.7 A directed qualitative content analysis is a deductive approach focused on the explicit and implicit characteristics of textual content in addition to counts and frequencies. It starts with a theoretical framework, codebook, and definitions.

scheme. Explain how you developed your coding scheme, and how you coded the content that resulted in categories and subcategories, and how these generated themes. Discuss any quality criteria used to support your interpretations and conclusions. Trustworthiness can be enhanced by pilot testing your coding scheme, having your coding definitions reviewed by experts, and using illustrative quotes from the raw data to tie to aspects of your analytic process (Graneheim and Lundman, 2004).

Inductive and Deductive Quality Checks

Deductive Checks

Transparency – Explain the analytic procedures in detail so others can judge the process. You can put supplemental details on a website associated with the research. Also, be transparent about the researcher's methodological orientation to better understand underlying assumptions and how the research process was carried out.

Index Themes to Data – Coded data chunks that make up themes and subthemes should be locatable. This can be done by line numbering textual material and assigning the theme to the relevant data location(s).

Multiple or Independent Coders – Deductive approaches can accommodate multiple or independent coders. However, with multiple coders coding accuracy can be checked with interrater reliability scores. Independent coders should code and recode with periods between to compare consistency.

Audit Trail – Another way to maintain research quality is to conduct audit trails of the developing analysis. This documentation tracks revisions and explains other process decisions.

Illustrative Quotes – In the final report, direct quotes from the collected data provide evidence that the analysis is firmly rooted in the data.

Inductive Checks

Transparency – Explain the analytic procedures in detail so others can judge the process. You can put supplemental details on a website associated with the research. Also, be transparent about the researcher's methodological orientation to better understand underlying assumptions and how the research process was carried out. Reflexivity – Reflexive techniques, such as journaling, can examine and question the assumptions underlying the themes or its organization including the researcher's background and experiences.

Audit Trail – Audit trails are documentation that tracks revisions and explains other process decisions.

Illustrative Quotes – In the final report, direct quotes from the collected data provide evidence that the analysis is firmly rooted in the data.

Academic Writing Examples

Example 1

Just what kind of impact do smartphones have on varsity athletes? Researchers DesClouds and Durand-Bush (2021) looked at collegiate athletes' positive and negative experiences using focus group interviews. They found that experiences included stress, distraction, and disengagement. Notice how direct quotes from participants are used to provide a data-based analysis. The following excerpt examines how stress and smartphones usage was viewed by athletes. For how the data as analyzed and the study's full results, go to the article (Figure 8.8).

Results

The results are presented in three sections: general usage, negative usage, and positive usage. All three sections pertain to varsity athletes' perceptions of the positive and negative experiences of smartphone usage in and around the sport context. Participant identification codes are provided with each citation (F = Female, M = Male; T = Track and Field, B = Basketball, Rw = Rowing, X = Nordic Ski, R = Rugby, Sw = Swimming, L = Lacrosse, S = Soccer, F = Fencing), and numbers indicate the focus group in which the athlete participated. For example, a female rugby player from the third focus group was coded as RF-3.

Negative Usage

Negative usage pertained to any experience of smartphone usage deemed debilitative to self-management, optimal functioning, performance, and/or well-being. The three main sub-themes pertaining to negative usage were (a) stress, (b) distraction, and (c) disengagement.

Figure 8.8 Researchers DesClouds and Durand-Bush (2021) looked at varsity athletes' positive and negative experiences using smartphones.

Stress

The athletes experienced smartphones as a source stress induced by feelings of obligation, pressure, and FOMO, which all appeared to be intertwined. Stress was induced both by features of the smartphone and obligations associated with the smartphone. FOMO was a major component of stress induced by smartphones. Athletes reported feeling more comfortable when their phones were easily accessible: "I guess it's just a comfort thing, to have it there" (LM-5). Uniquely, athletes reported stress when separated from their phone, for fear of missing out on essential information or updates from their team and coach. One athlete mentioned, "Quite often we'll have to look at our phone to see when our event is, or to double check 500 times to make sure that it still says the same thing, always double checking" (TM-1). The athletes also discussed feeling disappointed about missing out, induced by the social scarifies they have to make as varsity athletes. This feeling was easily exacerbated by their smartphones, which allowed non-athlete peers to put pressure on the athletes to disregard their sport commitments for social events. Athletes commented that their smartphones allowed pressure from the outside world to be brought into various performance situations (e.g., messages from professors during practise), and conversely, pressure from the sporting world intruding in personal situations (e.g., messages from coaches during down time). As one athlete explained:

I find I can't handle the social media at competitions, when I'm already stressed out. I just find texting people and messages to be way too stressful for me. None of my friends who are not at the track care about how my events are going… To me, that's like the outside world at that point, and I don't really want to deal with that. I just want to deal with what's happening at the competition. (TM-1)

A major catalyst of stress was obligation – a pervasive and often overwhelming negative feeling of urgent responsibility. Participants revealed that smartphone usage, and even the mere presence of a smartphone, fostered a feeling of obligation to be accessible at all times, to provide immediate responses, and to provide continuous updates, including on performance outcomes.

I find it stressful sometimes, on Messenger and in a {text} conversation, if I don't want to reply, but have already seen it, it's like: Oh my god! It says I've seen it, I HAVE to reply now. Then, you get stressed out. (TF-1)

Participants noted that while this feeling of obligation is likely not unique to athletes, it is intensified for varsity athletes, due to the demands of their coaches in particular. The athletes felt that communication from their coaches was something they could not ignore or save for later. Thus, the athletes agreed that the smartphone communication habits of their coaches would directly implicate their own smartphone habits and sense of obligation to stay connected. One athlete explained, "{As an athlete}, I think the requirements of how often you should check your phone are higher… more serious. You don't have a choice if your coach is emailing you; he's not going to wait" (BF-1).

Moreover, several athletes felt that a unique aspect of social media in their lives was the pressure to properly represent their institution. As one athlete explained:

Every team has started an Insta{gram} or Twitter. I think everybody's trying to push that on us…and that differs from the regular student body. We don't even have a choice, really. We're just already implicated… Public space is a public space. So we're implicated whether we want it or not. (RF-2)

Obligation to the university made a number of athletes feel that they had to be active on social media, even if they preferred not to be. The athletes also discussed their obligation to be ever-aware of their social media presence, modelling respectable behaviour. Notably, some athletes felt their university's representation of them on social media was a direct reflection of the institution's support (or lack of support) for their sport. Some athletes described how the university's social media made them feel disregarded and overlooked by the institution. One athlete described being "bumped" out of the way by more popular sports:

We got double banners, beat {our rivals} … We got one post {on social media}, which was then bumped 5 min later by a men's game {happening} in 3 weeks… We just did something huge; we creamed them. And we get bumped. (XF-3)

Example 2

Patients' expressions about patient-centered care were described in van Diepen and Wolf's (2021) quantitative and qualitative content analysis of patient tweets (Figure 8.9). Below are the results for the qualitative content analysis. For the complete analysis and report, check out the full article.

3.3 Care should be person-centred

This first theme, with 253 tweets (59%), was an overall positive expression of PCC and emphasized the importance of PCC (person-centered care) in health care. The tweets in the theme of "Care should be person-centred" were overwhelmingly positive about this type of care and how it can change people's lives when practised. In particular, posting content on how health care should be person-centred seemed popular and surpassed the mentions of real-life experiences of PCC (see Figure 8.2).

Half of the tweets (n=127) focused on "the vision of PCC." These tweets represented a desire for a more PCC approach, which was often explicitly sought for groups that can be made vulnerable, such as the elderly, people with disability and the LGBT+ community.

"Integrated, person-centered care & accessible, high-quality #community support should CAN be pillars of our health system. People regardless of their 'ability', what they've been through, where they are now -deserve care suited to their needs. #StateOfCare #ACEs (Organizations & Companies)

"Person-Centred Care for LGBTQI people is our #1 priority! #lgbt #lgbtqi #lgbtcare #cqc #healthcare #socialcare" (Health-care facility)

Another sub-theme, with 91 tweets (36%), addressed the facilitation of PCC by health-care professionals. These tweets contained references to

Figure 8.9 Parents' experiences with communication in the pediatric surgical setting were described in Claus et al. (2021) study.

acts of person-centredness from the perspective of the health-care provider. Often these tweets demonstrated elements of PCC that were possible to achieve in the context of the health-care facility.

"REPLY @#### Uniforms can be a useful visual aid for a person who needs assistance. However, I sometimes wear regular clothes when helping those who hate 'white suits' - so there is an argument, but it all comes down to person centred care. Being flexible and adaptable is key." (Health-care professional)

The third sub-theme, with 35 tweets (14%), highlighted individuals receiving PCC. These tweets expressed a sense of thankfulness that they received this type of care, as PCC is not common practice.

"Took me back to my Input days…. feeling especially lucky that all my physio contacts in primary and tertiary care were exactly this. Compassionate, holistic and completely person centred. I hadn't realised this may have been exceptional at the time; 15 years ago (Individual)

@'health service' brilliant & outstanding outpatients experience today with person centred consultant rheumatologist ####. Gave time & great care to my daughter thank you" (Individual)

3.4 PCC is challenging to realize

One hundred seventy-five (41%) tweets had a more critical perspective on PCC. The tweets in this theme of the challenges of realizing PCC have shown the everyday difficulties with this model of care. The largest sub-theme, with 74 tweets (42%), communicated how contradicting interests or traditions affected the possibility of providing PCC. These tweets contained content emphasizing that moving on from words is complicated.

"REPLY @#### The political class (Lib Lab) don't understand what 'person-centred care' is. They are locked into provider-centred care systems – unions will accept nothing else on the ALP (American Labour Party) side; the AMA (American Medical Association) will accept nothing else of the Coalition. It will require a 3rd pol force to achieve it." (Individual)

One-third (n=57) of the tweets in this theme discussed the challenges when implementing PCC. These tweets underlined the effort that goes into realizing a PCC environment for patients.

"@### @### @### This is really important for care providers to read. we don't believe murals are person centred and therefore we don't use them. They are often disorienting for individuals causing unnecessary distress, as highlighted. Than{k} you for sharing #carehomes #dementia" (Health-care facility)

"@#### @### @### @### I work in Aged Care and the sad truth is we just don't have enough time to treat people as they should be. Person Centred Care models are fine but without the time and a proper amount of staff you just can't deliver it." (Health-care professional)

The last sub-theme pointed out the lack of access (25% and n=44) to individual PCC encounters. A number of these tweets underscored that health-care providers said they provide PCC but that the reality was different and that patients did not actually have access to PCC.

"I honestly can't believe I am about to go through another social care complaints procedure due to not adhering to the care act, or person centred care planning. I despair. Do SW (social workers) not look at the work being done by SWE (Social Work Education)" (Individual)

"@###### Since mum was diagnosed 9 months ago, we have not received person centred care. We have been to 8 group meetings and had

a nurse allocated to us who has changed recently. We are fighting our way through trying to find help and services. Please DM if you need any details." (Individual)

Activities

Coding Exercise

There are many techniques for data coding, but the codes themselves are usually short multiword labels describing data chunks. In this exercise, the research question focuses on teaching factors and non-teaching factors.

1. For the following paragraph, how would you code the interview transcription of a student explaining her experience in a biology classroom?
2. How could you organize and condense the information?

Interviewer: How would you describe your Biology 101 classroom experience?

Student Respondent #7: I was pretty nervous because I don't like science. I nearly failed biology in high school. This teacher though was pretty funny so that helped make it easier to stay awake and listen. She was hard but you could tell she LOVED biology, which was cool. The labs were really fun, too. The equipment and space were all new so that was nice. When I didn't understand the homework, the teacher didn't get mad and just kept explaining it in different ways until I got it. One thing that really bothered me though was the cost of the book and the lab fee. Those were way too expensive! That's not the teacher's fault though. Overall, it was a pretty good class.

Coding a Full Interview

A research project interested in how corporations address racial discrimination could include CEO interviews. Use USA Today's transcript with PayPal CEO Dan Schulman (Guynn, 2021) to code for this research question: How do CEOs address racial discrimination?

1. Familiarize yourself with the data by reading the interview twice.
2. Code the data relating to the research question by condensing sentences or paragraphs with short multiword labels.
3. What main themes emerged? What might be the central organizing idea?

Resources

- Thematic Analysis: A Reflexive Approach, The University of Auckland,
  https://www.psych.auckland.ac.nz/en/about/thematic-analysis.html
- Thematic Analysis Part 1 (Braun, Clarke & Hayfield) (part of a series)
  https://www.youtube.com/watch?v=37VjRn6nlXg
- Thematic Analysis: An Introduction
  https://www.youtube.com/watch?v=5zFcC10vOVY
- Mozdeh – (Time series, sentiment, and content analysis of social media software).
  http://mozdeh.wlv.ac.uk/
- Mozdeh social media analytics with Twitter – 8 minute demo
  https://www.youtube.com/watch?v=GkxcldNZbzI

References

Adu, P. (2019). *A step-by-step guide to qualitative data coding.* Routledge. https://doi.org/10.4324/9781351044516

Auerbach, C. F., & Silverstein, L. B. (2003). *Qualitative data: An introduction to coding and analysis* (Ser. Qualitative studies in psychology). New York University Press.

Bazeley, P. (2021). *Qualitative data analysis: Practical strategies* (2nd ed.). SAGE Publishing.

Braun, V., & Clarke, V. (2012). Thematic analysis. In H. Cooper, P. M. Camic, D. L. Long, A. T. Panter, D. Rindskopf, & K. J. Sher (Eds.), *APA handbook of research methods in psychology, Vol. 2. Research designs: Quantitative, qualitative, neuropsychological, and biological* (pp. 57–71). American Psychological Association. https://doi.org/10.1037/13620-004

Braun, V., Clarke, V., Hayfield, N., & Terry, G. (2019). Thematic analysis. In Liamputtong P. (Ed.), *Handbook of research methods in health social sciences* (pp. 843–860). Springer. doi:10.1007/978-981-10-5251-4_103

Braun, V., & Clarke, V. (2013). *Successful qualitative research: A practical guide for beginners.* SAGE. Publications.

Braun, V., & Clarke, V. (2019). Reflecting on reflexive thematic analysis. *Qualitative Research in Sport, Exercise and Health*, *11*(4), 589–597. https://doi.org/10.1080/2159676X.2019.1628806

Braun, V., Clarke, V., Hayfield, N., Terry, G. (2019). Thematic Analysis. In: Liamputtong, P. (eds) *Handbook of Research Methods in Health Social Sciences*. 843–860, Springer, Singapore. https://doi.org/10.1007/978-981-10-5251-4_103

Braun, V., & Clarke, V. (2006). Using thematic analysis in psychology. *Qualitative Research in Psychology*, *3*(2), 77–101. doi: https://doi.org/10.1191/1478088706qp063oa.

Braun, V., & Clarke, V. (2019). Reflecting on reflexive thematic analysis. *Qualitative Research in Sport, Exercise and Health*, *11*(4), 589–597.

Braun, V., & Clarke, V. (2019). Thematic analysis: A reflexive approach. https://www.psych.auckland.ac.nz/en/about/our-research/research-groups/thematic-analysis.html

Claus, L. E., Links, A. R., Amos, J., DiCarlo, H., Jelin, E., Koka, R., Beach, M. C., & Boss, E. F. (2021). Parent experience of communication about Children's surgery: A qualitative analysis. *Pediatric Quality & Safety*, *6*(3), e403. doi: https://doi.org/10.1097/pq9.0000000000000403.

DesClouds, P., & Durand-Bush, N. (2021). Smartphones and varsity athletes: a complicated relationship. *Frontiers in Sports and Active Living*, *2*. https://doi.org/10.3389/fspor.2020.560031

Graneheim, U. H., & Lundman, B. (2004). Qualitative content analysis in nursing research: Concepts, procedures and measures to achieve trustworthiness. *Nurse Education Today*, *24*(2), 105–112.

Guynn, J. (2021, Jul 15). 'Values cannot be words on a wall': PayPal CEO Dan Schulman on why corporations must end racial discrimination. *USA Today (Online)* https://www.usatoday.com/in-depth/money/2021/07/15/george-floyd-racial-justice-paypal-ceo-dan-schulman/7859266002/

Hsieh & Shannon (2005). Three approaches to qualitative content analysis. *Qualitative Health Research*, *15*(9) 1277–1288. DOI: 10.1177/1049732305276687

Krippendorff, K. (2018). *Content analysis: An introduction to its methodology* (4th ed.). SAGE Publishing.

Mozdeh (n.d.) http://mozdeh.wlv.ac.uk/

Saldaña, J. (2015). *The coding manual for qualitative researchers* (3rd ed.). SAGE Publishing.

Thelwall, M. (2020, Sept. 8). Mozdeh social media analytics with Twitter – 8 minute demo [Video]. YouTube, https://www.youtube.com/watch?v=GkxcldNZbzI

QUANTITATIVE DATA ANALYSIS

Figure 8.10 With quantitative analysis, it's easy to drown in a sea of numbers.

Making Sense of Quantitative Data

Full disclosure: math and statistics are not my idea of a fun time. But I do appreciate their essential role in making sense of quantitative data. If you are math phobic or have avoided statistics, you can still generate meaningful analysis with some basic statistical operations. These are explained through freely available stats websites. If you are a beginner, I suggest starting with Prof. Essa and Dr Nic's Maths and Stats YouTube videos and the websites Statistics How To and Social Science Statistics. Other useful sources are provided in this chapter's resources section.

Getting Started

Quantitative data results sections in most journal articles are short and to the point, but don't let that brevity fool you. A lot of work goes into analyzing and presenting data findings/results. This chapter explores ways to organize, analyze, and write your quantitative findings, and includes an in-depth look at choosing the right analysis and visualization techniques. Be sure to check out the end-of-chapter resources for some help with statistics.

A written summary of data findings/results that often includes tables and charts. The results section follows the methods section. Writing your study's results clearly and well is important, and the graphics support the narrative while helping the reader visualize the data.

Basic Organization – Skip the background information, and start the results section with a restatement of the research problem. Next, logically order your results in one of two ways: 1) by research question(s), or 2) from most important to least important. Don't report irrelevant findings/results, things the research uncovered that aren't connected to the study and its questions.

Summarize Your Data – Analyze and summarize variables in aggregate form, as one whole thing – not one by one. Researchers studying product placement in ten current movies would summarize all the name-brand items in all ten, not tally what showed up in each film. Include aggregates of product placement categories, such as auto/trucks, food, etc.

Sentence Format and Content – Write results in complete sentences in past tense. Don't explain descriptive or statistical tests except to mention what analytical tools they used. When reporting percentages, use numbers and percent signs: 84%, not "84 percent." When a sentence starts with a percentage, though, spell it out: "Eighty-four percent of …"

Writing Voice – The results section can be written in first- or second-person voice. For example, if you did the research by yourself, first-person is best: "I examined 500 Instagram posts…" If you have a research partner, "We examined 500 Instagram posts…"

Non-Textual Elements – You can include non-textual elements (tables, charts, figures, photos, etc.) in the text or at the end of your paper as an appendix, but don't do both. If you use these graphic items in the results section, make sure they're next to the text they help explain, and label them in order: Figure 1, Figure 2; Chart 1, Chart 2, etc. In the text, reference them like this: "Our research showed that product placement occurred in 84% of the scenes in the 10 films examined (see Figure 8.1)." A complete heading at the top of each non-textual element should fully describe the nature of the data.

Don't Speculate – Avoid speculating beyond the basic data results. What you *think* the data means goes in the *discussion section*, after the results section.

Characteristics of Numerical Data

Here's a simple way to think about the two kinds of research data: Quantitative data (which measures quantity) is made up of mostly numbers, and it needs to be organized and summarized before it's analyzed. Qualitative data (which measures qualities, or characteristics of things) allows researchers to consider *variables* (how one thing's different from another) and *classify* (group) things based on attributes and characteristics (a thing's particular qualities). Quantitative variables do the same thing, but with numbers instead of words.

Quantitative variables are either discrete or continuous.

Discrete data focuses on observing and recording frequency – how many times did something happen? – and this data is numeric (numbers, not words), finite, and countable, starting from zero, 1, 2, 3 … and on up! Discrete data items count a characteristic, item or activity as a complete unit that can't be broken down further. For example, the number of Instagram posts created in a week is finite (it has a definable limit) because it could be 50 or 80 posts, but not 50½ or 80.7. The number of posts is finite (it has a definable limit), it's countable, and its value ranges from zero to a positive number.

When discrete data has a categorical variable with two or more categories, words are used to describe this qualitative categorical data. For example, gender can be described as male, female, transgender, or nonbinary. These gender options are numerically labeled to categorize them but the numbers don't have numerical value (1-male; 2-female, 3-transgendered, 4-nonbinary). In other words, 4-nonbinary is not greater than 1-male. The numbers are labels to classify information. Nominal and ordinal levels of measurement are categorical, discrete data. Simple statistical operations are used to analyze this data.

Continuous data has numeric value and can be meaningfully broken down into smaller parts such as fractions (1/4, 1/2) or decimals (.25, .50). For example, money is continuous because you can break it down into meaningful parts. Interval and ratio levels of measurement are continuous data. Ratio is the ultimate form of data measurement.

Continuous data is summarized with measurements of central tendency and measures of variability.

Levels of Measurement

Different types of research questions will provide different types of data – categorical or numerical – that control what type of statistical analysis you can perform (Schneider, 2010). Data is classified by four levels of measurement: nominal, ordinal, interval, and ratio (NOIR). Nominal and ordinal are categorical (qualitative) data, and interval and ratio are numerical (quantitative) data (Figure 8.11).

Nominal Level – A nominal variable, which has no mathematical value, is categorical because it can classify (group) things together. For example, in a research question asking what brand of smartphone the subject owns (1 – Apple, 2 – Google, 3 – Samsung or 4 – other), the numbers representing the brands have no mathematical value; they represent categorical information – the brand. Math operations for these questions are limited to frequencies, percentages, and computing the mode.

Ordinal Level – An ordinal variable, which rank orders items, is a mix of numerical and categorical data. At this level, we can say one attribute is more or less than another one. The mathematical operations available are computing the median and the mode, the range (the spread of a data set), and interquartile range (the middle half of a data set). The range can be calculated by subtracting the lowest value from the highest value.

Likert scale questions ("On a scale of 1 to 5 …") are at the ordinal level of measurement but are often analyzed at the interval level.

Interval Level – An interval variable has numeric value, which equal distance between the attributes, but no true zero, as well as rank order. While they're not common in communication research, temperatures and IQ scores are at the interval level. You can add, subtract, compute the mean, median, and mode, calculate the range, interquartile range, standard deviation, and variance.

Ratio Level – This is the highest level of measurement. The data has numeric value and its attributes are rank ordered, equidistant; and there's a true zero point. The main difference between ratio and interval is ratio's true zero point. Measuring someone's height (interval) cannot include a height of zero inches. You can, however, have zero children (ratio).

At this level you can add, subtract, multiple and divide; compute the mean, median, and mode; and calculate the range, interquartile range, standard deviation, and variance. Except in advanced statistical operations, interval and ratio-level data can be calculated similarly (Schneider, 2010).

Options for Analyzing Numerical Data

Let's examine the most basic ways to organize, summarize, analyze, and visualize data for descriptive statistics and statistical relationships. The level of measurement will dictate what options are available, and analytic options for each level of measurement are described in the next sections.

Measures of Frequency – Frequencies include counts and percentages. They show how frequently something occurs.

Measures of Central Tendency – The idea behind measures of central tendency is to locate one number that most represents the data set – the average (Snapp, 2006). The three measures of central tendency are mean (average value), median (the midpoint), and mode (the most frequently occurring value). A normal distribution is represented with a symmetrical bell curve, which is highly desired for calculating probability (Figure 8.12).

Measures of Dispersion – Measures of dispersion (spread) basically describe how variable your data set is. Normal bell curves tell us that the data is less likely to contain extremes (outliers). The more symmetrically distributed the data (bell curves), the easier it is to use statistical tests and draw conclusions. Two problems can affect calculating probabilities – the skewness and the kurtosis of the distribution. The skewness issue examines the symmetry of distribution; normal distributions, the symmetrical bell curve, are best for data analysis.

Measures of Position – Measures of position provide percentile and quartile ranks. Common measures of position are box and whiskers plots, percentiles, quartiles, and z-scores.

When You Have Nominal (Categorical) Level Data

If your data is qualitative, it is categorical in nature; the numbers don't have numerical meaning, and the data is discrete. Nominal and ordinal variables are categorical data that can be organized and visualized with a description or stats. Here are some univariate statistic options for nominal variables:

Frequencies and Percentages – Frequency means how many times a number appears. To visualize these frequencies and percentages, distribution tables display numbers and percentages for each variable.

Data
4 Levels of Measurement

1. Ratio Level — FREQUENCIES, ADD, SUBTRACT, MULTIPLY, MODE, MEDIAN, MEAN, DIVIDE, RANGE, STANDARD DEVIATION, %, VARIANCE, MATH STUFF. DATA CAN BE CLASSIFIED, IS ORDERED, EQUALLY SPACED, AND HAS A TRUE ZERO! EXAMPLE: # of children you have...

2. Interval Level — EQUAL SPACES. FREQUENCIES, MEAN, MEDIAN, MODE, RANGE, ADD, %, SUBTRACT, MATH STUFF, STANDARD DEVIATION, VARIANCE. DATA IS ✓CLASSIFIED ✓ORDERED ✓EQUALLY SPACED. EXAMPLE: TIME ON A 12-HOUR CLOCK. BUT... NO TRUE ZERO

3. Ordinal Level — Rank Order. %, MODE, MEDIAN, FREQUENCIES, RANGE, MATH STUFF. EXAMPLE: RANK YOUR FAVORITE FOOD 1. CHOCOLATE — CAN'T LIVE WITHOUT 2. CAKE — DELICIOUS 3. CANDY — ALSO YUM! DATA CAN BE CLASSIFIED AND ORDERED

4. Nominal Level — MODE, %, FREQUENCIES, MATH STUFF. EXAMPLE – HAIR COLOR – Numbers are used as labels to classify

Figure 8.11 In statistics, there are four levels of measurement, each with cumulative properties. The highest level of measurement, ratio, can categorize, rank, and infer equal intervals between nearby data points, and there is a true zero point.

Figure 8.12 A bell curve visualizes the shape of data conforming to a normal distribution.

Measures of Central Tendency – Measures of central tendency are important because they tell you how your data clusters around a central value, the typical value. If the data is nominal, not numerical, the only measure of central tendency you can use is the mode – which will show the most common value in your data set.

Chi-Square Tests – Sometimes referred to as the "goodness of fit," the chi-square test is a statistical hypothesis test. It can test for relationships between two categorical (nominal) variables and can tell if the sample data represents the full population. A chi-square test can be conducted on a contingency table.

Visualizing Categorical Data

Categorical data can be visualized as tabular (table) and graphs.

Frequency Distribution Table – As the name suggests, it tells us how often something occurs (the counts). The table just organizes it. In a spreadsheet, column 1 lists the variable's attributes; column 2 represents the frequency (count) for each attribute with a total at the bottom (Figure 8.13).

Relative Frequency Distribution Table – This adds an additional column to the frequency distribution table and assigns the percentage of each attribute to the whole. It should add up to 1 (100%).

Cumulative Relative Frequency Table – Another variation, it adds another column after the relative frequency that keeps a running count of the cumulative percentage. It also adds up to 1 (100%).

FREQUENCY TABLE

	FREQUENCY	%
In a sample of 200 online newspapers how many featured at least one environmental story?	50	25%

n = 200 (based on 200-online-newspaper sample examined)

	FREQUENCY	%
How often were environmental stories featured as one of the top 10 stories?	30	30%
How many environmental stories used the phrase "climate change"?	70	70%

n = 100 (based on the 50-newspaper sample, a total of 100 environmental stories were published during a one-week period)

	FREQUENCY	%
For each environmental story that used the phrase "climate change" how frequently was it connected to human-caused factors such as burning fossil fuels, cutting down forests and raising livestock?	35	50%

n=70 (based on the 70-story sample that mentioned climate change)

Figure 8.13 Frequency tables summarize the number of times something appears and its percentage based on the total. "N" refers to the total number of things in the sample. In this example of 200 online newspapers only 50 newspapers featured one or more environmental story. These 50 newspapers published 100 environmental stories during one week. Of these 100 stories, 70% used the term "climate change," in the stories that mentioned climate change, 35% mentioned human causes for climate change.

Contingency Table (Cross Tab, Two-Way Table) – To show the frequency distribution for two or more variables at once to see if there's a relationship, this is a good way to simplify data and see patterns. Use the pivot table in Microsoft Excel to create a contingency table, a table that shows the frequency distributions for two or more categorical variables.

Bar Graphs – Great when you want to compare the amounts or frequency of groups or track changes over time. Especially useful for nominal levels of measurement with discrete variables, bar graphs are good for looking at one variable at a time.

Pie Charts – Use these when comparing parts of a whole; they're good for visualizing one variable at a time. Pie charts show the various attributes of a single variable, and the slices must add up to 100% (Figure 8.14).

Box Plots and Histograms – If your data is purely categorical, meaning the data has no quantitative value, it's not recommended that you use box plots or histograms. If the data has a quantitative element, a boxplot is an option. Likewise, histograms, which show the distributions of variables, should be used with continuous quantitative data.

When You Have Ordinal (Rank-Ordered) Level Data

Ordinal variables have a meaningful order, but there's no way to know if the distance between each is the same. They are categorical (qualitative), but sometimes researchers treat ordinal variables as numeric.

For ordinal variables, the following basic analytic options available are:

Frequencies, Percentages – Frequency distribution tables can display numbers and percentages for each variable. For ordinal-level data, the cumulative percentage is useful because the data is ordered in descending values.

Measures of Central Tendency – Ordinal variables can use measures of central tendency to find the mode and the median – but not the mean. The mode is the most commonly occurring number in the data set.

Range – Range measures variability, the difference between the maximum and minimum values, in an ordered distribution of the values of a variable.

Interquartile Range – Interquartile range shows the spread of the data. Quartiles split the data into four quarters, and the range describes the middle 50% of values when data is ordered from lowest to highest value.

Two Sample Statistical Test – Ordinal data from two samples, such as an experimental treatment/control group data, can use the Mann-Whitney U Test (sometimes called the Wilcoxon Rank Sum Test) to compare the sum of rankings scores for null hypothesis testing. When you have two independent samples, it tests whether one variable tends to have higher values than the other.

Rank-Based Non-Parametric Test – Bivariate statistics measure exactly two variables. Spearman's rank-order correlation can be applied to ordinal, interval, or ratio data using two variables as long as they are in the same relative direction. Remember, *all* correlations do not

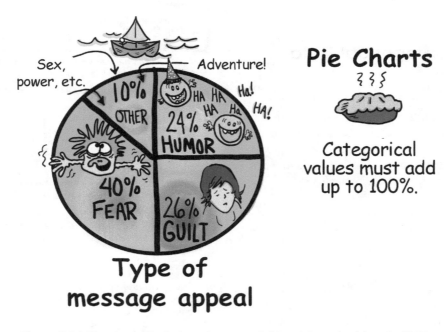

Figure 8.14 Pie charts illustrate only one variable and must add up to 100%.

equal causation, but a *positive correlation* means that an association exists between variables.

Visualizing Ordinal Data

Pie Charts and Tables – Pie charts and frequency distribution, relative frequency distribution, cumulative relative frequency, and contingency tables are options to display data on individual or groups of variables (see When You Have Nominal Level Data, above).

Histogram – A histogram looks like a bar chart, except that the bars have no spaces between them to stress that categories have an inherent order. In some instances, such as Likert scales with five values – strongly agree, agree, neither agree/disagree, disagree, strongly disagree – this scale is sometimes treated as a continuous variable. Histograms, in these instances, can be used to visualize Likert scales. However, a stacked bar chart would be the best representation for the Likert scale.

When You Have Interval or Ratio (Continuous) Level Data

Continuous data is at the interval and ratio level of measurement, and it has a true zero point or an arbitrary zero point. This level of data allows for more powerful statistical tests and greater precision. Here are some common options:

Frequencies and Percentages – Frequency distribution tables can display numbers and percentages for each variable. Visualization options include frequency distribution, relative frequency distribution, cumulative relative frequency, and contingency tables (see When You Have Nominal Level Data, above).

Measures of Central Tendency – Measures of central tendency are important because they tell how data cluster around a central value, the typical value. Normal bell curves tell us that the data is less likely to contain data extremes (outliers). The mean, median, and mode are all useful to analyze continuous data. Of these three, the most accurate is the mean, when there are no extreme outliers. If you have extreme outliers, use the median.

Measures of Spread – Measures of spread (also called measures of dispersion) tell us how variable (inconsistent) our dataset is. If the values are close together, there is low variability – good for making predictions about a population. It's important to know the measures of central tendency and spread to get a full picture of your dataset. Measures of spread include range, quartiles, variance, and standard deviation.

Range – Range measures the spread, the difference between the maximum and minimum values, in an ordered distribution of the values of a variable. Extreme outliers can really influence the outcome.

Quartiles – Quartiles describe a range of a dataset in four defined intervals that measure the spread above and below the mean. Quartiles can calculate the interquartile range, which measures the spread (variability) around the medium. The interquartile range is helpful because it eliminates the influence of outliers.

Variance – *Variance* measures the spread of a dataset. The variance is the average squared deviation from the mean.

Standard Deviation – Measuring the spread around the mean, standard deviation is the average amount of variability in your dataset. It's good for detecting the presence of outliers.

Regression Analysis – A linear regression helps make a prediction between two continuous variables (independent and dependent). Scatter plots can visualize this data.

Correlation – This is a type of nonexperimental research (no manipulated variables) that tests for relationships between two variables. The most common use in communication research is the Pearson r test. A positive correlation using the Pearson r's coefficient (r) is any value over 0. A value of 1 is a perfect correlation. The best way to visualize a correlation is to use a scatter plot.

Multivariate Statistics – Multiple regression extends a linear regression and uses a minimum of two independent variables and a dependent variable. There has to be a linear relationship between the independent and dependent variables.

Visualizing Interval/Ratio Data

Pie Charts and Tables – Pie charts display data for single variables. Tables, such as frequency distribution, relative frequency distribution, cumulative relative frequency, and contingency, help organize and display information about several variables.

Stem and Leaf Plot – Helpful when you have discrete and continuous data at the ordinal, interval or ratio level of measurement, this technique shows the shape of the distribution for a categorical variable, and it shows the order property of the real numbers. A stem and leaf plot's main advantages are that it can be done by hand, and it displays all data. It's best when you have a small number of data values. Each value is split in two parts: a stem (vertical) and a leaf (horizontal). The stem contains the first digit, and the leaf contains the rest, sorted from lowest to highest.

Histogram – Used with discrete or continuous numerical data measured at the interval level, this type of chart shows the shape of the distribution, and it's also helpful in identifying outliers. Histograms are best for plotting the distribution of a single group. For continuous data, a histogram will visually portray your counts of data with no gaps (spaces) between the bars.

Scatter Plot (X-Y Plot) – When you want to show the relationship between two numeric variables, use a scatter plot, also called a correlation plot. They can show possible relationships (correlations) between the variables. A positive correlation will have a positive line (as the value of *x* increases, the value of *y* increases; a negative correlation happens when the variable moves in opposite directions; when value of *x* increases, the value of *y* decreases; or when *x* decreases, *y* increases. Sometimes, there is no relationship between the two variables; there is no linear pattern in the data – the points are scattered everywhere.

Data Visualization Considerations

Data visualization helps a reader see the data patterns and make quick inferences (Rajaretnam, 2015). There are lots of techniques for visualizing data including tabulated and graphed data options. Here are some common ones, and tips for using them:

- **Word Cloud** – If you have qualitative data (textual data) such as responses from an open-ended survey question, word clouds are helpful. This visualization tool allows you to show the frequencies of words within a selected text. Most software programs allow you to adjust the font size, weight, and colors (Figure 8.15).

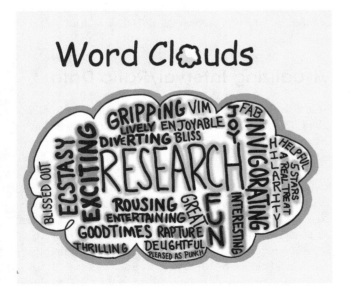

Figure 8.15 Sometimes noting how many times words and phrases appear in documents can show something important about data. Online word cloud generators use size to show frequency – the bigger the word or phrase, the more often it appears in the document. In this example, students described their research experience in various glowing terms.

- **Pie Chart** – For data with nominal or ordinal level variables, making a pie chart is easier than making an actual pie! Just identify each slice with a specific color, percent label, and title. If you have several slices (values/attributes for a variable), such as five, six, or more parts, you should consider using a different graph. Pie charts use categorical or qualitative data.

- **Bar Graph** – Bar graphs are for variables at the nominal or ordinal level of measurement. Place a space between each bar value; there should be no connected points. Generally, the *x*-axis displays the categorical values while the *y*-axis shows numerical values. A bar chart contains at least two variables, including one quantitative and one categorical. For example, you could show the frequency of certain types of film shots (extreme close-up, close-up, medium close-up; medium shot, medium long-shot; long shot, and very long shot) used in one or more films (Figure 8.16).

- **Line Graph** – Line graphs connect continuous data points using straight lines. They're useful for identifying trends over time and visualizing relationships between variables and multiple data sets. If there are several lines, they should be different colors.

- **Area Graph** – Similar to a line graph, but an area graph's plotted line is filled with color. Area graphs are useful for trend analysis and for visualizing quantitative continuous data. Multiple data sets can get confusing so it's best to limit what you analyze, or make your colors transparent so that you can see what's underneath.

- **Histogram** – Histograms can graph a continuous variable within data intervals. It is useful when working with data values of 100 or more (Holmes et al., 2018). Data is split into bins; an example could be a person's lifetime split into intervals of 10 years. Histograms can be used at the interval or ratio level of measurement and can show the shape (distribution) of the data. Unlike bar graphs, histograms have no gap between any two bars.

- **Box Plots** – Box plots (also called box-and-whisker plots) contain a visual representation of the distribution and spread of data – how tightly the data is grouped. These can be used at the interval level for a data set. Your data is divided into quarters with the box representing the interquartile range (the middle 50%), and outliers are represented as individual points outside the box.

- **Scatter (X-Y) Plot** – Scatter plots are used when you think two interval or ratio level variables are related. When using a scatter plot, the "line of best fit" helps the reader see the relationship between the two variables. Scatter plots are best when you have a lot of data points to show.

- **How to Remember X-Y Variables** – When creating a graph, the x-axis, the horizontal part of the chart, measures the independent (controlled) variable. The *y-axis*, the vertical part of the chart, measures the dependent variable. The DRY-MIX acronym is a helpful reminder of how to plot our data correctly: **D**ependent, **R**esponding **Y**-axis, **M**anipulated, **I**ndependent **X**-axis.

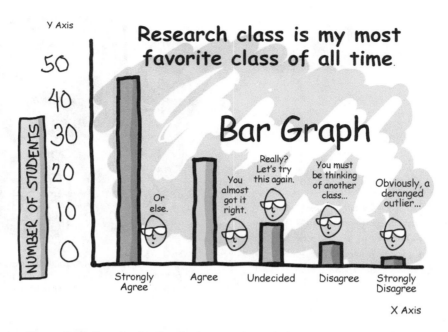

Figure 8.16 Bar charts visualize comparisons between categories of data.

Academic Writing Examples

Example 1

Here is an excerpted portion of the results section from Cassady et al., (2006) content analysis study about branded soft drinks in popular American movies (Figure 8.17). To see the entire results section, go to the full article.

Figure 8.17 A content analysis study examined the prevalence of branded soft drinks in popular American movies (Cassady et al., 2006).

Results

Twenty-one percent of the movies were rated G for general audience or PG for "parental guidance" and so were appropriate for all ages (Table 1). The majority of movies were action (32 of 95 {34%}) or comedies (24 of 95 {25%}), although all genres were represented. Thirteen percent of the movies were children's movies, such as animation, fantasy, or family. The majority (80 of 95 {85%}) were set between 1960–2000, the period when soft drink consumption was rising rapidly in the U.S.

The prevalence of branded soft drinks

Forty-five percent of movies (43 of 95) included at least one depiction of soft drinks, and the majority of these movies with soft drinks showed at least one portrayal of a branded soft drink (31 of 45 {72%}, Brands from four companies were depicted in these 31 movies: the Coca-Cola Company's brands Coke, Diet Coke, and Sprite; Pepsi-Cola Company's brands Pepsi and Diet Pepsi; Cadbury Schweppes' brands Dr. Pepper and 7-Up; and ampm's Big Gulp. Of these four companies, Pepsi and Coca-Cola accounted for 85% (26 of 31) of the movies with branded soft drinks (Figure 8.1). Wayne's World was the only movie that included brands from competing companies (Pepsi and Dr. Pepper). Three other movies showed more than one brand of soft drink, but the brands were owned by the same company.

There was no relationship between movie rating and portrayals of branded soft drinks. Some genres were more likely to portray branded soft drinks (p = 0.0136). For instance, comedies were more likely to include a branded soft drink compared to horror or drama movies. Examples of youth-oriented comedies that included the most depictions of soft drinks include Home Alone 2, There's Something About Mary, and Wayne's World.

There was no statistically significant difference between the amount of time branded and unbranded soft drinks appeared on screen. The median time unbranded soft drinks appeared was 38.5 seconds (95% CI 14.6–94.2), while the median time branded soft drinks appeared onscreen was 62.02 seconds (95% CI 35.5–111.4). While these differences are not statistically significant, they are in the anticipated direction: Branded soft drinks were on screen over 60% longer than unbranded soft drinks.

Portrayals of branded soft drinks compared to other branded beverages

We also examined whether there was a difference in brand appearance and actor endorsement for branded soft drinks compared to other branded beverages. For this analysis branded soft drinks were grouped into one category and were compared to three other categories of branded beverages: other non-alcoholic drinks (e.g., water, juice, milk, coffee, tea); beer; and other alcoholic drinks (e.g., wine, liquor, mixed drinks).

Branded soft drinks appeared in a significantly greater proportion of movies compared to the other 3 beverage categories (Table 2). Branded soft drinks appeared in 15 times more movies than branded non-alcoholic beverages (33% vs. 2%; $p = 0.0001$), five times more movies than branded beer (25% vs. 5%; $p = 0.0004$), and in four times more movies than branded other alcoholic drinks (28% vs. 7%; $p = 0.0006$).

This result is notable given that the relationship is reversed for unbranded beverages. Unbranded non-alcoholic drinks appeared in 20 times more movies than unbranded soft drinks ($p = 0.0001$). Unbranded beer appeared in movies two times more often than unbranded soft drinks ($p = 0.028$). Unbranded alcoholic drinks appeared 11 times more frequently than unbranded soft drinks ($p = 0.0001$) …{excerpted}.

Actors were more likely to consume unbranded beverages other than soft drinks. For instance, ten times the percentage of movies were actor endorsed for unbranded non-alcoholic beverages compared to unbranded soft drinks (44% vs. 4%, $p < .0001$). The same pattern is present for actor endorsement of unbranded alcohol compared to unbranded soft drinks ($p = 0.0001$).

Example 2

Here is an excerpt from a content analysis study results section (Al Bawab et al., 2018) that examined how newspapers in the United States and the United Kingdom covered health care apps (Figure 8.18).

Results

A total of 220 (151 UK and 69 US) relevant newspaper articles were retrieved. Health care apps were most frequently reported on in the Daily Mail and The Guardian (UK newspapers) and in the New York Times and the Washington Post (US newspapers). An exponential rise in published scientific articles (PubMed) on health care-related apps was noted during the study period. A total of 26.4% (58/220) and 19.1% (42/220) of the retrieved newspaper

Figure 8.18 A content analysis study examined how newspapers in the United States and the United Kingdom covered health care apps (Al Bawab et al., 2018).

articles appeared in the features and main news sections, respectively. General information about health care apps was the main theme coved by the newspapers (45.9%, 101/220). Most of the articles represented a societal point of view (72.3%, 159/220). The main focus of the articles was on general health matters (48.2%, 106/220) and specific disease matters (36.8%, 81/220). Diabetes was the most frequently mentioned disease in the articles. A high proportion (91.4%, 201/220) of the articles mentioned benefits of using health care apps mainly for personalized care, whereas 24.1% (53/220) of the articles commented on related risks such as anxiety and confidentiality issues. Almost half (45.9%, 101/220) of the articles mentioned potential facilitators to the use of apps; less than 10% (16/220) discussed barriers. Most of the articles (83.6%, 184/220) were judged as having balanced judgment on the present topic and more than half (60.0%, 132/220) of the articles were judged to be of generally low quality.

Activities

Data Visualization

Tables, charts, and graphs can visualize your data findings/results. Take the following data excerpted from Al Bawab, AlQahtani and McElnay (2018) study results and visualize it. For the variable theme, create a pie chart and a frequency table using the following data:

Within the 220 articles selected, the most frequent areas covered in the newspapers were general information about health care apps (101 articles; 45.9%), sport and fitness apps (63 articles; 28.6%), and disease-specific apps (20 articles; 9.1%). The remaining articles (36 articles; 16.4%) covered a range of topics, such as apps as sources of information, diet/healthy food apps, and apps used to communicate between health care professionals and between patients and health care professionals. This data is excerpted from Schimmelpfennig's

(2018) study results: The last research question pertains to the portrayal of models in advertisements. Of the 2,877 ads analyzed, 1,651 (58%) feature a person, while 1,226 (42%) only depict the brand's logo, the advertising text, the advertised product, or other objects.

The study finds that 121 (7%) of the ads that portray a person feature a celebrity, 149 (9%) feature other endorsers, and the remaining 1,381 (84%) ads depict anonymous models. While 401 (14% of all the advertising units) show anonymous models in the background or very small in size as some kind of extra in the ad scenery, 1,226 (43% of all the advertising units) show blow-ups of the models or feature them very prominently in the foreground.

Quantitative Analysis

Using your own research project, think about how to quantify data. How can your research topic be explored quantitatively? Example: A content analysis of newspaper coverage of climate change.

1. Develop three questions related to your research topic or research question. Example: How often do newspapers cover climate change?
2. Identify the level of measurement for each question.
3. Identify the statistics that can be used to analyze the information.
4. How would you visualize your data?

Resources

In-depth quantitative data analysis instruction is beyond the scope of this text. Fortunately, there are many helpful resources that provide step-by-step instructions for statistical operations. Here are my favorites:

- Introductory Statistics
  https://openstax.org/details/books/introductory-statistics?Book%20details
- Introductory Business Statistics
  https://openstax.org/details/books/introductory-business-statistics
- Dr Nic's Maths and Stats
  https://www.youtube.com/user/CreativeHeuristics
- Prof. Essa Basic Statistics (Descriptive Statistics)
  https://www.youtube.com/c/ProfEssa
- Prof. Essa Excel for Statistics
  https://www.youtube.com/c/ProfEssa
- Statistics How To: Statistics for the Rest of Us – Basic Statistics
  https://www.statisticshowto.com/statistics-basics/
- Social Science Statistics – Tools for Descriptive Statistics
  https://www.socscistatistics.com/descriptive/
- Excel Help and Learning
  https://support.microsoft.com/en-us/excel
- ExcelFunctions.net
  https://www.excelfunctions.net/excel-statistical-functions.html
- SPSS Beginner Tutorials
  https://www.spss-tutorials.com/basics/

References

Al Bawab, A. Q., AlQahtani, F., & McElnay, J. (2018). Health care apps reported in newspapers: Content analysis. *JMIR mHealth and uHealth*, 6(10), e10237. https://doi.org/10.2196%2F10237

Cassady, D., Townsend, M., Bell, R. A., & Watnik, M. (2006). Portrayals of branded soft drinks in popular American movies: a content analysis. *International Journal of Behavioral Nutrition and Physical Activity*, 3(1), 1–8. https://doi.org/10.1186/1479-5868-3-4

Dr Nic's, Maths and Stats (n.d.) https://www.youtube.com/c/CreativeHeuristics

Holmes, A., Illowsky, B., & Dean, S., & OpenStax College. (2018). *Introductory business statistics*. OpenStax College. https://openstax.org/details/books/introductory-business-statistics

Rajaretnam, T. (2015). *Statistics for social sciences*. SAGE Publishing.

Schneider, R. A. (2010). *Basic statistics for social workers*. University Press of America.

Social Science Statistics (n.d.) https://www.socscistatistics.com/

Statistics How To (n.d.) https://www.statisticshowto.com/

van Diepen, C., & Wolf, A. (2021). "care is not care if it isn't person-centred": A content analysis of how person-centred care is expressed on Twitter. *Health Expectations: An International Journal of Public Participation in Health Care and Health Policy*, 24(2), 548–555. doi: https://doi.org/10.1111/hex.13199

9

Writing the Discussion Section

Figure 9.0 A research discussion section offers you an opportunity to give your opinion on what the results mean.

DOI: 10.4324/9781003214489-9

The Discussion Section

Your study's results and discussion sections are what people often read first. This section is your interpretation about the significance of your research findings/results. But it's more than just that. While not a literal dialog, the discussion section allows you to explain to your reader why your results are important, how the results connect to previous research, and how the results might be used in the real world. You also lay out any of the study's weak points and suggest possible future research that could further explore your research topic and question(s). Remember, you need to write for the non-researcher – explain everything clearly so it's easily understood (Figures 9.1 and 9.2).

Organizing the Discussion Section – Write a straight-forward summary of key findings/results, their significance, possible real-world applications, any connections to previous research/theories, and any limitations (Wolcott, 2008). The organization of this section can vary, but here is a suggested order:

1. Summary of key findings/results
2. Comparison to previous research
3. Theoretical connections
4. Significance of findings/results
5. Applications of findings/results
6. Study limitations
7. Next steps

How Researchers Really Read Research

Figure 9.1 Results and discussion sections are the most eagerly read portions of a study.

How to Write the Discussion

Summary of Findings/Results – Recap your key findings, but do it briefly since these have been detailed in the results section. Any conflicting data should be detailed.

Comparisons – Situate your study's findings/results within the research literature. "Situate" is research-speak for "compare your findings to other studies." Explain how what you discovered was similar or different.

Discussion in Research

Figure 9.2 A research study discussion isn't a two-way conversation. Still, a researcher addresses the reader explaining the research's significance, possible implications, connections to other research, and any weaknesses.

Theoretical Connections – Since a theory proposes an explanation of something, and your research came up with evidence to support or oppose it, you need to discuss connections to the theory – one way or the other.

Significance of the Findings/Results – Imagine people who've read your findings/results thinking: "So what? Who cares?" This is where you tell readers why they should care about your findings. You've already explained how your study fits into other research and connects with the theory; now you explain the significance of your key findings. With qualitative data, this means telling the story about people's lived experiences or how they manage or do things. It allows interpretation based on your thorough knowledge of the data. If you relied on quantitative data, you'll focus on what certain variables tell us about a phenomenon. Maybe there's a significant relationship between two variables. Still, not all findings are significant, so describe their importance realistically. And if any of the numbers point in a different direction, report that conflicting data, too.

Applications of the Findings/Results – Applying what you learned to real-world situations will help you answer the "Who cares?" question, the real significance of your findings.

Depending on the specifics, you might explain how the study results could solve practical problems and/or increase understanding, or just general suggestions. And make sure you explain how additional research might help – specifically or generally – if your findings leave some questions unanswered.

Study Limitations – Nobody's perfect! That includes researchers and their work, so a warts-and-all approach that lays out what wasn't so perfect about your study helps build trust with your readers (Figure 9.3). The limitations section should explain any problems encountered while conducting the research, at every step of the process: design, data collection, and analysis. Ask yourself: If I could do it again, what could I have done differently to improve the study's quality? Let's consider some potential problems:

- **Prior Research** – Lack of prior research studies can hamper a researcher's understanding of phenomena and ways to measure them.
- **Resources** – Lack of time and other resources can negatively impact the ability to observe, collect, and analyze data properly.

Figure 9.3 All research studies have some weaknesses (limitations). Researchers explain what those are in the discussion section of their research report.

Researcher Issues – Personal beliefs and attitudes can negatively affect every step of the research process. Researcher misconduct, such as falsifying data, can destroy a study's quality. Conflicts of interests – relationships with people and organizations – can affect the design and results of the research. Inexperienced researchers are prone to mistakes at every stage of the research process.

Participant Issues – Participants may act differently in a study or not participate. Participant's self-reported data can be inaccurate due to impaired memories.

Concepts and Variables – Abstract concepts are hard to measure; a variable might not measure what you say it measures.

Sampling Issues – The sample may be too small, or unrepresentative of the population.

Data Access – Access to data can limit overall data quality.

Coding Issues – Coding techniques may be inadequate; coders may be inconsistent over time; multiple coders may code differently.

Next Steps – What next? The last part of the discussion section can include suggestions for future research: to answer unanswered questions, study other (and different) populations, or use new ways to observe and measure what's happening.

Academic Writing Examples

Example 1

Micro influencers' effect on delivering a flu vaccination program was examined by Bonnevie et al. (2020). Survey data found greater improvement in knowledge and positive perceptions of the flu vaccine. The discussion focused on the implications of their study (Figure 9.4). Go to the article to read the full discussion section that includes the study's limitations.

Discussion

Results from this study of a campaign to affect social norms regarding seasonal flu vaccine among African Americans and Hispanics demonstrated a greater improvement in knowledge and positive perceptions of the flu vaccine among respondents sampled from the campaign area versus those in the control area in the post-campaign follow-up survey. Notably, respondents in the campaign area reported significantly higher agreement with social norms and perceptions of community attitudes conducive to receiving the flu vaccine than those in the control area at follow-up. Additionally, the differences detected in the campaign group were generally significantly higher in the follow-up period versus baseline. Finally, at follow-up, those in the campaign area who reported exposure to campaign posts were significantly more likely to have received the flu vaccine and report positive flu vaccine perceptions than those who did not report exposure to campaign posts.

Regarding the feasibility of using an influencer-based campaign to promote flu vaccination, the examination of digital metrics demonstrated high levels of engagement, signaling that this type of campaign can reach large numbers of people with a relatively limited amount of resources. Although it was not a main focal point of this study, another study undertook a qualitative analysis of comments on Stop Flu influencer posts over the course of two years of implementation, finding that on average 94% of comments that were made on influencer posts were of a positive nature (Bonnevie et al., 2020). This finding suggests that individuals will engage in a positive way with vaccine promotion messaging if it is presented from individuals that they already admire or follow. This is particularly important because flu vaccination (and vaccination in general) is a topic that is often subject to heavy debate, and digital campaigns can easily become grounds for the spread of false information and negative sentiment from individuals opposed to vaccinations (Karlamangla, 2019; Hoffman et al., 2019, and Dubé et al., 2013). The health community must react to these negative trends by utilizing new technology and innovative methods to communicate information in places that are less likely to be flooded with anti-vaccination messages, and in ways

Figure 9.4 Micro influencers' effect on delivering a flu vaccination program was examined by Bonnevie et al. (2020).

that will most resonate with at-risk audiences. Targeted messaging is also a critical piece of native advertising and producing effective behavior change campaigns. This study shows that targeted messaging for flu vaccination can be engaging for both English and Spanish–speaking populations. We theorize that the higher rate of engagement within the Spanish-speaking community may result from individuals not being accustomed to seeing health information in Spanish and in a style that resonates with them, so they felt more compelled to engage with the content, compared to those who viewed the English-language content.

In addition to showing the potential to reach African Americans and Hispanics in both English and Spanish, this study revealed other potential audiences that may be ideal to target for future flu vaccination campaigns. Baseline results from the campaign area showed that nearly 25% of respondents had already received the flu vaccine for the upcoming year, while just over 30% intended to do so, and around 15% were unsure. However, the follow-up showed final vaccination coverage around 45% of the sample. This suggests there are at least two groups that may be an ideal audience to target for future campaigns: those who intend on getting the vaccine (but do not), and those who are unsure if they will get the vaccine. Future studies should examine the feasibility of using an influencer-driven model to reach that group who express intention or hesitancy, but may be more receptive to receiving the vaccine. This methodology also has promising implications in communicating information about other topics that are hotly debated, including other non-seasonal vaccinations, particularly in light of recent measles outbreaks (CDC, 2019).

Example 2

In Buckton et al.'s (2018) study, newspaper coverage of sugar-sweetened beverage taxes in the UK, the researchers list three study limitations (Figure 9.5).

This study's findings are subject to a number of limitations. Firstly, while double-coding and inter-rater agreement were used to validate the coding instrument to foster consistency of interpretation and application, the final dataset was not double-coded, such that we can present no statistical measure of consistency of coding. However, the rigorous double-coding of a subsample of articles, and continued dialogue between both coders during that process, ensured that the final coding instrument was validated. Thus facilitating consistent interpretation and application of codes in final coding, within the limitations imposed by the inherently interpretive process of coding text content (Krippendorff, 2013; Daubler et al., 2012). Secondly, our findings reflect commentary exclusively presented in newsprint and cannot be generalised to broader media, particularly social media sources. Finally, the focus on manifest content analysis means that we may have over-looked subtleties in the debate, especially the nuanced way arguments representing multiple codes were constructed by stakeholders in supporting or opposing a point of view. These limitations notwithstanding, this is a comprehensive, robust study of newsprint representations of the policy debate around SSB taxation and the SDIL, which brings up to date earlier work in the area in both the UK and United States (Elliott-Green et al., 2016; Niederdeppe et al., 2013).

Figure 9.5 In Buckton et al.'s (2018) study of newspaper coverage of sugar-sweetened beverage taxes in the UK, the researchers listed three study limitations.

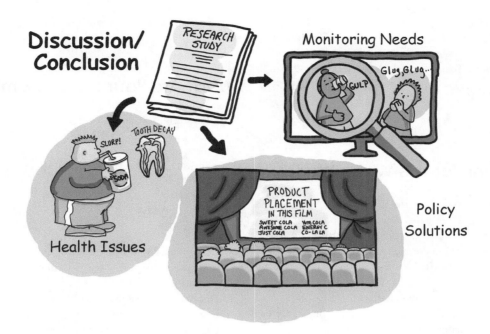

Figure 9.6 Discussion sections can include a subsection called a conclusion. Cassady et al. (2006) content analysis of branded soft drinks in American movies used its conclusion to include final thoughts about the study, including concerns about obesity's association with soft drinks, the need for ongoing monitoring of soda product placement in films, and possible policy solutions to alert consumers to such advertising.

Example 3

Here's part of the conclusion section from researchers Cassady et al.'s (2006) content analysis study about branded soft drinks in popular American movies, especially films aimed at children. As noted above, researchers have flexibility in how they organize the discussion/conclusion information (Figure 9.6). Notice how this conclusion section adds suggestions for future research and policy options for the movie industry, rather than placing them in the discussion section. Again, there is flexibility in your discussion and conclusion sections.

Conclusion

Until recently, the negative health consequences of soft drink consumption were limited to dental caries as identified in the current research. As soft drink consumption skyrocketed, the concern about soft drinks has shifted to obesity and its associated health consequences. Cross-sectional (Troiano et al., 2000) and longitudinal studies (Berkey et al., 2004; Ludwig et al., 2001) have linked soft drink consumption with obesity. Higher consumption also is associated with lower milk and higher total energy intakes (Harnack et al., 1999). For these reasons, health researchers and policy makers should consider product placement in movies and its potential influences on children.

Future research: Monitoring product presence in movies

This study provides a useful baseline to continue monitoring the presence of branded soft drinks in popular movies. As pressure increases to limit aggressive marketing of soft drinks to children, we speculate that the soft drink industry may choose to increasingly rely on more subtle forms of advertising, including product placement in movies. Monitoring product placement of soft drinks in movies should continue in order to track any changes in product placement strategies and methods. For instance, a new technology allows the U.S. version of a movie to feature one branded product, while depicting another branded product in the movie's overseas distribution. The 2004 movie Spider Man 2 featured Dr. Pepper in its U.S. distribution, and the beverage Mirinda for the overseas audience (Goldsmith, 2004).

Policy options: What to do about product placement?

The soft drink industry's payment for product placement in movies is legal, although inherently misleading when the promotional intent of the placement is not revealed. Regardless of whether product placement affects health or not, the public has the right to know when advertising is occurring in movies. Disclosure requirements shown during the movie credits would be one way to inform viewers about the financial relationship between the soft drink companies and movie producers. This solution would have little effect, however, since few moviegoers stay until the end of the credits. A more effective disclosure strategy would be to flash "Product placement paid by {name of company}" on the movie screen each time a branded product appears. While a more effective warning, it is unlikely that movie producers or soft drink producers would agree to this disclosure strategy.

The Writers Guild and the Screen Actors Guild have called for a code of conduct that includes disclosure at the beginning of each movie when advertising has been incorporated into the script (Marr, 2005). Disclosure at the beginning of each movie would inform the public that they will be subjected to advertising without interrupting the flow of the movie. It remains to be seen, however, whether voluntary disclosure would occur.

Activities

Implications for the Wider World

Generally, it's easy to discuss the significance of research findings/results. The hard part? Explaining how the findings could connect to policy, practice, or theory – and what direction future research should take. Briefly discuss how your research findings might be used to affect:

1. Policies, governance, or human behavior
2. Professional practice guidance to do things differently or reinforce what existing practice
3. Theory, either support, constrain or change it

4. Further research, identified knowledge gaps, further support

What Are Your Study's Limitations?

Problems big and small can show up at every step of the research process. Using the issues identified earlier in this chapter, consider your own study's limitations. Write a short description of the issue(s) that may affect your study.

Resources

- Discussion Phrases Guide (APA) https://apastyle.apa.org/instructional-aids/discussion-phrases-guide.pdf
- Discussing Your Findings (APA) https://www.apa.org/gradpsych/2006/01/findings
- Organizing Your Social Sciences Research Paper – Discussion https://libguides.usc.edu/writingguide/discussion

References

Berkey, C. S., Rockett, H. R., Field, A. E., Gillman, M. W., & Colditz, G. A. (2004). Sugar-added beverages and adolescent weight change. *Obesity Research, 12*(5), 778–788. doi: https://doi.org/10.1038/oby.2004.94.

Bonnevie, E., Rosenberg, S. D., Kummeth, C., Goldbarg, J., Wartella, E., & Smyser, J. (2020). Using social media influencers to increase knowledge and positive attitudes toward the flu vaccine. *PLoS One, 15*(10), e0240828. doi: https://doi.org/10.1371/journal.pone.0240828.

Buckton, C. H., Patterson, C., Hyseni, L., Katikireddi, S. V., Lloyd-Williams, F., Elliott-Green, A., Capewell, S., & Hilton, S. (2018). The palatability of sugar-sweetened beverage taxation: A content analysis of newspaper coverage of the UK sugar debate. *PLoS One, 13*(12), e0207576. doi: https://doi.org/10.1371/journal.pone.0207576.

Cassady, D., Townsend, M., Bell, R. A., & Watnik, M. (2006) Portrayals of branded soft drinks in popular American movies: A content analysis. *International Journal of Behavioral Nutrition and Physical Activity. 3*(4), 1–8. doi: https://doi.org/10.1186/1479-5868-3-4.

Centers for Control and Disease Prevention. FluView: National, regional, and state level outpatient illness and viral surveillance. Centers for Control and Disease Prevention; 2019. [cited 2020, April 1]. https://gis.cdc.gov/grasp/fluview/fluportaldashboard.html

Discussion phrases guide (n.d.) American Psychological Association. https://apastyle.apa.org/instructional-aids/discussion-phrases-guide.pdf

Discussing your findings (n.d.) American Psychological Association. https://www.apa.org/gradpsych/2006/01/findings

Däubler, T., Benoit, K., Mikhaylov, S., & Laver, M. (2012). Natural sentences as valid units for coded political texts. *British Journal of Political Science, 42*(4), 937–951. DOI:10.1017/S0007123412000105

Dubé, E., Laberge, C., Guay, M., Bramadat, P., Roy, R., & Bettinger, J. A. (2013). Vaccine hesitancy: an overview. *Human vaccines & immunotherapeutics, 9*(8), 1763–1773. https://doi.org/10.4161/hv.24657

Elliott-Green, A., Hyseni, L., Lloyd-Williams, F., Bromley, H., & Capewell, S. (2016). Sugar-sweetened beverages coverage in the British media: An analysis of public health advocacy versus pro-industry messaging. *BMJ Open, 6*(7), e011295. pmid:27436666

Goldsmith, C. (2004, Dec. 6). Dubbing in product plugs: How 'Spider-Man 2' made Dr Pepper a star in the U.S. and Mirinda a star overseas. *Wall Street Journal*, sect. B:1. https://www.wsj.com/articles/SB110228925774491481

Hoffman, B. L., Felter, E. M., Chu, K. H., Shensa, A., Hermann, C., Wolynn, T., ... & Primack, B. A. (2019). It's not all about autism: The emerging landscape of anti-vaccination sentiment on Facebook. *Vaccine, 37*(16), 2216–2223. https://doi.org/10.1016/j.vaccine.2019.03.003

Karlamangla, S. (2019). Anti-vaccine activists have doctors 'terrorized into silence' with online harassment. *The Los Angeles Times*. https://www.latimes.com/local/california/la-me-ln-vaccine-attacks-20190317-story.html

Krippendorff, K. (2013). *Content analysis: An introduction to its methodology* (3rd ed.). SAGE Publishing.

Ludwig, D. S., Peterson, K. E., & Gortmaker, S. (2001). Relation between consumption of sugar sweetened drinks and childhood obesity: A prospective, observational analysis. *Lancet, 357*, 505–508. 10.1016/S0140-6736(00)04041-1.

Marr, M. (2005, Nov. 14). Hollywood writers push back against product placements. *Wall Street Journal*, sect. B:8. https://www.wsj.com/articles/SB113192942392196060

Niederdeppe, J., Gollust, S. E., Jarlenski, M. P., Nathanson, A. M., & Barry, C. L. (2013). News coverage of sugar-sweetened beverage taxes: Pro- and antitax arguments in public discourse. *American Journal of Public Health*, *103*(6), e92–e98. doi: https://doi.org/10.2105/AJPH.2012.301023.

Organizing your social sciences research paper (n.d.) University of Southern California. https://libguides.usc.edu/writingguide/discussion

Troiano, R. P., Briefel, R. R., Carroll, M. D., & Bialostosky, K. (2000). Energy and fat intakes of children and adolescents in the United States: Data from the National Health and Nutrition Examination surveys. *The American Journal of Clinical Nutrition*, *72*(5), 1343s–1353s.doi: https://doi.org/10.1093/ajcn/72.5.1343s.

Wolcott, H. F. (2008). *Writing up qualitative research* (3rd ed.). SAGE Publishing.

10

Formatting the Paper

Figure 10.0 Following formatting and style rules keeps everyone happy!

DOI: 10.4324/9781003214489-10

Formatting Your Paper

Paper formatting refers to guidelines provided by various writing styles. The goal of paper formatting is consistency and clarity. When someone picks up your formatted paper, they should be able to easily navigate it and recognize various style characteristics, such as citations.

The most popular citation writing styles are the American Psychological Association, Modern Language Association (MLA), and Chicago/Turabian style are the most popular. Not only do they provide citation and reference guidance but they provide writing guidance including how to format your paper.

American Psychological Association Style

An academic writing style provides standards for writing, organization, and citing reference materials. Academics and researchers in the social sciences and business disciplines tend to favor APA style; its guide is called the *Publication Manual of the American Psychological Association,* (American Psychological Association, 2019).

APA's handouts and guides are available on its website (APA Style Handouts and Guides, n.d.) Below are links to some of them, including the handouts and guides landing page. (Figure 10.1):

- APA's Handouts and Guides
  https://apastyle.apa.org/instructional-aids/handouts-guides
- APA's Style and Grammar Guidelines
  https://apastyle.apa.org/style-grammar-guidelines
- APA's Sample Papers
  https://apastyle.apa.org/style-grammar-guidelines/paper-format/sample-papers
- APA's Style Blog
  https://apastyle.apa.org/blog
- Purdue University's Online Writing Lab (OWL)
  https://owl.purdue.edu/owl/research_and_citation/apa_style/apa_style_introduction.html

Figure 10.1 The American Psychological Association (APA) has developed a number of useful quick guides to help users apply APA style to their research. These are available at APA Style's website: https://apastyle.apa.org/instructional-aids/.

Formatting at a Glance

APA recommends typed, double-spaced on standard-sized paper (8.5″ × 11″) with 1″ margins on all sides, a text size between 10 and 12 pt., and a standard font such as Times New Roman. *Don't use hard-to-read fonts.*

Title Page (separate page)

Abstract (separate page)

{Main Body}

Title of research (followed by introduction to your topic)

Literature Review

Method

Results

Discussion

{End Matter}

References (separate page)

Tables (separate page)

Figures (separate page)

Appendices (separate page)

Title Page – The first page of your paper will be the title page. Here are the formatting considerations for student papers:

- **Title** – Describe your research and include the variables. Use bold, upper and lowercase letters centered and double-spaced in the upper half of the page.
- **Author's Name** – Under the title: first name, middle initial(s), last name.
- **Department** – Under author name, department name and institutional affiliation (Department of X, University of Y).
- **Class Name** – Include the course prefix and full name
- **Instructor's Name** – Separate line
- **Date** – Provide a full date (month, date, year) on a separate line

Abstract – The abstract section is the next page after the title page. Heading should be 12 pt., upper/lower case, centered on its own line, not bolded. No extra line space separates the heading from the 250–300-word text (Figure 10.2).

Introduction Section – This section starts with the full title of your paper, centered, not bolded, and double-spaced (like everything else). Follow this title with introductory material

Figure 10.2 An abstract summarizes in one or more compact paragraphs your research's essential elements, including the research purpose, data collection method, and key findings.

that precedes the literature review section, which uses a level one heading.

Page Numbering – APA style says student papers need page numbering – inserted in the top right corner, starting with the title page – but not page headers.

Section Headings – Headings help organize your information. This guide offers specific help with what goes into each section of your report. For example, the literature review has several parts:

- **Section Headings** – APA uses five heading levels; you'll probably need the first two or three. Level one refers to the main section headings for: Literature Review, Method, Results, Conclusion, Discussion. Note that the abstract, introductory material section, and reference sections are handled differently.
- **Level One Headings** – Level one headings occupy a separate line starting with the Literature Review section and followed by Method, Results, and Discussion/Conclusion sections. Level one headings are 12 pt., upper/lower case, bold, and centered.
- **Level Two Headings** – More headings can help organize more complicated materials. Level two headings occupy their own line, are 12 pt., upper/lower case, bold, and flush.
- **Level Three Headings** – If you need to subdivide the material within your level two heading section, a level three heading is 12 pt., bold, indented .05 inches from the left margin, is upper/lower case, and ends with a period. Text follows the heading's period.

Additional Heading Levels – two more heading levels are available if you need them. Take at a look at the APA style guide for more information.

164

Abstract

Writing the Abstract – An abstract summarizes in one or more compact paragraphs your research's essential elements. Writing it well is important because the abstract is the second-most common download indicator (after research title) in databases. People look at title, then abstract, to figure out whether they want to read further. And research conference organizers often use abstracts rather than full papers to decide on presenters.

The abstract section is the next page after the title page. Heading should be 12 pt., upper/lower case, centered on its own line, not bolded. No extra line space separates the heading from the 250–300-word text. And even though it's the first thing in the paper, the abstract is the last thing you write. Use the past tense, and include:

- **Research Purpose** – The study purpose relates to your research question and/or hypothesis. State concisely what your research wanted to understand, describe, or explain.
- **Method Used** – In a few words, describe key features of your research design such as sampling, data, collection method, and materials.
- **Major Findings/Results** – Highlight 1–3 major finding(s) from the study, briefly explaining its/their significance.
- **Implications** – Explain how your results might have consequences for policy, practice, or theory.
- **Keywords** – Appearing below the abstract, keywords are ordinary words or phrases that best describe your research and help others find it in databases. APA recommends 3–5 keywords.

References

Reference Section – Your paper should contain a number of in-text citations that credit the work and ideas of other people. All in-text citations should be represented in your reference section. Here are some basic formatting guidelines:

- The reference section should start on a separate page. This section is an exception to the section heads in the body of the paper.
- The word "References" should be centered and not bold.
- Double space your references.
- The first line of each reference should be flush left, with additional lines indented. This can be automatically formatted as a "hanging indent."
- Entries should be in alphabetical order; do not number references.

Reference and In-Text Citation Basics – In APA style, a reference page contains full details about sources mentioned in the body of the paper, one reference entry for every unique in-text citation. In-text citations and references formatting vary, so be sure to cite a source, such as APA's Publication Manual or its website section titled Reference Examples (Reference Examples, n.d.)

In-Text Citation – A brief notation of a reference, an in-text citation appears in the body of your paper and signals to the reader that the information comes from an outside source. The basic format for an in-text citation that paraphrases information is: (Author's Last Name, Publication Year). Examples:

(Smith, 2021).
    Smith (2021) states…

Follow directly quoted material with the citation: (Smith, 2021, p. 4).

Reference – A reference provides complete publication information, and the general format is: Author's Last Name, Author's First and Middle Initials. (publication year). Title of article. Title of Periodical [in italics], issue number, pp–pp [pages]. An example:

Smith, P.G. (2021). How to write a research paper. *The Journal of Research Writing, 7*(3), 143–162.

Tables and Figures

Tables usually contain numerical values, while figures include charts, photographs, drawings or other kinds of illustration. Tables and figures should illustrate and clarify your work, and there are two options for placing them: embedded in the text after their mention, or on a separate page after the reference section. Don't flood your paper with tables and figures. Be selective in what you choose to visualize. Refer to APA style for further guidance.

Tables – *Tables* should have a number and title heading (e.g., Table 1 Demographics) with number and heading on separate lines and should include headings for columns and rows.

Figures – If your data visualization isn't a table, it's a figure. Similar to table labels, a figure requires a number and title. For example, "Figure 10.1 Chocolate Types" could label a pie chart about chocolate bar varieties. The number and heading are on separate lines.

Supplemental Information/ Appendices

You may want to supplement your research with material that's too long to include in the body. Things like survey forms, informed consent statements, participant instructions, tests, coding forms, and lists can all be appendices. At the end of the research report, after references and any tables and figures, each appendix gets its own page. On the line below "Appendix" is the title; both lines are centered and bolded. If there are multiple appendices, label them with sequential letters: Appendix A, etc.

Academic Writing Examples

Example 1

A research article examined factors that related to digital native news media failures (Buschow, 2020). He explained why the research is important, its overall data collection, key findings, and implications for the future (Figure 10.3).

Abstract:

Digital native news media have great potential for improving journalism. Theoretically, they can be the sites where new products, novel revenue streams and alternative ways of organizing digital journalism are discovered, tested, and advanced. In practice, however, the situation appears to be more complicated. Besides the normal pressures facing new businesses, entrepreneurs in digital news are faced with specific challenges. Against the background of general and journalism specific entrepreneurship literature, and in light of a practice – theoretical approach, this qualitative case study research on 15 German digital native news media outlets empirically investigates what barriers curb their innovative capacity in the early start-up phase. In the new media organizations under study here, there are – among other problems – a high degree of homogeneity within founding teams, tensions between journalistic and economic practices, insufficient user orientation, as well as a tendency for organizations to be underfinanced. The patterns of failure investigated in this study can raise awareness, help news start-ups avoid common mistakes before actually entering the market, and help industry experts and investors to realistically estimate the potential of new ventures within the digital news industry.

Figure 10.3 One study examined digital native news media failures (Buschow, 2020). Its abstract provided a brief overview on how the study was conducted and included the main reasons for digital native news media failure.

Figure 10.4 A study about the debate on sugar-sweetened beverage taxation in newspapers (Buckton et al., 2018) used a more detailed subdivided abstract.

Example 2

This abstract for Buckton et al.'s (2018) "The Palatability of Sugar-Sweetened Beverage Taxation: A Content Analysis of Newspaper Coverage of the UK Sugar Debate" uses a slightly different format that subdivides the abstract into three sections (Figure 10.4):

Abstract

Background

Excess sugar consumption, including sugar-sweetened beverages (SSBs), contributes to a variety of negative health outcomes, particularly for young people. The mass media play a powerful role in influencing public and policy-makers' perceptions of public health issues and their solutions. We analysed how sugar and SSB policy debates were presented in UK newspapers at a time of heightened awareness and following the announcement of the UK Government's soft drinks industry levy (SDIL), to inform future public health advocacy.

Methods & findings

We carried out quantitative content analysis of articles discussing the issues of sugar and SSB consumption published in 11 national newspapers from April 2015 to November 2016. 684 newspaper articles were analysed using a structured coding frame. Coverage peaked in line with evidence publication, campaigner activities and policy events. Articles predominantly supportive of SSB taxation (23.5%) outnumbered those that were predominantly oppositional (14.2%). However, oppositional articles outnumbered supportive ones in the month of the announcement of the SDIL. Sugar and SSB consumption were presented as health risks, particularly affecting young people, with the actions of industry often identified as the cause of the public health problem. Responsibility for addressing sugar overconsumption was primarily assigned to government intervention.

Conclusion

Our results suggest that the policy landscape favouring fiscal solutions to curb sugar and SSB consumption has benefited from media coverage characterising the issue as an industry-driven problem. Media coverage may drive greater public acceptance of the SDIL and any future taxation of products containing sugar. However, future advocacy efforts should note the surge in opposition coinciding with the announcement of the SDIL, which echoes similar patterns of opposition observed in tobacco control debates.

Activities

Writing an Abstract

Abstracts help people find your paper. They're usually 300 words maximum, so every word counts. Include these items in one paragraph when writing the research paper's abstract: Research purpose, method used, major findings, implication of findings, and keywords.

Getting to Know APA Style

The APA style for most reference listings is fairly straightforward. For more detailed information, access the APA website – or the *Publication Manual* for complicated style issues.

1. Using the APA's Social Media guidance at https://apastyle.apa.org/style-grammar-guidelines/references/examples#online-media, provide a reference citation for a Facebook, TikTok, Twitter, or other social media post.
2. Using the APA's Audiovisual Media guidance at https://apastyle.apa.org/style-grammar-guidelines/references/examples#online-media, provide a reference citation for a YouTube reference.

Resources

- Handouts and Guides, APA Style. https://apastyle.apa.org/instructional-aids/handouts-guides
- Article Reporting Standards, APA Style. https://apastyle.apa.org/jars
- Style and Grammar Guidelines, APA Style. https://apastyle.apa.org/instructional-aids/handouts-guides
- In-Text Citations, APA Style. https://apastyle.apa.org/style-grammar-guidelines/citations
- Reference Examples, APA Style. https://apastyle.apa.org/style-grammar-guidelines/references/examples
- Discussion Phrases Guide, APA Style. https://apastyle.apa.org/instructional-aids/discussion-phrases-guide.pdf
- Abstract and Keywords Guide, APA Style. https://apastyle.apa.org/instructional-aids/abstract-keywords-guide.pdf

References

American Psychological Association (2019). *Publication manual of the American Psychological Association: The official guide to APA style* (7th ed.). American Psychological Association.

Annotated student paper sample (n.d.) American Psychological Association. https://apastyle.apa.org/style-grammar-guidelines/paper-format/student-annotated.pdf

APA Style Handouts and Guides (n.d.) https://apastyle.apa.org/instructional-aids/handouts-guides

Buckton, C. H., Patterson, C., Hyseni, L., Katikireddi, S. V., Lloyd-Williams, F., Elliott-Green, A., ... & Hilton, S. (2018). The palatability of sugar-sweetened beverage taxation: a content analysis of newspaper coverage of the UK sugar debate. *Plos one*, *13*(12), e0207576. https://doi.org/10.1371/journal.pone.0207576

Buschow, C. (2020). Why do digital native news media fail? An investigation of failure in the early start-up phase. *Media and Communication*, *8*(2), 51–61. doi: https://doi.org/10.17645/mac.v8i2.2677.

Figure set up (n.d.) American Psychological Association. https://apastyle.apa.org/style-grammar-guidelines/tables-figures/figures

General writing FAQs (n.d.). Purdue Online Writing Lab. https://owl.purdue.edu/owl/general_writing/general_writing_faqs.html

Handouts and guides (n.d.) American Psychological Association. https://apastyle.apa.org/instructional-aids/handouts-guides

Reference examples (n.d.) American Psychological Association.

11

Presenting Your Research

Figure 11.0 It's showtime!

DOI: 10.4324/9781003214489-11

Beyond the Research Paper

Hard work pays off – the paper is done! Don't let it gather dust. Instead, share what you've discovered. The two basic approaches for presenting research are oral presentation and poster presentation. There are also options for publishing your paper.

Spoken Research Presentations

Whether you present in a classroom or at a conference, time is limited. Spoken presentations are usually 15–20 minutes, and research conferences follow pretty strict schedules. Make sure you ask about time limits, including a question-and-answer period, and plan accordingly.

What Gets Included? – Don't try to cover everything, and don't get bogged down in the literature review. Provide context and describe the research design. Focus on the most important and interesting parts of your research – findings/results, their significance, and possible implications.

- **Research Elements** – Briefly state why your research topic is important, followed by a quick review of theoretical framework, research question, hypothesis (if you had one) and the research design (method, sampling, etc.).
- **Results** – The presentation's main attraction – what you found out – should be clearly organized. Present data results from most important to least important, or organized according to your research questions.
- **Discussion** – Describe what's most significant about your findings/results and any possible implications or applications for practice and/or theory.
- **Limitations and Future Research** – End the presentation with the study's weaknesses and any recommendations for future research.

Slide Presentation – Often spoken presentations incorporate a PowerPoint or Slides show. Keep these simple guidelines in mind (Figure 11.1):

- **Title page** – Include the full title of your research paper, your name, and academic institution.
- **Readability** – Fewer words are better. Follow the "6 × 6 rule," no more than six lines on each slide and no more than six words on each line.

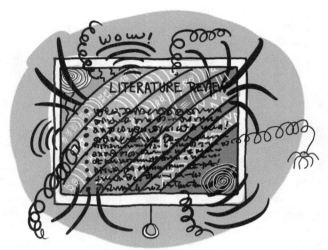

The unreadable but pretty slide

Figure 11.1 For slide presentations, limit the amount of text per slide and avoid unreadable fonts, bad contrast (dark text on dark backgrounds), and annoying animation add-ons.

- **Color Contrast** – Avoid dark text on dark background colors. Use plain, neutral, light-colored backgrounds.
- **Text Font and Size** – Make sure the font you use is easy to read – no fancy script fonts! Remember, when you prepare a presentation, you're seeing the words on your computer screen much closer than someone sitting in class or a conference room will be, so make text 24 pts. or larger.
- **Bullet Points** – Don't use complete sentences – just key phrases or thoughts.
- **Data visualization** – Label data in visuals clearly – keep it simple! Simple, easy-to-read (and understand) charts and tables are best.
- **Transitions/Animations** – Limit the use of slide transitions and animations – or, better yet, don't use them at all. They take attention away from the story you're telling.
- **Examples** – Use examples to illustrate your findings/results. Be sure to remove any information that could identify your study participants (e.g., blur user names in social media posts and faces in photos).
- **Review** – As obvious as this sounds, check your slides for misspellings and omissions. Ask a friend to look them over.

Spoken Presentation – Make your research presentation come alive by doing a few simple things (Schulze & Barton, n.d.):

- **Practice, Practice, Practice!** – Do a practice presentation. You'll find just how fast 15-20 minutes goes by. Use your cell phone's timer function when practicing, and get ready to delete some slides!
- **Don't Read the Slides** – The words on the slides (remember "6 × 6?") are for your audience to read – not you. The story you tell needs to include those words, but the last thing you want to do is read your slides (Figure 11.2). Know your presentation so well that you can look at the audience while you're talking, because eye contact helps establish your credibility, and it helps tell the story memorably.
- **Speaker Notes** – Notes that briefly outline or bullet information is best. Don't use text-heavy notes because your eyes will be on those notes rather than your audience.
- **Show Enthusiasm** – Put some energy into your presentation, because if you're bored the audience will be, too. Gesture, smile, change the pitch and tone of your voice from low to higher and back again – figure out what works for you when you practice, and use it.
- **Slow Down** – It's easy to talk too fast when you're nervous or excited. Slow down! Pausing for emphasis and asking a rhetorical question ("And what did the results show?") now and then can keep the pace right for the audience.
- **Questions** – Most presentations end with a brief question-and-answer session. Have a copy of your research handy if you need to refer to it. If you don't know the answer to a question, it's fine to say, "I don't know the answer to that, but it's a good question and I'll explore it further," or something similar.
- **Technology Check** – Check the technology setup ahead of your presentation. Back up your presentation; email yourself a copy or create a Google folder and save it there.

Poster Presentations

An alternative to oral presentation, the poster presentation provides a visual and textual representation of your research. Some first-time researchers find being part of a poster session

Figure 11.2 Engage your audience by establishing eye contact often. Don't read your slides. If you must, use note cards.

with multiple presenters less stressful than an individual presentation (Figure 11.3).

Poster presentation sessions are held in a designated area with tables, walls, and/or standing boards available for poster displays. Researchers stand next to their posters and talk with individuals or small groups who stop by. Usually, each presenter briefly summarizes the study's key points, adding to what's shown on the poster, and then answers questions. It's a great way to build experience in presenting and discussing research, one that supports newcomers.

Designing a research poster offers a creative option for presenting your research. Here are some research poster suggestions (Creating a Poster, n.d.):

- **Format** – Determine the type of poster format your session requires. For example, is it tabletop, wall, or cork board display? Tabletop posters can be made of lightweight foam core boards inserted into various stands or a self-standing trifold corrugated board. Another option is a single-sheet laminated poster. Check your university's printing center capabilities for ideas.
- **Size Requirements** – Generally, a single-sheet poster is 48 inches wide and 36 inches tall, but the venue might have other requirements – so always check to be sure.
- **Content** – Focus on your research results with some context (introduction, methods, discussion, limitations, and conclusion). Just like with slides, the fewer words the better.
- **Layout** – Most academic posters are subdivided into three columns, with research title, your name, and institution's name on top. The left column includes the introduction, method, and research question(s). The center column, usually twice as large as the left and right columns, displays results. The right column contains conclusion, limitations, and further information.
- **Text Size** – 72 pt. for the main title, 48 pt. for headings, at least 24 pt. for body text, and use an easy-to-read font (no script!). Don't try to make too much text fit; you want to make it easy for people to read – even from several feet away.
- **Color** – Backgrounds should be either dark with white/light colored text or white/light colored backgrounds with black/dark colored text.
- **Visuals** – Visual data such as charts, tables, or other illustrations are a great idea.
- **Handouts** – A one-page summary of your research handout with contact information can help spread your work to others.
- **Draft and Revise** – Start with a sketch or digital mockup of the poster. Ask your teacher about layout and content, and always ask someone to edit your poster content (Figure 11.4).

Research Conference Presentations

After presenting your research to your class, consider presenting it at an academic conference. Why? A conference presentation looks great on your résumé, builds confidence in your

Research We'd Really Like to See!

Figure 11.3 Poster presentations should provide the essential elements of your research study.

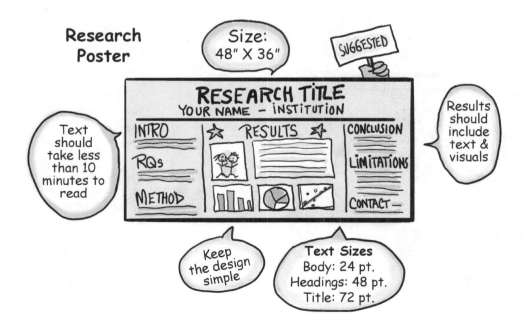

Figure 11.4 Make your research poster the standard size, and stick close to the typical format – unless you have a good reason to do something a bit different. Bottom line: make sure you include key research elements – and emphasize the data results.

research ability, provides feedback in a supportive environment, and can help you network with other researchers.

Campus Student Research Conference – Most universities have student research conferences. Find out how to enter – it might be as simple as filling out a brief form and providing your project abstract. Check nearby colleges for opportunities to present your research at their student conferences. Again, these conferences offer a supportive environment and provide helpful feedback that can improve your research.

Beyond the Campus Research Presentation – Regional, state, or national research conferences commonly offer undergraduate research opportunities. Google "undergraduate research conferences" and the name of your city or state, and you should see results. (Also, check out the Council on Undergraduate Research, https://www.cur.org/.) Faculty in your academic department often belong to national, regional, and state organizations that offer research conferences, so ask your teacher about those opportunities (Figure 11.5).

Publishing Options

Academic Publishing Options – Beyond presenting your research, you can try to get it published. There are two basic options: academic and professional (industry) publishing.

- Directory of Open Access Journals (DOAJ) provides open access to more than 16,000 peer-reviewed journals.
- Communication Institute for Online Scholarship (CIOS) maintains a listing of communication-focused journals.
- Undergraduate Research Commons features undergraduate student work published by colleges and universities.

Figure 11.5 Research conferences often provide opportunities for graduate and undergraduate research presentations. These presentations offer a supportive environment and valuable feedback.

Figure 11.6 Evidence-based research can show up in lots of places – not just peer-reviewed academic publications. Old-school print, e-magazines, traditional and online media often feature research-related stories.

Professional Publication Options – Did you know there's an industry magazine called *LNG Industry* that's all about the business of liquefied natural gas? How about gaming? Take your pick: *Gambling Times*, *Gaming & Leisure*, *Casino Journal*, *Casino Life*, *Casino Player*, *GGB Global Gaming Business*, *Indian Gaming*, *Gambling Insider*, *Card Player*, and *Strictly Slots*, among others. There is a publication for nearly every industry, business, and hobbyist interest under the sun, and they all need content! (Figure 11.6).

Industry and nonprofit organizations are always looking for interesting editorial content for their magazines, websites, newsletters, and blogs. If your research touched on something of interest to a particular industry or topic, it's worth checking to see providing if a summary of your research to a relevant organization would interest them.

How to Pitch Your Research for Publication – Anyone can ask to publish in a non-academic publication. It's as easy as sending a pitch (a query email) to a publication's editor. Here's how it works:

1. Carefully select a publication that aligns with your research topic. Check to see if the publication has published material related to your research topic.
2. Use a descriptive subject line in your email to grab the editor's attention.
3. Address the letter to the editor by name.
4. Editors are busy people, so get to the point: Explain who you are and what you propose to write.
5. Keep it short, and include your study's most interesting findings/results.
6. Explain how the study results might be relevant to the publication's audience, and give an example or two.
7. Write in the style of the publication – not academic style.
8. End with a sentence that thanks the editor for his/her time and indicates you'll follow up in a few weeks.

Finding Industry Publications – Thousands of industry publications and organizations are looking for interesting articles for their publications, including websites. Find trade publications using your college's library database resources:

- **ABI/INFORM** – Search this database by trade journals in its Source Type menu box.
- **Business Source Premier** – You can limit your database search to trade journals. Under "limit your results" pick "Trade Publication."
- **Business Source Complete** – Select "Trade Publication" within "Publication Type."
- **Business Insights** – Use its "Search within Results" for "Trade Journals."
- **General OneFile** – Use its "Limit to" function in "Publication Subject" to "Business and Industry."
- **Nexis Uni** – This database has thousands of newspapers, magazines, trade press, and trade journals.

Activities

Design a Research Poster

Your first research conference presentation may be in a poster session, standing next to a poster on a wall or tabletop with others in a room doing the same thing. Using your research paper, create a mockup of your research as a poster presentation:

1. Design a poster in a horizontal orientation (48 × 36 in.) for your research project.
2. Use the poster formatting instructions provided in this chapter as your guide.
3. Select the information from your research paper for the poster. It may need to be modified to shorten the content. Use 24 pt. or larger for body text, 48 pt. for headings, and 72 pt. for the main title. Select a font that's easy to read.

Write a Pitch Letter

Thousands of professional and industry publications are looking for content that interests their readers. Design a pitch letter for a professional publication focused on your research area.

1. Many academic institutions issue news releases, short summary documents that provide the key findings/results of published research by faculty. Do a search of your university's news archives, and read some of these research study news releases. This will give you an example of a layperson's approach to academic writing.
2. Do a library database search, an internet search, or consult *Writer's Market* in your library to find publications that match your research topic. Find three possibilities or more. Write them down.
3. Become familiar with the publication and how your research will interest its readers.
4. With the names of your publications, go to their websites and follow the "writer's guidelines" for submitting your story idea.
5. In your story pitch or letter of inquiry, explain your story idea, how it fits the publication's readers' interests, some of the study's key findings/results, and any credentials that qualify you for the writing project (Krueger, 2016).

Resources

- 3 Guidelines for a Good Story Pitch
  https://www.poynter.org/educators-students/2016/3-guidelines-for-a-good-story-pitch/
- Council on Undergraduate Research
  https://www.cur.org/
- Creating a Poster
  https://writing.wisc.edu/handbook/assignments/posterpresentations/.
- Internship and Research Opportunities
  https://www.cur.org/engage/undergraduate/research/
- Locating a Research Mentor Guide
  https://www.cur.org/assets/1/7/Locating_a_Research_Mentor_Guide.pdf
- Paper and Presentation Opportunities
  https://www.cur.org/engage/undergraduate/presentation/
- Undergraduate Research Commons
  https://undergraduatecommons.com/

References

Creating a poster (n.d.) University of Wisconsin-Madison Writing Center. https://writing.wisc.edu/handbook/assignments/posterpresentations/

Krueger, V. (2016, July 12). 3 guidelines for a good story pitch. Poynter. https://www.poynter.org/educators-students/2016/3-guidelines-for-a-good-story-pitch/

Schulze, P., & Barton, L. (n.d.) How to give a good presentation. Council on Undergraduate Research. https://www.cur.org/assets/1/7/How_to_Give_a_Good_Presentation__CUR.pdf

Index